FASTPITCH

. . .

The UNTOLD HISTORY
of SOFTBALL and the WOMEN
Who Made the Game

. . .

ERICA WESTLY

TOUCHSTONE
New York   London   Toronto   Sydney   New Delhi

Touchstone
An Imprint of Simon & Schuster, Inc.
1230 Avenue of the Americas
New York, NY 10020

First Touchstone hardcover edition June 2016

TOUCHSTONE and colophon are registered trademarks
of Simon & Schuster, Inc.

For information about special discounts for bulk purchases,
please contact Simon & Schuster Special Sales at 1-866-506-1949
or business@simonandschuster.com.

The Simon & Schuster Speakers Bureau can bring authors to
your live event. For more information or to book an event,
contact the Simon & Schuster Speakers Bureau at 866-248-3049
or visit our website at www.simonspeakers.com.

Interior design by Kyle Kabel

Manufactured in the United States of America

10 9 8 7 6 5 4 3 2 1

Library of Congress Cataloging-in-Publication Data is available.

ISBN 978-1-5011-1859-3
ISBN 978-1-5011-1861-6 (ebook)

For female athletes, past, present, and future

CONTENTS

FASTPITCH

PROLOGUE

For most of the year, the weeds are so overgrown that you can't even make out the chain-link fence, let alone the field. If you happened to drive by it, which would be unlikely, given its isolated location on the outskirts of a residential area, you probably wouldn't notice it at all. Only if you walk up close to the fence and peer carefully through the dense plant life do the dugout and the wooden bleachers where thousands of fans used to sit become visible. The field is a Superfund site now, sealed off by the Environmental Protection Agency after piles of asbestos and other toxic pollutants were found buried there. But for more than three decades, it was Memorial Field, home to the legendary Brakettes softball team. Women used to come from all over the country just for the chance to play there.

Raybestos, the company that owned the team, built the field for its employees in the 1940s. It was within walking distance of the company's manufacturing facility on Frog Pond Lane so that workers could go straight to practice when their shifts were over. It had state-of-the-art field lights and a giant scoreboard, making it nicer than many minor league baseball stadiums. A restaurant, fittingly called the Frog Pond Restaurant, even opened up down the road and began advertising itself as the place to go for food and wine "before, between, and after the games."

Stratford, Connecticut, was an unlikely location for a champion

1

softball team. Historically, the other top teams came from the West Coast or large Midwestern cities such as Detroit or Chicago, where the sport was the most popular. Stratford, meanwhile, was a small town nestled between Long Island Sound and the Housatonic River, primarily known for its lighthouse and Shakespearean namesake. But Bill Simpson, the eccentric owner and general manager of the Raybestos facility, had become enthralled with fastpitch. He had never been much of an athlete himself, although he lettered in soccer and tennis as a student at Williams College. Once he saw his first fastpitch game, he was hooked, however, and he was determined to have the best men's and women's teams in the nation.

The Cardinals, the Raybestos men's fastpitch team, were good, but it was the Brakettes, named after the brake linings that the company produced, who made sports history. Between 1958 and 1978, the team won fifteen national championships and made the finals all but one time. They were the New York Yankees of softball. For women, who had been banned from baseball and had few athletic options at school, the Brakettes represented a rare opportunity to not only play sports, but play at a competitive level. Girls found out about the team through word of mouth—in those days every town seemed to have at least one fastpitch enthusiast—and if they made the cut, they would move up North, get a job, usually at Raybestos, and find a place to live. Many stayed with the team for years, even decades.

Fastpitch wasn't the only company-sponsored amateur sport—companies also had leagues for bowling, basketball, volleyball, and even sailing in some states—but it was by far the largest, with hundreds of thousands of men's and women's teams across the United States in the 1940s, '50s, and '60s, and was the most popular with fans. It was also one of the oldest company sports. The trend dated back to the early 1900s, when factories adopted fastpitch as a way to keep workers in shape and boost morale.

Then, in 1933, fastpitch became a spectator sport, when it made its national debut at the Chicago World's Fair. After that, the company teams started selling tickets to their games, and they quickly became community events. People went to cheer on their coworkers and neighbors, spreading out blankets on the grass if there weren't enough seats in the stands. Having men's and women's teams meant twice the number of games to attend and doubled the chances of victory. When the teams won, the entire town celebrated.

The level of play of top teams such as the Brakettes was orders of magnitude above that of today's company softball teams, most of which are of the laid-back slowpitch variety. The top fastpitch players were akin to professional athletes: they trained year-round, and for many of them, the sport was the main focus of their lives. Women cleaned and ironed their team uniforms with such care an onlooker might assume they were handling priceless works of art. Many put off marriage and school and left their families behind to play on the best teams. They spent their spring and summer weekends traveling to and from regional and national games, usually by car or bus and often on their own dime.

Fastpitch was the first team sport that women got to play seriously. It wasn't a gimmick or a show, and it was stable and established, which meant that players could develop their skills over time and not have to worry about whether the league would still be around the next year. The women who played on the Brakettes and other strong fastpitch teams were among the most prominent female athletes of the twentieth century. They appeared on television shows, such as CBS *Sports Spectacular*, and helped pave the way for Title IX, the 1972 law that required American schools that receive federal money to provide athletic opportunities for female students. They were also some of the first female athletes to have their own professional sports league.

Today, fastpitch is primarily a women's high school and college sport. The competitive adult teams made up of male and female workers are long gone, along with most of the companies that sponsored them. Raybestos's downfall was particularly dramatic. In the late 1970s, town and state officials discovered that the company had been using its softball field, along with several other areas in town, to dump asbestos waste from its manufacturing facility (the *bestos* in the company name stood for "asbestos," the main component of the brake linings). Ten years later, the company was bankrupt and facing a slew of lawsuits. Investigations revealed that Raybestos had been exposing the townspeople to asbestos, lead, and other toxins for decades. In the 1940s and '50s, the company even gave residents free samples of asbestos-laced sludge from its factory and encouraged them to use it as fill soil in their yards.

The Stratford cleanup effort, considered one of the most extensive in US history, has taken more than two decades and cost tens of millions of dollars. Few of the town's residents have kind words to say about Raybestos these days. The Brakettes emerged from the scandal unscathed, however. The team still exists, albeit in a much-reduced form. Most of the players on the roster are college students from the New England region, and most of the fans in the stands are their families rather than townspeople. The season only lasts two months, from early June to early August, and afterward, the players go back to school or transition into coaching jobs or other careers. It's a temporary stop on the way to somewhere else rather than the permanent destination it once was.

Other influential fastpitch teams from the company-sponsored era live on in memorial names—for example, the Erv Lind Stadium in Portland, Oregon's Normandale Park, which commemorates the championship-winning Erv Lind Florists softball team. Many more have been forgotten, though. Florida used to have some of the country's strongest fastpitch teams, but in the 1990s, parents had to sue just to get the state's high schools to offer the sport. School administrators resisted the change, saying they didn't have people on staff who knew the game well enough to coach it. Had baseball not been so unwelcoming toward women, fastpitch might not be around today at all.

Softball was invented in the 1800s as an indoor game, played with a broomstick and a balled-up boxing glove. In the sport's nearly 130-year history, it has been, at various points, an Olympic sport and a traveling vaudeville act and has been called many names—mush ball, lightning ball, kitten ball—but above all, it was inclusive, not just of women, but of people of all different shapes and sizes and from all different walks of life. It was an everyman's game that also appealed to outsiders and amassed tens of millions of fans around the world without ever becoming mainstream.

Although few realize it today, fastpitch had a profound effect on the way Americans consume and participate in sports. Softball players couldn't generally expect to get rich. They played for themselves and their teams, and if they were good enough, they got to travel around the country and sometimes even overseas. The story of fastpitch is the story of these players, who lived in relative anonymity but accomplished extraordinary things.

CHAPTER 1

Softball is by no means fashioned only for males. Women not only play it well, they add grace and charm to a sport that is rapidly gaining popularity to surpass any other American game.

—Arthur Noren,
Softball with Official Rules

. . .

B ertha packed her suitcases neatly and deliberately, as she always did, making sure to keep her glove and other athletic gear separate from the skirts and blouses she would be wearing to the office. The next morning she would be moving across the country to a town nearly three thousand miles away where she knew no one. A man in Connecticut had offered her a job with his company if she would play on his softball team, and to her great surprise, she had accepted. It was 1956, and she was thirty-four years old, and her daughter and only child, Janice, was thirteen.

Before the job offer, Bertha hadn't considered leaving California. With the exception of a few years spent in Texas during World War II, she had lived there her whole life. She grew up in a small farming town outside Fresno and had a long list of friends and family in Orange County, where she had established herself as one of the best fastpitch pitchers in the country. She had led her team, the Orange Lionettes, to multiple national titles, and her success had made her a local celebrity. Fans would stop by her house looking for autographs, and MGM studios had hired her to teach Lana Turner how to pitch for the 1947 movie *Cass Timberlane*, which also starred Spencer Tracy.

Bertha was happy playing for the Lionettes, but it was rumored that the team would soon be losing its sponsorship. Some of her teammates were considering joining other California teams. Bertha was ready for a more drastic change, though. Bill Simpson, the man from Connecticut, was serious about softball, and he had a lot of money to spend on it. He had already paid for her to fly out to visit the town, an almost-unheard-of extravagance at a time when a cross-country plane ticket cost upward of $200, or nearly $2,000 in today's dollars. He had also assured Bertha that she and the team would be provided with the highest-quality uniforms and equipment available.

She had never played for what could be called a well-funded team before, and although money was hardly her main concern, she had to admit she liked the idea of it. Moving to New England would mean saying good-bye to summer days at Laguna Beach and pitching for a team that had barely played in a national tournament, let alone won one. She enjoyed a challenge, however, and what better way to prove that she was the best than to take a small team few people had heard of and turn it into a national champion?

By spring, Bertha and Simpson had a formal arrangement: She would spend her summers in Connecticut, working for him and playing on his softball team. Then, when the softball season was over, she would return to California and work in his company's Los Angeles office. That way, she could avoid the New England winters, and Simpson wouldn't be breaking the softball league's residence rules, which prohibited teams from bringing in out-of-town players just for the season, even though that was exactly what he was doing. She and her daughter, Janice, would come out to Connecticut as soon as the school year had ended. Her husband, Jim Ragan, would be staying back in Orange County, at least for the time being.

Simpson would be taking care of all of Bertha's housing and travel expenses. He also agreed to bring over Jo An Kammeyer, Bertha's catcher from the Lionettes, and to give her a job at the company, too. Softball players didn't usually receive such VIP treatment, but it wasn't unprecedented. Fastpitch may have been an amateur sport, but it was fiercely competitive. Many of the teams came from towns that were too small to have professional sports, even at the minor league level, and the teams were seen as a chance for their communities to get state and national recognition. Companies that sponsored the teams began hiring workers for their softball skills, and as the competition level ratcheted up, they started to look beyond the local talent pool and recruit players from other towns and other states. Simpson had already acquired a few out-of-state players for his company's men's fastpitch team, and it had netted him a national title. Now he was bringing in Bertha to do the same thing for his women's team.

Few would have pegged Bertha as an athlete if they met her on the street or at the office. She wasn't particularly tall or muscular, and with her flawless makeup and dark, salon-quality curls she came across as someone who abhorred dirt and never broke a sweat. On the softball field, though, her physical and mental toughness were instantly apparent. As a pitcher, she could be relentless. Even if her team was ahead by ten runs, she would continue to attack, throwing strike after strike. She did not subscribe to the win-some/lose-some approach to sports. She went into games expecting to come out on top; to her, anything less than a resounding victory was unacceptable. She never got angry, though, or showed any other outward signs of frustration. In fact, opponents were often unnerved by how calm and collected she seemed.

She had been an elite softball pitcher since she was in high school, and after more than fifteen years of practice, her technique was impeccable. She also kept mental notes on each batter she faced in order to exploit their weaknesses. At one game, she threw a pitch that sank toward the dirt so quickly, the opposing batter fell to her knees trying to hit it. "Don't do that again!" the batter called out to her somewhat playfully. Bertha smiled, then threw the exact same pitch, with the exact same result. It wasn't personal. She figured out the most efficient way to defeat her opponent and then executed that plan. As another player put it, "To prepare for a game she would press her uniform, have her hair done, and watch your batting practice. You didn't have a chance."

She held the national records in almost every pitching category: most strikeouts thrown, most no-hitters, most consecutive scoreless innings, most perfect games. She was widely considered to be one of the best softball pitchers of all-time, maybe even *the* best. Growing up with brothers on a farm had gotten her into baseball at a young age, but as a girl, Little League and other organized forms of the sport were off-limits to her. When she switched to softball at age thirteen, she had to play with girls five years older than her to get any real competition.

By age fifteen she had joined an adult team, and by age seventeen she had been recruited to play for the Lionettes, one of the best women's softball teams in California. Her older brother Sam would drive her down to Orange County as soon as the school year ended, and she would spend the summer traveling with the team, staying with the coach and his wife or with whichever teammate had a couch available that week.

After she graduated from high school, she moved to the town of Orange permanently. The softball season lasted for five months and included about eighty games if a team made it to the national tournament, which the Lionettes almost always did. It was never enough for Bertha, though. After a season ended, she would train on her own and wait anxiously for the next one to begin. It was much, much more than a hobby.

For Bertha and other women who were serious about sports in the 1940s and '50s, competitive fastpitch teams were a lifeline. Hardly any high schools or colleges offered women's sports programs, and those that did tended to emphasize socialization over athleticism. Swim meets featured punch and cookies, and the governing motto was "Play for play's sake." Being a top female athlete meant pushing hard when the other women around you were only half-trying and defying coaches who told you to slow down and take it easy. It took enormous determination and courage.

Most of the women who succeeded came from working-class backgrounds. They needed to earn a living, and they knew better than to believe the Victorian notions that prevailed at the time, which warned that strenuous physical activity put women at risk for infertility and premature death. Company-sponsored teams such as Simpson's gave them a steady job and a chance to realize their athletic potential all in one.

Janice had cried for days when she first found out about the move. She wanted to spend the summer playing with her friends and staying over at her grandparents' house as she usually did, not being stuck in some strange town on the other side of the country. But Bertha told her about all the adventures they would have—that they would be like explorers, learning about the East Coast together—and that seemed to change Janice's perspective a little.

They left Los Angeles on a clear, sunny day. The city's airport was much smaller back then, and flying out of it didn't require much of a process. Bertha and Janice said their good-byes, stepped through a waist-high metal gate, and within seconds were walking onto the plane. As they found their seats, they realized that two of Bing Crosby's sons were across the aisle from them. Celebrity sightings were common when one flew out of Los Angeles back then. At those prices, who else but movie stars and millionaires could afford to fly?

Bertha felt fortunate to be flying instead of driving, which would have taken a week or longer and would have required navigating a circuitous route of small highways, given that the interstate freeway system didn't yet exist (that would soon change, however, as President Eisenhower signed the Federal Highway Act later that year). Still, flying from Los Angeles to New York in 1956 was by no means an easy journey. It took a good eight hours, and because commercial planes were then powered by pistons instead of jets, the flights were notoriously loud and bumpy. Bertha didn't mind the noise that much, but the turbulence gave her terrible motion sickness. As Janice and the other passengers craned their necks to look out the windows at the Grand Canyon and other sights, she closed her eyes and tried to sleep.

They arrived in Stratford, the town where Bertha's new team was based, early enough in June that the air still turned chilly at times. You could start the day basking in the sun in short sleeves only to find yourself bundled up in a sweater by evening. The humidity was high that week, though, so it actually felt hotter to Bertha and Janice than Southern California did. Fortunately, the house that Simpson had arranged for them was right on Long Island Sound, with ocean breezes coming through the windows at night.

Bertha knew that adapting to the Connecticut climate was

going to be a challenge, but she was also excited about living in a place so different from what she knew. Stratford was the quintessential New England town, with tall stone churches and narrow, winding streets flanked by leafy oak trees. Its most famous landmark was a stout red-and-white-striped lighthouse that had been there since the 1800s. Bertha felt as if she'd stepped into the setting of a classic American novel such as *Little Women* or *Moby-Dick*.

Her favorite part of living there, though, was the large clapboard house where she, Janice, and Jo An, her catcher, would be staying that summer. It had high ceilings, a spacious kitchen, and, best of all, was mere steps away from the ocean. The water was frigid, and the beach was small compared to the ones in California, but it was perfect for sunbathing and breathing in the sea air. Most of their neighbors were tony New Yorkers who fled to Connecticut in the summers to escape the city heat. Bertha could only imagine what they thought of her and Jo An, clomping up and down the stairs in their softball cleats. She doubted if any of them ever came to one of their games even though the field, like most other locations in town, was a quick drive away.

Most of the town locals knew of and supported the team. About thirty thousand people lived in Stratford in the 1950s, and nearly all of them worked at either Sikorsky, which built helicopters, or Raybestos, Bill Simpson's company, which manufactured car-brake linings. Like many New England towns, Stratford had started out as a Puritan outpost, founded in the 1600s, but was becoming increasingly industrial as the early twentieth century wore on. Its proximity to New York and Boston made it an ideal manufacturing center. The factories moved in, and the sheep that had once freely roamed the town's streets moved out.

The shift away from rural living had been welcomed by most Stratford residents. Farming in that part of the country had always been difficult. The factories brought workers indoors, and an element of excitement and pride was attached to the products they made. Igor Sikorsky, a Russian immigrant, had essentially invented the modern helicopter, and his Stratford manufacturing plant was the sole helicopter supplier for the US military for many years. He also built an airport on the outskirts of town that became the site of many historic test flights.

Raybestos was less flashy, but its product was arguably just as significant. The brake linings that the company helped originate in the early 1900s made cars much safer to drive and were one of the reasons that the Model T, and car ownership in general, became popular. They were also used in military tanks during the two world wars and in race cars (Mario Andretti later appeared in company advertisements). The Brakettes, the team Bertha had been hired to pitch for, were named after them, and it was considered an honor.

Both Sikorsky and Raybestos were respected by the Stratford community and thought to be good companies to work for, but Raybestos had a slight edge because of Simpson. Comfortably in middle age, he was laid-back, friendly, and seemed to genuinely care about his employees' well-being. He bought Christmas presents for their children and attended their funerals when they died. Perhaps because he'd inherited the company from his father, or perhaps he was just quirky—he was known for his odd fashion choices, such as a cashmere blazer that some of the secretaries liked to pet as if it were a cat—but he often appeared to be more interested in the plant's sports teams than its profits. He was rumored to have sunk thousands of dollars of his own money into the Raybestos softball teams, not to mention the numerous other sports-related activities that the company sponsored: bowling, basketball, tennis, archery, and even a sailing-knot camp for kids.

· · ·

Between playing for the Brakettes and their clerical jobs at the Raybestos factory, it didn't take long for Bertha and Jo An to become part of the Stratford community. Bertha wasn't particularly interested in cars, but she enjoyed working at the company, and her job duties, which mostly consisted of organizing paperwork, weren't that different from what she'd been doing in California. She didn't make any lifelong friends at work, but she was outgoing, and she liked to socialize. Silence was great for tasks that required intense concentration, such as pitching practice, but otherwise she preferred being part of a group, the more talkative and lively the better.

Not surprisingly, she spent the most time with the employees who were associated with the company's softball teams. The guys who played on the men's softball team would come with their families to watch the women's games and vice versa. Afterward, they would all flock to Danny's Drive-In for hamburgers and hot dogs. It was an easy routine to fall into, and everyone seemed to get along with one another.

Bertha still considered California home, though, and at times she longed to go back. She particularly missed the food. One night that summer, she and Janice were craving tacos so badly that they drove all the way to Manhattan on a quest to find them. The best they could do was a South American restaurant that didn't serve tacos and also wasn't very good. They would have tried making them at home, but there didn't seem to be anywhere to buy tortillas other than the kind that came in a can. Salads, too, were a letdown. In California, Bertha always made green salads, with fresh-picked lettuce and ripe tomatoes, but the only salad people in Connecticut seemed to like was coleslaw.

Still, Bertha was enjoying Stratford. She loved Long Island Sound, and she couldn't get over how effortlessly green New England was. The forests were lush and thick in a way that she'd never seen out West, and all she had to do to have a beautiful lawn was let it rain and mow the grass—none of the elaborate watering and fertilizer regimens she'd learned in Southern California was necessary. Initially, she had thought of the move as a temporary experiment, but as the summer progressed, she was beginning to think she might like living there long term.

Janice would need more convincing. She still missed her friends and family back in Orange and couldn't help but think about all the fun they were having without her. Bertha made sure that Janice had plenty of activities to keep her busy, though. She signed her up for tennis lessons and, as promised, took her on several East Coast adventures. At every break in the softball schedule, they would hop in the car Simpson had given them to use for the summer and head out on an excursion. They toured the House of Seven Gables in Salem, Massachusetts, went through Amish country in Pennsylvania, and visited the Lincoln Memorial in Washington, DC. They marveled at how close together everything was in the East, not like in the West, where it took the better part of a day just to drive to the next state.

When Bertha had to travel with the Brakettes, she would arrange for Janice to stay with her teammates' families. Some of the younger players became like sisters to Janice, and their parents were happy to incorporate her into their summer plans. One of the families had a lake house, which Janice enjoyed visiting. What she loved most, though, was spending time with her mom at the house on Long Island Sound. The two of them often cooked dinner together, and Janice learned to do the grocery shopping so that all the ingredients would be ready when Bertha and Jo An got home from work. Before bed, Janice and Bertha would trade stories about whatever new tidbits they had picked up that day—maybe a new idea for a place to go on a day trip or a funny variation of the New England accent that they hadn't heard before. They really were like explorers, Janice realized.

· · ·

With the Brakettes, Bertha's role was as the seasoned expert. Her job was to teach the team the ways of the West Coast teams that had dominated women's softball for the past decade. In exchange for her efforts, Simpson had given her free rein over the team. One of the first things she changed was the uniforms, which featured baggy cotton pants modeled after the ones male players wore. Bertha could put up with playing in variable weather conditions, but she refused to play in pants. It had to be shorts, she insisted, and not just any shorts: they needed to be made of shiny "jockey satin" and have custom-tailored tops to match. She was used to playing in this attire. Plus, she thought it was important for women's uniforms to look attractive, which, to her, meant formfitting. It wouldn't have occurred to her that not all the players on the team cared about their appearance or what their uniforms looked like.

By the time Bertha was done with them, the Brakettes' uniforms looked remarkably similar to the Lionettes'. The main difference was the color scheme: the Lionettes' uniforms were white and Creamsicle orange, while the Brakettes' were white and red to match those of the Cardinals, the Raybestos men's softball team. The shorts were short, and the shirts were tight. In fact, they weren't really shirts at all, but shirt-leotard hybrids, held in place by two pieces of fabric that buttoned together at the crotch. The shirts also featured a flared collar and pocket and were separated from the shorts by a fashionable but otherwise functionless white belt.

The whole ensemble was shiny, to the point that it was almost blinding under the field lights. Not all the players liked wearing it—some objected on stylistic grounds, while others, quite understandably, were wary of the injuries that sliding on hard-as-concrete dirt in bare legs could cause—but most felt it was a small concession, given the quality of pitcher they were getting in return. Besides, nearly all the top women's softball teams wore shorts in the 1950s. The trend had started on the West Coast, but it had become so widespread by the late forties that newspapers considered it noteworthy if a team wore pants. Bertha also told her new teammates that they shouldn't be sliding unless it was an important game; otherwise, it wasn't worth the risk of getting injured.

Bertha could tell from her first practice with the team that there was some talent on the roster. What they lacked, she decided, was confidence. Getting her teammates to think of themselves as national rather than regional, great instead of merely good, became her first priority after she got the uniforms changed. Bernie Kaplan, a longtime Raybestos employee, was technically the team's coach, but Bertha was its philosophical leader. She knew better than anyone that confidence was more about attitude than skill. She had a decent arm, but her pitching prowess came from psychology, not strength. She believed that she could outsmart every batter she faced, and she was so determined to do so that she usually succeeded.

She was at least ten years older than the other women on the team. Some were fresh out of high school. Joan Joyce, a pitcher-in-training, was only fifteen, just two years older than Janice. Still, Bertha's teammates shared a common history. Like her, they had been kicked off boys' baseball teams growing up and had been disappointed by the other athletic options available to them. They didn't need to be pushed so much as given permission to push themselves. They needed someone to tell them that it was okay to be competitive and to try as hard as possible. Bertha gave them permission not only to try, but to strive.

Sometimes, Bertha would invite the team over to the beach house in the evenings to discuss techniques and strategies. She knew everything there was to know about the West Coast teams that they would have to beat if they wanted to win a national championship. In addition to several California teams, there were the Phoenix Ramblers and the Salt Lake City Shamrocks, both of which were sponsored by retail stores, and the Portland, Oregon, Florists, who were sponsored and coached by a local florist. The Brakettes usually only saw these teams once a season, if that, but Bertha had been playing against them regularly for years. She knew what it felt like to defeat them, and she told her new teammates that they soon would, too.

Bertha pitched most of the Brakettes' games that summer, and the team breezed through their regional season, winning 38 out of 43 games. The more they won, the more the town of Stratford turned out to watch them. The bleachers at Memorial Field could accommodate about four thousand fans at the time, but the crowds at the Brakettes' games that season were often twice that size. The away games proved the biggest obstacle for Bertha. The Raybestos field was similar in quality to what she was used to playing on in California, but many of the other ones in the New England area were in rough shape. Some of them weren't even flat, and Bertha had to train herself to look down periodically during games so that she didn't trip and fall.

In September the time came for the Brakettes to see how they fared against the best teams in the country. Simpson paid for the team to fly down to Clearwater, Florida, to compete in the national tournament. It was a definite upgrade from the days-long bus trips Bertha was used to taking with the Lionettes. Simpson also met the team at the Raybestos factory before they went to the airport and handed each player an envelope that contained a congratulatory letter and $10 for "incidental expenses during the trip."

The Brakettes had played in the national tournament before,

but they were always eliminated fairly early. This time, though, they almost made it to the finals. Bertha pitched all of the six games that they played. Kammeyer wasn't able to be her catcher, however. She had broken her ankle sliding into third base during a game before the tournament—she hadn't heeded Bertha's warning about that—and so was there only as a spectator. Micki Macchietto, an eighteen-year-old newcomer to the team, was put in as her replacement, and she did quite well. Her hitting also helped the team win a crucial game against the Portland Florists.

Then the night before the finals, the Brakettes lost to the Buena Park Lynx, a Southern California team Bertha knew inside and out. Bertha was disappointed by the loss, which knocked the Brakettes out of the tournament. It had been an extremely close game, though. It went into extra innings and only one run was scored; a walk and a triple had done it. She was proud of her teammates' performance, and she tried to convince them of this, but it was no use. They knew how much she had wanted to win, and they felt they'd let her down.

The Lionettes, who hadn't lost their sponsorship after all, won the 1956 title. Bertha was happy for them—if anyone was going to win besides her team, she wanted it to be the Lionettes—but it stung a bit. She wondered if maybe she'd made the wrong choice. She knew that she probably only had a few playing years left, and she didn't want to spend them losing. Even though she had already accomplished so much in her softball career, she wanted to end it on a high note. Still, she wasn't going to give up on her new team just yet. She decided she would give it at least one more season. After all, she told herself, she hadn't won her first tournament with the Lionettes, either.

Simpson promised her that he would do even more to support the team the next summer, starting with scheduling more competitive regular-season games and bringing in a more experienced coach. By spring, Bertha was looking forward to returning to Connecticut. She would be staying in the beach house again, and Simpson had given her permission to bring another former Lionette with her (she chose Beverly Connors, her friend, who was also a great batter and infielder). Janice graduated from eighth grade that year, and she wasn't surprised when she opened her present from her mom: a brand-new suitcase.

CHAPTER 2

Its shorter distance has made softball play possible in large cities where the real estate and building business have gobbled up most of the vacant lots on which our fathers and grandfathers played baseball.

—Morris Bealle, *The Softball Story*

. . .

Softball wasn't always so serious. It developed informally and haphazardly, and for decades it didn't even have a name. George Hancock, a reporter for the *Chicago Board of Trade* newspaper, is credited with the sport's invention. He and a group of friends had gathered in the gymnasium at the prestigious Farragut Boat Club to watch the annual Thanksgiving Harvard-Yale football game, which in 1887 meant waiting for the results to come via telegraph on a ticker-tape machine. The game was close, but Yale eventually won, 17–8, giving Harvard its only loss of the season.

The exact details of what happened next are difficult to verify, but according to historians, one of the Yale fans celebrated the victory by grabbing a boxing glove off the floor and tossing it in the air, to which one of the Harvard men responded by smacking the glove down with a broomstick. The incident might have turned into a fistfight had Hancock not been there, but he was intrigued by the idea of playing baseball with a boxing glove and convinced the other men to try it out with him. Their impromptu game wound up lasting several hours. Hancock organized a few other indoor baseball games around Chicago that winter, and by spring the sport had become so popular that people began taking it outdoors.

Baseball was still the dominant sport in the United States in the late nineteenth century, but the bucolic landscape that had given rise to the game was fast disappearing. Baseball was said to have originated in the American colonies as a hybrid of the British games cricket and rounders; it was meant to be played on vast expanses of grass. Elysian Fields, where the first known organized baseball game took place in the 1840s, was a wide, open pasture in New Jersey that didn't even have an outfield fence. Even though most of the players came from Northeastern cities, such as New York and Philadelphia, the parks where they played were always in the more rural outskirts. Such spaces were becoming a rarity by the late 1800s, though, when American cities began expanding at a rapid pace. The empty fields that had surrounded New York and other urban centers before the Civil War were being swallowed up by factories and residential neighborhoods.

Chicago's transformation into a metropolis was particularly sudden. In the early 1860s, it had been a quiet agricultural city with a population of only about one hundred thousand. The railroad totally changed its dynamic, however. It became the central commercial hub that connected the raw materials of the West and Midwest with the industrial cities of the Northeast. Meatpacking plants and steel mills arose where once there had only been farms and swamps, and people from all over the Midwest began moving to the area in droves. By 1890, the city's population had reached 1.1 million. It was said that no other city in the Western world had ever grown so big so quickly.

The urban setting and cramped living quarters created a need for a new kind of recreation, a game that could be played in tight spaces and on any surface, be it grass, dirt, or concrete. Softball provided an easy solution because it was highly adaptable, and it resembled a sport people already knew and liked. Compared to baseball, it was also fast paced—games often finished in under two hours—which made it a good fit for factory workers who were short on free time.

By the early 1900s, softball had a strong following in Chicago and was starting to spread across the Midwest and the Northeast. "In New York, prominent men play even in the snow of winter and enjoy it," a Connecticut newspaper reported in 1915. Hancock published a set of rules for his version of the game, which he continued to call indoor baseball, but they were vague and also weren't widely distributed, leaving people to come up with their own interpretations. The size of the ball and distance between the bases varied from place to place, as did the name of the game. In Minneapolis, where the sport was popular with firemen, it was called kitten ball because they played with a ball of yarn wrapped in leather. In other cities, it was known by such names as mush ball, big ball, town ball, and playground ball.

The main constants were that the ball was larger than a baseball and the pitching was underhand, which seemed to evolve naturally from using a larger ball. Otherwise, there were all sorts of differences, from the number of innings played to the way points were tallied. A set of "playground ball" rules from 1908 even allowed batters to run around the bases in either direction. With so many competing versions of the sport, teams from different states had trouble playing each other. Sometimes teams from the same state couldn't even agree on the rules. Finally, in the late 1920s, the Young Men's Christian Association (YMCA) helped to standardize the game, instituting a more concrete set of rules and giving it a single name: softball.

The YMCA and other religiously affiliated groups liked softball because they saw it as a wholesome alternative to baseball, which, like most professional sports in the early twentieth century, was associated with heavy drinking and gambling. And few organizations were more influential in American sports in the 1920s than the YMCA. Not only was it the main source of recreation in many communities, but it had recently given the country two new sports—volleyball and basketball—that were becoming immensely popular.

The YMCA, along with the American Physical Education Association and a few other national recreation groups, narrowed the ball-size options down to two—twelve inches or fourteen inches in circumference—and set the number of innings at seven, two less than baseball, which helped ensure that games stayed short. There were still regional variations. For example, in Chicago, a gloveless version of the sport called for a sixteen-inch ball. Softball was gradually shedding its improvised beginnings, though, and was advancing on the path toward legitimacy.

Meanwhile, factories embraced softball as a way to keep workers active and in good spirits. Industrialization and the cities that came with it were no longer new, but they were still recent enough to worry people about the harms of working indoors, surrounded by metal and glass instead of trees and sky. Physical activity, especially team sports, was believed to help workers maintain their humanity. "The machine age has given us more routine, mechanized jobs. These jobs demand a righting of an outraged biological balance through some form of play," wrote Stuart Chase, an economist and social theorist, in the 1928 essay collection *Whither Mankind: A Panorama of Modern Civilization*.

After the stock market crashed in 1929, softball gave the newly jobless a cheap way to pass the time. Games would start up spontaneously in the streets, but cities also organized them in the hopes that sports would help ward off violence and other disorderly behaviors. Games were held in the parks and playgrounds that had been built in large numbers during the mid-1920s, when cities were flush with cash and wanted to give children places to play. Because softball only required about two hundred square feet of space, about half the size of a baseball field, many parks were able to hold multiple games at once.

In 1933, the first national softball tournament was held, in Chicago, as part of the 1933 World's Fair. Even though it was the height of the Great Depression—Chicago's unemployment rate had recently reached an alarming 40 percent—millions of people turned out to explore the fair. The theme was "A Century of Progress," to commemorate Chicago's centennial, and the motto, "Science Finds, Industry Applies, Man Conforms," inspired a host of futuristic attractions. Attendees could tour a "House of Tomorrow" that featured electric doors and an airplane hangar, and they could soar above the fairgrounds in the gondola-like SkyRide, which transported people 210 feet in the air between two bridge towers.

Softball was a late addition to the fair and wasn't included in the official program. Leo Fischer, the sports reporter who organized the tournament, used most of the $500 budget he was given to promote the event and had to get extra money from his newspaper's publisher, William Randolph Hearst, to provide trophies for the winning teams. A fourteen-inch ball was used, probably in part to accommodate Chicago players, who were used to playing with a sixteen-inch ball, and twenty-four teams participated: sixteen men's and eight women's.

The three-day tournament didn't receive much press coverage outside of the *Chicago American*, where Fischer worked. Other sports events at the fair, such as the horseshoe-throwing contest, seemed to garner much more attention. The softball games were free, though, and they were played on Northerly Island, near where the Hall of Science, one of the fair's most popular attractions, was located. By the end of the tournament, a combined 350,000 spectators had reportedly watched the games.

The tournament's success led to the formation of the Amateur Softball Association, a full-time organization to govern the sport in the United States and Canada. Fischer became the group's president, and he and the other members decided that Chicago would host a national tournament every year, starting in 1934. That fall, teams representing twenty-five different states and Canada competed for the national title, and Fischer's operating budget had gone up to more than $5,000. By the 1935 tournament, teams from thirty-five states participated, and by 1936, forty-one states were represented.

Fifty years after its invention, softball had become as complicated and sophisticated as its parent sport: it was no longer just a community game to get people moving and boost worker morale. Male players began switching over from baseball, and many found that they preferred softball. Others liked that softball allowed them to spend most of their time playing sports without being a professional athlete, which wasn't viewed as a respectable career choice at the time.

By the late 1930s, tens of thousands of competitive softball teams had formed across North America, nearly all of them sponsored by local businesses or civic organizations, such as the YMCA. Even the White House had a softball team, which played in upstate New York during the summers (President Roosevelt was said to coach from the third-base line). "It's a curious game, this softball, that has already the greatest following of any single pastime in the land," Lowell Thomas, news reporter and radio personality, wrote in a 1937 article.

As the sport grew more competitive, the smaller, faster twelve-inch ball became the standard, which, in turn, made the pitching more advanced. The mushy, boxing-glove-size balls that Hancock and other early softball players used didn't give pitchers many options beyond gently lobbing the ball to batters. With the more structured twelve-inch ball, however, a variety of throwing styles were possible. Some pitchers liked to send the ball in from the side as if they were throwing a low discus. Others began experimenting with different windups, such as the windmill, in which one circled the ball around one's shoulder like a swimmer doing the backstroke. The ball was thrown hard, and when it hit you, it hurt, as anyone who got in the way of a pitch soon discovered. The sport's name, though only about a decade old, was already outdated, based on equipment and throwing styles that were no longer used.

Slowpitch softball, which retained the lobbing pitching style from the early 1900s, was still played, but it was seen as a game for children and senior citizens. Fastpitch, or fastball as it was known in Canada and parts of the Midwest, became the mainstream form of the sport. The underhand pitching was the main component that set it apart from baseball, not just in appearance but from a technical standpoint as well. Baseball players who thought they would be able to cross over to the sport and get hits right away were sorely mistaken.

The ball used in fastpitch may have been larger and thrown slower than the one used in baseball, but the distance between the pitcher and batter was about twenty feet shorter. By the time a softball pitcher stepped forward and threw the ball, he or she was often mere steps away from the hitter—almost close enough to shake hands, some said—which could be disorienting, especially to players who weren't used to it. It also meant that batters had less time to react to the pitch: hitters barely had a chance to swing the bat, let alone decipher what type of pitch was coming their way.

And the underhand delivery gave softball pitchers a wide

range of pitches to choose from, including some that didn't even exist in baseball. There were knuckleballs, multiple types of curveballs, drop balls that plummeted toward the dirt, and their inverse, rise balls, which looked like enticingly hittable pitches but then abruptly snapped up above the batter's swing. The rise ball was the pitch that baseball players usually struggled with most. Unique to softball, it was made possible by the underhand throwing motion, which allowed pitchers to release the ball low. In baseball, where pitchers throw overhand and stand on an elevated mound, the release point is inherently high, which means the ball can go down in the strike zone but never up. A 1936 newspaper article depicted the challenge of being a softball batter in comic-strip form: "Why waste the effort swinging?" read the speech bubble above the illustrated batter as strike three blew past him. "With that guy hurlin' I couldn't hit it even if the ball were the size of a balloon."

Baseball players had so much trouble facing softball pitchers that pitting them against each other became a popular form of entertainment. Vaudeville was dying out in the 1930s, but barnstorming sports acts, such as the Harlem Globetrotters, which traveled from town to town, challenging local teams, were still doing well. Crowds loved to watch powerful baseball sluggers struggle with a task that seemed as if it should have been easy for them. It had a humanizing appeal, much like the widespread but untrue rumor that Einstein had flunked math as a kid, which began circulating around the same time.

One of the most high-profile matchups of a baseball hitter versus a softball pitcher occurred in 1937, when Babe Ruth faced John "Cannonball" Baker at a children's charity event in New York. Ruth was in his early forties and had been retired from professional baseball for two years. Baker, on the other hand, was only twenty-five and at the top of his game. Still, people expected Ruth to get a hit of some kind. Instead, he struck out miserably. After swinging and missing at fifteen pitches in a row, Ruth allegedly turned to the catcher and said, "If you're catching those, you might as well catch them in front of the plate because I can't hit them."

In baseball, it was often possible to wait for pitchers to tire themselves out, but softball pitchers rarely got fatigued and hardly ever had to be replaced by relief pitchers. Throwing underhand is less stressful on the arm, and fastpitch games are shorter, with only seven innings to baseball's nine. As a result, pitchers dominated in softball even more so than they did in baseball. Home runs were rare, while pitchers' duels—low-scoring games that mostly consisted of pitchers trading strikeouts—were common. A softball team without a strong pitcher had little chance of winning games.

Fastpitch batters did have an advantage over their baseball counterparts when it came to baserunning, though. The smaller infield—sixty feet between the bases instead of the ninety feet in baseball—meant that it didn't take much of a hit to get on base. Tapping the ball with the bat, or bunting, became the cornerstone of many softball teams' offensive strategies. In baseball, bunting was usually a sacrifice play, meant to advance a runner who was already on base. In fastpitch, however, a well-placed bunt could easily get a batter to first base and possibly to second in the event of a missed throw. Softball infielders had a shorter distance to cover than their baseball counterparts, but the fast baserunning forced them to be even more precise. A small fielding mistake that would be of no consequence in baseball could lead to a run scored in softball.

Base stealing also became an important offensive weapon for fastpitch teams. Softball players weren't encouraged to steal bases during the sport's early years. A rule even prohibited runners from leaving their base until after a pitch had crossed home plate.

That changed when the pitching improved in the mid-1930s, and the Amateur Softball Association was eager to facilitate more offense. Although players couldn't take both feet off the base, as they can in baseball, they were allowed to start running as soon as the ball left the pitcher's hand, which made stealing much easier.

The speedy baserunning made fastpitch games more exciting—it was the reason the sport was called lightning ball in some places—and it meant that the best batters were often the scrawniest players on their teams, which reinforced softball's status as an everyman's game. "The small wiry player with instantaneous reflexes and quick get-away is the star of softball," Morris Bealle proclaimed in *The Softball Story*.

The fields where softball was being played were changing, too. After experiencing the grandeur of the World's Fair, players didn't want to go back to playing on abandoned lots, and they didn't have to. Companies began building proper fields for the softball teams they sponsored, complete with bleachers and lights, and outfitting the players with uniforms and manufactured equipment.

The Midwest and Northeast, where the nation's industrial cities were concentrated, tended to have the best softball teams of the 1930s. They had the most money and a ready supply of players who had experience with the game. Rochester, New York, had a championship-winning men's team sponsored by the Eastman Kodak company, which was headquartered there. The team's star player was a bespectacled sheet-metal worker named Harold "Shifty" Gears. Other top teams of the decade included the Ke-Nash-A's, who were sponsored by the Kenosha, Wisconsin–based Nash Motors company, and the Carpenter Steelies from Reading, Pennsylvania.

There were always smaller teams mixed in with the industrial powerhouses, though, and it wasn't unheard of for the national title to go to a team sponsored by a local restaurant, hotel, or retail store. The well-funded teams may have made softball more competitive, but the proliferation of small-community teams drove the sport's growth. Teams that couldn't afford to build their own fields could easily make do with the available public parks if necessary, and they didn't have to win at the national level to be popular.

The lower cost of fielding teams and organizing games benefited spectators, too. Many Americans were still recovering from the Depression and needed affordable entertainment options. The cost of a softball game was rarely more than twenty-five cents and was often free, which was cheaper than a movie or a professional baseball game. The more fans came to the games, the more new teams formed. In Portland, Oregon, which had fourteen different adult softball leagues, fans could get a season pass for twenty-five cents. By 1938, the city had an estimated three softball players for every baseball player, leading a reporter for the *Oregonian* newspaper to wonder if it was still accurate to call "old-fashioned baseball" America's national sport.

CHAPTER 3

Several years of playing and coaching softball have convinced me that it is truly a grand game. Only those who
are all thumbs and never can catch a ball without jam-
ming a finger fail to fall victim to its charms.

—Viola Mitchell, *Softball for Girls*

. . .

At first, there were many more men's softball teams than
women's. For example, just fourteen women's teams competed at the 1935 national tournament compared to forty-two
male teams. That disparity was gradually disappearing, though.
Women had been playing softball almost since its inception, when
it was primarily an indoor game. Because softball, like basketball,
was a newer sport, it was easier for women to break into than
sports, such as baseball and football, that were seen as traditionally male.

And unlike in basketball, which didn't offer a national tournament for women until about twenty years after the first men's
competition was held, women had always been included in the
national softball tournament. "We didn't think it would go very
well, but we didn't want to slight the ladies. They could have
their chance if they wanted it," Leo Fischer, the sports reporter
who organized the World's Fair tournament, later said. Women's

softball players also played by the same rules as their male counterparts—the only significant difference was that the pitching distance was slightly closer—whereas women's basketball was considerably different from the men's version: dribbling was limited and each side had six players instead of five, only three of whom could cross the half-court line.

The result was that softball became one of the few sports that women in the 1930s were permitted to play and the only major team sport that put men and women more or less on equal footing. The number of women's teams increased, and crowds turned out to watch them, partly for the novelty of seeing women play sports but also to support them. Americans were starting to become more accepting of female athletes in the thirties, thanks to the recent celebrity achieved by tennis player Helen Wills Moody and by Babe Didrikson Zaharias, who won three track-and-field medals at the 1932 Olympics and then became a champion golfer. It also helped that softball was a community game. Fans were less likely to have a problem with women playing sports when they knew the women personally as coworkers and neighbors.

By the late 1930s, women's softball was more popular than men's in many places. "Women's softball has grown tremendously despite the comparatively small amount of newspaper and radio plugging it has received," a writer for *Esquire* magazine observed. "A young lady who works at the neighborhood plow plant or dairy outdraws Hedy Lamarr or Ann Sheridan in many a community where these females are competitively billed as entertainment. When the local young lady known as Butch, Spike, or Mickey can do that, you may be sure that she appeals to fundamental instincts."

Cities embraced women's softball, too. In the summer of 1938, it even moved back indoors, when Madison Square Garden in New York City started hosting biweekly women's softball games. The host team, the New York Roverettes, would challenge visiting teams from all over the country. These exhibition games, which were sanctioned by the Amateur Softball Association but weren't part of the regular softball season, drew crowds of nine thousand or more at seventy-five cents a ticket. The *New Yorker* published a short article on the games that summer. "I believe anything done well by girls will sell in New York," the magazine quoted the Roverettes coach as saying, to which the editors added, "And we couldn't deny it."

One of the most popular players at the Madison Square Garden games was Freda Savona, a shortstop from Ohio. She had started out as a basketball player, but she chose to focus on softball when she got older because it offered more opportunities to travel and earn money. Before she was out of high school, Savona was winning national titles with the Cleveland-based National Screw & Manufacturing team. The team she played with at the Garden was sponsored by the Num Num Food Company, one of the first potato-chip manufacturers.

Savona wasn't that tall, but she was muscular and strong. Sometimes before games she would entertain the crowd by throwing balls from the outfield to home plate with pinpoint accuracy. Tris Speaker, a former player and manager for the Cleveland Indians, said her throwing arm was one of the best he'd ever seen in baseball or softball. She could also hit the ball hard and run fast—she was said to be able to run the hundred-yard dash in eleven seconds—which meant that she usually had the highest batting average on her team.

By the time she was recruited to play for the newly formed Jax Maids team in New Orleans, when she was twenty-one years old, the *Times-Picayune* newspaper wrote that she had already been written about so much "that it would be useless to elaborate further." She moved to New Orleans with her eighteen-year-old sister, Olympia. The New Orleans coach had originally only planned to recruit Freda, but when he got to Ohio, he saw Olympia clock a boy in the head with a snowball from a half a block away and decided he wanted her for the team, too.

Together, the Savona sisters helped turn the Jax Maids into a national sensation. The Jackson Brewery, the company that sponsored the team, sent them all over North America. During the 1939 season, the Savonas' first with the team, they traveled to New York to play at Madison Square Garden and also to Detroit, Louisville, and Toronto—pretty much anywhere that had a strong women's team. Before long everyone in softball knew the Jax Maids, or Brewers as they were sometimes called.

Playing for a company softball team wasn't usually lucrative, but it was exciting, even glamorous, compared to what most women were doing for work in the thirties. Only about 25 percent of women in the United States had jobs at all, and those who did were limited to the lowest-status, lowest-paying professions: sewing, teaching, clerical work, and domestic service. Female employees rarely received the kind of job protections their male counterparts were starting to get, such as a forty-hour workweek. Women were expected to work long hours without extra pay and were often the first ones terminated when an employer decided to make cuts.

Married women had an even tougher time finding work. The public works jobs that were part of President Roosevelt's New Deal program were preferentially given to men and were limited to one person per household. The only way a married woman could qualify for these jobs was if she could prove that her husband was physically incapable of working. Several private sector employers, such as banks, prohibited the hiring of married women outright. The consensus was that for a woman to work once she was a wife and mother was inappropriate, no matter how bad off her family's finances might be.

The situation was different for women who played softball,

though. Not only did they enjoy greater job security, but they were valued by their employers. Most were single, but more than a few were married with children. They received housing assistance if they needed it and were given high-paying secretarial positions even if they'd never used a typewriter before.

Then there was the travel. Few teams traveled as much as the Jax Maids did, but most at least took occasional trips to Madison Square Garden and to Chicago for the national tournament. For many of the women, the majority of whom came from humble backgrounds, just leaving their home state was an adventure. It was an opportunity to see famous landmarks, such as Radio City Music Hall and Niagara Falls, and to visit relatives they wouldn't have met otherwise because they lived too far away. They got to go out and explore at a time when many women barely left the house. It was like getting to step into someone else's life. All they had to do in return was play well and, ideally, win their sponsors a championship or two.

When the 1939 national tournament came around that September, there seemed little doubt that the Jax Maids would win. They had Freda Savona, along with three other players who had been on the Cleveland team that had won the '36 and '37 championships. By touring so much over the summer, they had also gotten to play against most of their potential opponents, whereas other teams would be going in blind. They were among the best-rested teams, too, having arrived in Chicago by train three days before the tournament was to start.

The national tournament had grown considerably in the six years since the 1933 World's Fair. Not only were there more teams from more parts of the country, but the competition was held at Soldier Field, Chicago's preeminent sports venue, and the gold trophies awarded to the winners had become so heavy that it took two men to lift them. Press coverage of the event had improved, too, and celebrities, such as clarinetist Benny Goodman, were known to attend the games.

There were so many teams—fifty-six men's teams and thirty-four women's teams, a total of ninety—that the tournament organizers had to hold marathon fourteen-hour sessions to get through the early rounds. If it rained, as it had in 1938, it could throw the whole schedule off by a day or more. The hardest part for the players was the single-elimination format, which meant a team was out after one loss. After saving up money for months and traveling long distances by car or train, the majority of the teams would get to play only one or two games before being sent home.

The players were willing to put up with the potential hardships and heartbreak, though, to compete in the tournament. There were other softball competitions, but none was as grand as the ASA's. It even featured an opening ceremony, during which all of the teams paraded around the field in their uniforms, holding their state flags, while a marching band played music. It wasn't quite the Olympics or the Major League Baseball World Series, but for many of the players it was close enough. Lining up with their teammates under the stadium lights at Soldier Field and looking out at the thousands of fans in the bleachers made them feel proud and significant. It was the kind of experience that stayed with people their whole lives.

The Jax Maids got through the early rounds of the tournament easily. They ran into trouble when they went up against the Phoenix Ramblers, however. The Jax had played the Ramblers in a three-game series earlier that month and won all three games. But when they faced them in Chicago, they couldn't seem to bring a run across the plate, despite loading the bases in the fifth inning. The Ramblers only got three hits off the Jax pitcher, but it was enough to score a run, which was all they needed to win.

The Jax were done; they would have to go back to New Orleans without even having made it to the semifinals. They'd had so many advantages coming into the tournament, but on the field they'd come up short.

The team that did win the women's trophy that year had a completely different background: they were poor, composed almost entirely of local players, and were from California, where softball was popular but wasn't nearly as established as it was in such places as Chicago and Cleveland. Had they not won the tournament the year before, they would have been considered underdogs. They were named after their sponsor, a local clothing retailer named J. J. Krieg, but he didn't give them much financial support. In 1938, after becoming the first softball team from west of the Mississippi River to win the national tournament, they found themselves stuck in Chicago with no money. Fans back in Alameda, their hometown, had to conduct a last-minute fund-raising campaign so that the team could buy train tickets home and pay off their hotel bill.

The Kriegs' experience at the 1939 tournament was equally rocky. While the Jax Maids were taking in the sights and relaxing after getting to Chicago early, the Kriegs were delayed by a missed train connection and arrived at the tournament a day late. They still had financial problems, too. They had enough money to get home this time, but that was only because they had borrowed $1,800 from local businesses. They would have to do more fund-raising after the tournament to pay the money back.

They were a resilient team, though, and they had a phenomenal pitcher: the young Bessie Johnson, originally from Stockton, California. Her pitching was the main reason that the Kriegs had been able to defeat the hometown favorites, the Chicago Down Drafts, at the previous year's tournament. Despite the cold, drizzling conditions, Johnson had kept the Chicago players from getting a hit until the last inning, allowing her team to win the game,

3–0. In the final of the 1939 tournament, which the Kriegs played against the Louisville Dairy Maids, Johnson didn't give up a single hit and only walked two batters.

No doubt, the Jax Maids would have recruited Johnson if they could have. She seemed to have little interest in leaving California, though, and she wasn't alone. Even though softball was somewhat new to the state, it had taken off quickly, with dozens of competitive men's and women's teams already. The sunny, pleasant climate allowed players to practice outdoors year-round, and burgeoning industries, such as agriculture and logging, ensured that a steady supply of young people flowed into the region.

California also took recreation seriously and exuded an almost manic enthusiasm for all things athletic. By the 1930s, the state was producing top contenders in a wide range of sports, including football, tennis, golf, baseball, and rowing, and had begun introducing new ones, such as beach volleyball. It was as if playing sports were an obligatory part of living there—one that every man, woman, and child was expected to participate in, be they movie stars, housewives, or farm kids.

California didn't have any major professional sports teams until 1946, and as a result, its amateur sports scene thrived. Los Angeles hosted the Summer Olympics in 1932, and nearby Pasadena was home to the Rose Bowl, college football's premier event. California's universities boasted some of the most competitive athletic programs in the country and were also among the most progressive. UC Berkeley and Stanford made history in 1896 when they allowed their female students to play basketball against each other (most schools didn't allow intercollegiate play between women until the 1930s). A few decades later, UCLA became one of the first schools in the United States to have racially integrated sports teams. Its 1939 integrated football team included future sports legend Jackie Robinson, the first African American to play in Major League Baseball, and Kenny Washington, one of the first African Americans to play in the National Football League.

California had so many fastpitch teams by the 1940s that the Amateur Softball Association decided to split the state into two regions. The California teams weren't always the most talented in the nation, and they definitely weren't the richest, but they did have momentum. They had gone from nonexistent to elite in just a few years, and they were continuing to improve. It seemed only a matter of time before they took over the sport completely.

CHAPTER 4

The outdoor life and athletic training, when properly pursued, tends to increase the beauty of a girl.

—The Softball Story

. . .

Around this time, Bertha first joined the Orange Lionettes team. Softball had become so popular in California that it was almost impossible to avoid. Bertha hadn't found out about the sport until she was a teenager, though. On the farm where she grew up, the only girl among six brothers, they played baseball.

Her family was new to the United States, although they were practically old-timers in California, having preceded the Dust Bowl migrants from Oklahoma and Kansas by more than twenty years. Bertha's parents, Chetko and Andje Petinak, were from the same village in Bosnia-Herzegovina. Like so many immigrants before them, they came to the United States to seek a better life. They changed their first names to John and Anna and made their way to California in 1913 with the goal of living off the land. Then they settled in the tiny town of Dinuba, about thirty miles southeast of Fresno, to be part of the Serbian community there.

Bertha's father was a short but strongly built man with stern eyes and a neatly trimmed mustache. Her mother had been the village beauty. She had long dark hair that she usually pulled back into a bun, a full mouth, and large, almost haunting light brown eyes. Bertha was the fifth of their seven children and the first to be born in a hospital, although there was still no official record of her birth. Her parents and their neighbors only spoke Serbian at home, and she didn't learn English until she started school. Nearly all of her classmates at the two-room schoolhouse she attended were the children of immigrants—mostly from Europe but a few from Asia, too. In their dusty shoes and loose-fitting dresses and overalls, they were all immediately recognizable as rural and poor.

The Petinaks' farm was in the middle of the San Joaquin Valley, which was one of the most robust agricultural regions in the United States and remains the country's leading produce source to this day. They grew vegetables and all sorts of fruits, including grapes, figs, and pomegranates. They hardly ever had to go to the store except for staples, such as flour. The farm, a small operation, was meant for family use. They had few animals beyond a milking cow and a couple of pigs that they would butcher in the winter. To earn money, Bertha's father worked as a cattle rancher on other people's land.

The house they lived in was simple but inviting. It had three bedrooms and a sleeping porch that was occupied by at least one kid most nights. As the only girl in the family, it fell to Bertha to help her mother with the long list of indoor chores, which included baking bread from scratch, cleaning, and hand-washing and mending clothes. It was training for the adult life she was expected to lead one day.

On weekends, the Petinaks' already-full house would become even more crowded when their Serbian neighbors would come over for drinking and dancing. Bertha would help her parents roll up the rugs and move the furniture against the walls to clear space for the revelers and the various musical instruments they brought with them. She would watch, enchanted, as the men and women performed the folk dances they had learned in their native villages. On Mondays, she would go back to her regular routine of going to school and helping out around the house. It wasn't necessarily an exciting life, but she was never bored.

Then, in 1936, when Bertha was fourteen years old, her father died suddenly of what most suspected was a heart attack. Within a year, her mother was gone, too, at the age of forty-five. Ovarian cysts were the likely cause of death, although she was never properly diagnosed by a doctor. All the children were told was that she had hemorrhaged and bled to death. With no other family nearby, the authorities were planning to separate Bertha and her brothers, several of whom still lived at home. Pete, the youngest, was only ten years old. Obren Vuich, a neighbor and friend of their parents', had to plead with a judge to become their legal guardian so that the siblings could stay on their farm together.

Money, which had always been tight for Bertha's family, became even scarcer. There weren't any extra funds for recreation, not that Bertha had much room in her schedule for hobbies after running the household and going to school. What leisure time she did have was her own, though, and she chose to spend it playing sports. She had always loved playing baseball in the fields with her brothers, but her mother had made it clear that such unladylike behavior would not be tolerated when she got older. Bertha was devastated by her mother's death, but it was also liberating. She no longer had to ask permission to play sports or worry that she'd have to quit someday.

As a girl, Bertha wasn't allowed to play baseball at school. A grade-school teacher had bent the rules so that she could play with the boys, but high school was a different story. She attempted to sneak onto the school's baseball team as a catcher, figuring that the mask would hide her identity, but she was found out as soon as it was her turn to bat. She tried joining a local girls' softball team instead, but the level of competition was so far below what she had grown used to playing with her brothers that she found it a waste of time.

Eventually, she found a softball team that matched her abilities: an adult team sponsored by the Alta Chevrolet dealership in Dinuba. They had snappy satin uniforms with a large *D* for "Dinuba" on the shirts and an *A* for "Alta" on the shorts. They also played on a well-maintained field with electric lights, which were such a novelty at the time that most Major League Baseball stadiums didn't even have them yet. That softball fields were smaller and thus cheaper to illuminate than baseball fields was another reason that the sport caught on so quickly in small towns. In many communities, the lights alone were enough to draw a crowd.

Bertha immediately loved playing for the Chevrolet team. She lived for Saturdays, when she would wake up early, wash and iron her brothers' shirts for the week, then catch a ride into town to play in a game. At first, she mostly played shortstop, the infield position in between third and second base, but in 1938, when Bertha was sixteen, the team's main pitcher, a college student, was killed in a car accident on her way home from school. Bertha was asked to take over, and she remained the team's top pitcher for the rest of the season. From then on, it was the only position she wanted to play.

Strangely enough, another car-related injury brought Bertha to the Orange Lionettes the next spring, when she was a junior in high school. The Lionettes, so named because they were sponsored by the local Lions Club, were one of the best teams in Southern California, and their pitcher, Lois Terry, was especially admired. Her combination of raw athleticism and long blond hair earned her nicknames, such as the Blonde Bomber and the Blonde Terror, and a tour with a Hollywood all-star team two years earlier had won her national acclaim.

But in 1939, Terry aggravated an old shoulder injury while driving and was in so much pain that she couldn't sleep at night. Her doctor told her she had no choice but to sit out most of the season, leaving the Lionettes desperate to find a replacement. Bertha's Chevrolet team wasn't national or even state-tournament caliber, but word had spread that they had a good pitcher, which got the attention of Elwood Case, the Lionettes' manager. The day that he and some of the other Lions Club members came up to Dinuba to recruit her was the day that Bertha knew for sure that she wouldn't be spending her life on a farm.

Getting asked to join a high-profile team such as the Lionettes and to replace a pitcher of Terry's stature was a huge honor, and Bertha planned to make the most of the opportunity. She hadn't secured the position quite yet, though. First, she had to play a few games with the team. Then, if they liked what they saw, she would have a chance at pitching for them full-time. The *Orange Daily News*, the town's newspaper, devoted several paragraphs to her first appearance with the team. "Out of the grape country will come a youngster who will be trying out in the fastest league in girls' softball to help the crippled Lionettes over the hump," it announced.

As Bertha prepared to take the field with the Lionettes for the first time, she was so nervous that she thought she might throw up. Her older brother Sam, who had pitched for a minor league baseball team after high school, tried to reassure her and went with her to the game for moral support. She couldn't shake her nerves, though. Plus, some differences threw her off: the ball the team played with was a quarter of an inch smaller than the twelve-inch one she was used to, and the distance between the pitcher's circle and home plate was a foot longer. She wound up walking twelve batters, and the Lionettes lost the game, 9–4, even though they outhit the other team.

Her second game with the team went much better. They played against a team called the Optimist Doughnuts, and Bertha threw several strikeouts, leading a local sportswriter to describe her pitching as brilliant. By summer, she was pitching for the team regularly and was planning to move to Orange after she graduated from high school the following spring. She knew that she'd be able to find a job once she was living in Orange. While the team had no company sponsor to work for, Case often gave players jobs at the dry-cleaning business that he ran with his wife. He and the other Lions Club members had also helped pay for some of the players to attend secretarial school. With most of her brothers already out of the house, Bertha had little to keep her in Dinuba. She headed south at the first opportunity, ready to start her new life.

The town of Orange, where Bertha and most of her Lionettes teammates lived, wasn't that much larger than Dinuba. Its population in 1940 was only seventy-nine hundred, and it was still rural in parts. The one major difference was the town's proximity to Hollywood. Living so close to the glamorous film industry could make you feel connected to it even if you weren't, but for Bertha the connection was real. Hollywood was crazy for softball in the thirties and forties—Columbia Pictures even had its own team—and the Lionettes were among the biggest draws in town. Celebrities could often be found in the stands at their games, and Marty Fiedler, the sports promoter who ran the league the Lionettes played in, had direct ties to the movie business. The team's uniforms had a Hollywood connection, too, having been designed by a movie-studio seamstress.

Los Angeles was still coming into its own in the early 1940s. San Francisco was the more established city and was generally thought to be more cosmopolitan and sophisticated. But the excitement that surrounded the film industry gave anyone associated with it an air of intrigue or "oomph," as the *Esquire* magazine article on softball put it, and this led to opportunities that weren't available to players in other parts of the country. A Northern California team may have won the women's softball tournament in 1938, but it was a group of Los Angeles players, including several Lionettes, that was sent on an all-expenses-paid tour of Hawaii, Japan, and the Philippines that fall. They sailed across the Pacific Ocean on the SS *Chichibu Maru*, a luxurious Japanese passenger ship that featured a swimming pool and a gymnasium, and were gone for four months.

Bertha liked Orange because it was close to the city but was still far enough away to offer a small-town feel. Indeed, the town, which was founded in the 1870s and named for the main crop produced there, was small by design. It was meant to be a residential farming outpost where families could build a house, grow a few crops, and visit the centrally located town plaza for basic services. Its defining landmark was a large, circular, tiled fountain that sat in the middle of the plaza. On weekends, the town's inhabitants would gather around it to socialize and do their shopping for the week. It was the kind of place where everyone knew one another by their first name.

Orange City Park, where the Lionettes played most of their games, was just several blocks south of the town plaza. Only a few years old, it had been built in the mid-1930s by the Works Progress Administration, the New Deal program that financed the construction of roads and other civic facilities to create jobs during the Depression. In addition to the softball field, the sprawling forty-acre park included a small bandstand for concerts and a large swimming pool known around town as the Plunge. Not surprisingly, it was one of the most popular places in town.

Bertha rented a room from a young couple, Leo Mathis and his wife, Ollie, who had an apartment in the large Mediterranean-style building that overlooked the pool. Mathis was the manager of the Plunge and was able to get Bertha a job there as a lifeguard.

It didn't pay much, but it was a dream job to her. Swimming was one of her favorite activities—as a kid, she had spent many an afternoon swimming in the irrigation ditches near her family's farm—and she never got tired of sitting outside. She loved feeling the sun's warmth on her skin, and she was a true believer in the saying that everyone looked better with a tan.

As much as she enjoyed working at the pool, though, Bertha never forgot that she was in Orange to play softball. She took her responsibility as lead pitcher seriously and was eager to prove herself to her teammates, most of whom were older than she was. The Lionettes were an intense bunch. After games, they would get together as a group to go over what had gone right and what had gone wrong. Whether they had won or lost the game was immaterial; there was always room for improvement.

Bertha liked that her teammates were so dedicated and focused. Plenty of women played sports in California in the early 1940s, but highly competitive female athletes were still rare. A team such as the Lionettes functioned as a support group of sorts. Instead of toiling away on their own, as athletes in individual sports had to do, the players could draw inspiration from one another and propel each other forward.

The Lionettes also benefited from having strong local teams to play against. The Southern California softball league was a stand-alone entity in the 1930s and early '40s: it held its end-of-the-season tournament at the same time that the national tournament was taking place. The Lionettes had talked about skipping the Southern California tournament and playing in the national one instead—they wanted to see how they stacked up against such teams as the Jax Maids and the Chicago Down Drafts—but they hadn't done so yet. Traveling to the Midwest was expensive, and it wasn't as if the Los Angeles league wasn't competitive. In fact, many suspected that it was the strongest group of women's softball teams in the country.

The Lionettes' chief rivals in the league were the Peppers, sponsored by a Dr Pepper bottler; the Bank of America Bank Girls; Young's Market; Karl's Shoes; and the Nobby Knits, a team sponsored by a high-end clothing store on Hollywood Boulevard. The players on these teams were tough and pushed Bertha to develop new pitching tactics. She could throw hard, but not hard enough to regularly blow fastballs past batters. She needed a different approach, one that prized cunning and nerve over power.

Slowly, she began constructing her pitching persona. She learned to make slow pitches look fast and high ones look low. Then she further disguised them with the deceptive figure-eight windup, in which one swirled the ball behind one's back before flicking it forward, palm down. The finishing touch was her face, which she made sure was calm and composed at all times. She wasn't physically imposing enough to intimidate on looks alone, especially when she was younger, but her relaxed yet otherwise unreadable face unnerved batters. One reporter took to calling her the "poker-faced miss." She seemed to always know what was going on in the opposing batters' heads, but they couldn't get into hers.

The Lionettes had won the 1938 Southern California championship, with Lois Terry pitching. More than twenty thousand spectators had attended the game, held in South Central Los Angeles, and Al Jolson and Martha Raye, two of Hollywood's biggest stars at the time, presented the trophy. In the 1939 tournament, though, they were eliminated in the semifinals. Bertha felt responsible for the loss and was determined to win the title back for her team the next year. As September approached, she seemed poised to succeed. The Lionettes had gone up against all the best California teams in the weeks leading up to the tournament, and Bertha had pitched them to victory in all but one of the games.

She still threw wild at times, but she was becoming more confident and could tell that she was starting to gain the respect of her teammates. A sports columnist for the *Los Angeles Times* declared that she was the area's best softball pitching prospect since Lois Terry. Finally, the first day of the Southern California tournament, the day Bertha had been waiting for, arrived. The games were being held in Long Beach, which meant that the crowds would be smaller and no movie stars would be in attendance. The pool of competitors was also weaker because the Hollywood teams, such as Karl's Shoes, had decided not to participate in the tournament that year. Still, winning the trophy mattered to Bertha. It meant almost as much to her as an Olympic medal.

The Lionettes had to win three games to get into the tournament finals. Bertha gave up three runs in the first game, which was against a Santa Barbara team, but otherwise she was flawless. Then in the final game, against the Long Beach Woolworths, she only gave up two hits and also got on base all four times she went up to bat, helping her team win by ten runs. The victory earned the team a nearly four-foot-tall trophy that would go on display in Scotty's Malt Shop in Orange's central plaza. Each player also received a golden softball and a blue-and-white leather jacket with "1940 Champs" inscribed on the right sleeve. The prize that Bertha treasured most, though, was the feeling that she had earned her place on the team. She no longer felt like Terry's interim replacement.

In fact, Terry had already joined a different Los Angeles team, and by coincidence, the Lionettes played them in Orange the night after winning the Southern California tournament. Bertha's arm was tired after pitching nearly every night for the past week, but she held Terry's team to one run and three hits, and as a batter, she scored the Lionettes' winning run. Bertha had nothing against Terry personally, but it felt validating to go head-to-head with her and come out victorious. The Lionettes had faced Terry's team two other times that season and had won those games, too.

Up in Dinuba, four of Bertha's brothers were competing for a regional title with a men's softball team, although technically Pete, who was only thirteen, was just the mascot. They didn't fare as well as the Lionettes and lost their final game by eight runs. Sometimes Bertha felt guilty about not staying up there with them, but her older brothers wouldn't have heard of it. Of the seven of them, she had the best chance to make a name for herself in sports. They encouraged her to work hard and see how far she could go. Her success was their success, they told her.

Bertha spent most of the winter visiting her brothers. She also occasionally saw her uncle Marko, her father's eccentric older brother, who ran a chiropractic office in Los Angeles. Marko wasn't around that much, though. Unlike her father, who had pretty much stayed put once he'd settled in Dinuba, Marko was an avid traveler. He was a member of the Sierra Club and embarked on hiking adventures all over the world, which he chronicled in books of photography and poetry. Bertha didn't share her uncle's love of hiking in the mountains—she would rather walk on flat land that was preferably close to the ocean—but she could relate to his need to explore. She dreamed that one day she, too, would be able to say that she had seen the world.

First she needed to get a handle on her pitching, though. As the 1941 season got under way that April, she found herself struggling with accuracy again. All of the progress she had made during the previous summer seemed to have disappeared. She was throwing more walks than strikeouts, and the Lionettes lost several games. A local sportswriter called her a "slow starter who has not yet rounded into shape." She already practiced so much, but she pushed herself to work even harder, and her consistency had started to come back by the end of the summer. Still, the coach sometimes put her in right field and had a different player pitch, and some days she wondered if she would be asked to join the team the next year.

Bertha had decided to stay in Orange regardless of what happened with the Lionettes. She adored the town and enjoyed working at the pool. She had also recently acquired her first serious boyfriend. Jim Ragan had grown up in Orange, and his family was well-known in town. His father, John, was an insurance agent in the town plaza, and his uncle James was a local deputy sheriff. Jim was about Bertha's age and was a regular at the Plunge, where she worked as a lifeguard. Their courtship began at the slow pace that was typical of the time: a bouquet of flowers here, a night out dancing there.

Then, in December of that year, Japan attacked Pearl Harbor and the United States entered World War II. Jim, who had already been working as an airplane mechanic, enlisted in the army right away. The country hadn't shut down exactly—there were still Christmas and New Year's celebrations, and stores still tried to entice customers with postholiday sales—but the feeling of melancholy was inescapable.

In January, she and Jim drove across the state border to Yuma, Arizona, so that they could avoid California's required waiting period and get married as quickly as possible. Like many young couples across the country, they were eager to solidify their relationship before the war took the opportunity away from them. The 1934 song "For All We Know," which advised living in the moment because there may be no tomorrow and which Bertha and Jim used to dance to, had begun to feel eerily relevant.

A few months later, Jim went to North Carolina to complete his army basic training, and Bertha moved in with his parents, who had become like surrogate parents to her. She continued to pitch for the Lionettes, who played an abbreviated season that summer, but softball was hardly her focus. While the Jax Maids were in Detroit winning their first national tournament, Bertha was anxiously following the news. Jim and three of her brothers were in the army, and her younger brother Bobby had joined the navy. None of them had been sent overseas yet, but Bertha knew that could change at any moment, and she wanted to be prepared.

By the fall, every aspect of life in Orange seemed to revolve around the war effort. There was a massive movement to collect scrap metal. The town jeweler had already donated the five-hundred-pound metal clock that hung outside his store in the central plaza, and citizens were encouraged to bring in whatever extra metal objects they could find at home. "A discarded copper kettle could furnish 84 rounds of ammunition for some soldier's automatic rifle," an *Orange Daily News* article informed readers. The telephone company asked callers to keep their conversations brief and to refrain from using long distance unless absolutely necessary to keep the lines clear for war messages. Meanwhile, the town bank put out an advertisement suggesting that people give each other war bonds as Christmas presents. "War has made your Christmas shopping easy!" it exclaimed.

The government had also started to ration food and gasoline in order to divert resources to military bases and munitions factories. Women had to figure out ways to cook meals with less sugar, dairy products, and meat and were encouraged to grow their own vegetables at home in "victory gardens." In Los Angeles, the car capital of the United States, drivers were asked to limit travel as much as possible. "All pleasure driving may soon be prohibited," the University of Southern California student newspaper warned in September. Not long after that, even taking the bus was discouraged.

At night, during dimouts, streetlights and store signs went dark, and people who lived on the coast were asked to keep their shades drawn. This security measure was meant to protect American cities from military attacks and was being implemented on both sides of the country. The dimouts took on an especially ominous tone in Los Angeles because the area had already experienced an attack, albeit a minor one. On February 23, just a few months after the Pearl Harbor bombing, a Japanese submarine had shelled an oil refinery just north of the city. It marked the first time that a continental US location had been hit during the war.

Although the oil-refinery explosion caused no casualties, fears of a follow-up attack were high. The next night, a report of Japanese fighter planes above Los Angeles led to panic by soldiers and civilians alike: army antiaircraft gunners fired into the air wildly, trying to hit the planes, and motorists crashed into one another trying to flee the scene. It became clear the following day that there had been no fighter planes—the supposed attack had been a false alarm. But the anxiety generated by the incident lingered and helped lead to the evacuation and detention of more than 120,000 Japanese Americans, most of whom were from the Los Angeles area.

Kazui Oshiki Masuda, who had played with the Lionettes the summer before Bertha joined the team, was sent to an internment camp in Arkansas along with her husband and most of her family members. Three years earlier, she had been one of the Los Angeles softball players selected to go on the goodwill tour of Japan. It was one of the only times that she had visited her parents' homeland. Now Masuda was being imprisoned because of her Japanese heritage, and the ship that she and the other softball players had sailed on, the *Chichibu Maru*, had been commandeered by the Japanese navy (it would later be sunk by a US submarine). The 1938 tour and the cultural exchange it was supposed to foster seemed a lifetime away.

Indeed, the entire fabric of California appeared to be changing. Naval bases and shipyards had taken over the state's coastline, and the army and the Marines were using the central agricultural and desert areas to test airplanes and train new recruits. Orange County, where the town of Orange was located, became home to several military bases, such as the Santa Ana Naval Lighter-Than-Air Station, where giant blimps that tracked submarines were stored. In Los Angeles, it was said that warplane manufacturers, such as Douglas Aircraft, had become more influential than the movie studios.

Bertha found these sudden developments troubling, but she tried to stay positive. Worrying all the time wouldn't help anything, and it used up energy that she couldn't spare. She had recently found out that she was pregnant, and she knew that raising a child during a war was going to require every ounce of strength that she had.

CHAPTER 5

In this age, when streamlining is the order of the day, from automobiles to radios, from airplanes to munitions of war, the streamlined brand of baseball has definitely surpassed the orthodox version of America's national game.

—*The Softball Story*

. . .

In New Orleans, the Jax Maids were preparing to start what they expected would be their most successful season yet. They still had the Savona sisters, and they had continued poaching the best players from other teams until they had one of the most intimidating rosters in the country. Their lineup included players from Ohio, Texas, Oklahoma, and Alabama. Only a few were actually from Louisiana.

In 1942, when the Lionettes and other California teams were reducing their seasons, the Jax played ninety-eight games, of which they lost only six. That year they finally won their first national tournament after being favored to win it for three years. Going into the 1943 season, they would have the same players, and they would have even more of a financial advantage over their opponents as wartime restrictions forced more and more teams to scale back.

It wasn't that New Orleans hadn't been affected by the war at all. Food and gasoline were rationed there just as they were everywhere else, and the city's famed party atmosphere had become noticeably subdued. Even its annual Mardi Gras parades had become staid, the festive costumes and floats having been replaced by a couple dressed as Uncle Sam and the Statue of Liberty who urged people to buy war bonds. The Jackson Brewery, the Jax Maids' sponsor, still had plenty of money, though. Beer production had actually gone up during the war, thanks in large part to the high demand for it on US military bases.

All of the Jax players worked at the brewery, and they enjoyed a lifestyle that few other teams could offer. First, there was the brewery itself, which was in an ornate, castle-like building right in the heart of New Orleans's famed French Quarter. The jobs the players had there came with flexible hours and good pay, and the company was well liked. Its main product, Jax beer, was the most popular beer in town, and its iconic candy-apple-red signs with *JAX* spelled out in all caps could be found throughout the South.

The Jax were also considered the best-dressed women's softball team in the country—an impressed reporter noted that each player had "three sets of uniforms and two different jackets"—and they were probably the most well-traveled team, too. While other teams were mostly confined to regional competitions, especially during the war, the Jax continued to tour the country by train, playing exhibition games wherever they could. The only difference was that they could no longer have their own private train car because wartime travel restrictions prohibited it. At home, their games attracted thousands of fans (it helped that they almost always won). They had become a New Orleans institution that, like Mardi Gras and beignets, was beloved by locals and visitors alike.

Of course, the main reason that players wanted to join the Jax was the team itself. Often, the opportunity to play alongside a legend such as Freda Savona was enough to attract players who might not otherwise have considered moving to New Orleans. Then, by 1942, the Jax also had Nina Korgan, who had in the past year become softball's latest pitching sensation. Originally from Council Bluffs, Iowa, Korgan spent her early twenties bouncing around from team to team. She started in Nebraska, then moved on to teams in Kansas and Missouri. Everyone who played with her admired her pitching skills, but she didn't achieve widespread recognition until 1941, when she and a team from Tulsa, Oklahoma, called the Higgins Midgets, seemingly came out of nowhere to win the national tournament.

Korgan's performance at the '41 tournament wasn't just impressive; it was masterful. She threw 67 strikeouts in the 4 games she pitched and didn't give up a single run. Against the Jax Maids in the semifinal, she struck out 17 and only allowed 1 hit. Then in the final game against the Erin Brews, a brewery-sponsored team from Cleveland, she struck out 11 and only gave up 3 hits. That level of pitching dominance was hardly ever seen in baseball and, although more common in fastpitch, was still rare. At twenty-five years old, she had become famous overnight, and within days the Jax manager was persuading her to move to New Orleans.

Korgan was tall—at five feet ten inches she towered over most of her opponents—but in her pitching technique she got low to the ground, almost into a crouch. It was one of the reasons that her teammates called her Tiger. The low stance gave her a dramatic rise ball that shot up so quickly it was known to make hitters swing the bat over their heads, but it also exacted a physical toll: her throwing hand often dipped low enough to graze the dirt, sometimes so hard that it rubbed her knuckles raw. She put a lot of spin on the ball, too, but her main weapon was speed. Sportswriters used words such as "whirlwind" and "scorching" to describe her pitching, and one compared her arm muscles to a "rippling mass of steel ropes."

With Korgan pitching and the Savona sisters hitting, the Jax were almost unstoppable. They defeated the Phoenix Ramblers and the Garden City Maids, a top Chicago team, to win the 1942 national tournament. Their manager was so confident that they would retain their national title in 1943 that he sent the team a telegram saying that he wasn't going to book their return train tickets until after the tournament, adding, "Depending on results of championship play, you may have to walk."

While Korgan and her teammates waited for the 1943 tournament to start in Detroit, many of their former competitors were in a different part of the Midwest, playing in the new professional women's softball league that had formed there. The idea for the new league had come from Philip Wrigley, the chewing-gum magnate who owned the Chicago Cubs baseball team. He knew how popular women's softball was in both Chicago and Los Angeles, where he had sponsored teams that played with the Lionettes in Marty Fiedler's league in the 1930s. In fact, the 1938 Southern California tournament, the one that more than twenty thousand fans had attended, had taken place at one of his fields.

Wrigley wasn't necessarily a fan of softball—some said that he didn't even like baseball that much—but he appreciated a good business opportunity when he saw one. With the war threatening to reduce the professional baseball season, a women's softball league seemed like a good way to help boost ticket sales. The government was already bringing in women to fill traditionally male jobs at factories and shipyards. Why not do the same thing in baseball? Wrigley thought.

He heavily recruited players from the best Chicago and Cleveland teams, and a large number of them said yes. It was flattering to be chosen, and Wrigley's league paid well: the starting salary was $45 to $85 a week, which was more than what many of the women's parents earned. Originally, the league was going to be based in Chicago, but Wrigley scrapped that plan when he realized that the war wasn't going to disrupt Major League Baseball as much as he'd initially feared it would. Instead, the players found themselves sent to smaller Midwestern venues, such as Kenosha, Wisconsin, and South Bend, Indiana, where, not coincidentally, softball was already one of the most popular sports.

All of the players in Wrigley's league came from fastpitch, and it was initially called the All-American Girls Softball League. Even when the name changed to the All-American Girls Baseball League later that summer, they still used a larger ball and underhand pitching. Indeed, the main difference between its four teams and other women's softball teams was in appearance rather than playing style.

Wrigley's league was full of talented female athletes, but it was also largely a gimmick. Players were required to play in large pleated skirts and attend charm-school classes so that they would "embody the highest ideals of womanhood." They were also expected to wear makeup at all times and high heels whenever they weren't on the field. Wearing pants, drinking alcohol, and using rough language were all grounds for termination.

It called to mind the Bloomer Girls baseball teams that had toured the United States playing against men during the early 1900s, except with different marketing. The Bloomer Girls were considered a spectacle because they played sports and wore pants, which at the time was enough to get a woman branded as masculine. "The rumor, it is well to state in passing, that the shortstop of the girls was a man is utterly and entirely without foundation. The lady says she is a lady, and the real thing," a reporter for the *San Francisco Call* wrote after a game in 1901. "Some contend that Miss Maud's name is Willie or Dick," quipped Salt Lake City's *Deseret Evening News* about a Bloomer Girls pitcher. "She walks like a man and runs like a man and, furthermore, it would not be surprising to learn that one of the parlor chairs had been robbed of its stuffing to make her hair."

Wrigley, by contrast, promoted his league as ultrafeminine. He wanted his players to play hard but to look and act like nice, wholesome "beskirted" ladies. In addition to the mandatory makeup and high heels, players in his league were assigned chaperones even though most of them were in their twenties. Some of the chaperones were former athletes, but others had no interest in sports and cared more about enforcing the dress code. A player remembered one from the latter category yelling, in horror, "You don't have your lipstick on!" as she went up to bat.

Wrigley's marketing tactics worked, and attendance was reasonably high during the All-American Girls league's first season. He had created a product that tapped into a brand of patriotism that had become popular, one that prized innocence and virtue over being adventurous and bold. It seemed no accident that the players' modestly tailored, satin-free uniforms looked a bit like the ones that military nurses wore. The league's publicity campaigns further emphasized the players' commitment to home and country. Newspaper articles arranged by Wrigley featured photos of the players performing domestic tasks, such as making coffee, and always made a point of mentioning if they or their family members worked in the defense industry. At games, the players would also perform patriotic routines, such as lining up to form the *V*-for-"victory" symbol while the national anthem played.

The league's first season was deemed enough of a success that it expanded to six teams the next year. A few of the players Bertha knew from Los Angeles decided to join. Dottie Wiltse, a pitcher from the Nobby Knits, and Faye Dancer, from the Peppers, were said to have inspired characters in *A League of Their Own*, the 1992 fictional movie about the league. Other California players, including some former Lionettes, moved to Chicago to participate in a rival professional women's softball league called the National Girls Softball League.

Wrigley's softball league didn't play in Chicago and therefore wasn't competing with the city's softball teams for fans, but it did take many of their best players. Teams that had previously been among the best in the country weren't even qualifying now for the national tournament. Annoyed, some of the sponsors decided to start their own professional women's softball league. Despite its name, the National Girls league was hardly national in scope. All of its teams were based in the Chicago area and were named after local sponsors in the traditional softball fashion—for example, the Brach's Kandy Kids and the Tungsten Sparks, which were sponsored by a candy company and spark-plug factory, respectively. The league's primary purpose seemed to be to restore Chicago as a women's softball powerhouse.

Unlike the All-American Girls league, which incorporated elements of baseball, such as ninety-foot base paths, the Chicago league stayed true to softball, although, confusingly, it later changed its name to the National Girls Baseball League. It also offered players similar salaries to the other league's without requiring charm school or skirts. Instead, teams played in shorts or pants just as most other women's softball teams did. Many of the women from the All-American league wound up switching over. They had been willing to go along with Wrigley's theatrics because the games themselves were competitive, but that changed once they had another option. Suddenly, it was Wrigley's league that had to worry about losing players.

One of the teams in the Chicago league tried to bring Bertha on as a pitcher. However, she had absolutely no interest. In 1944, when the league held its first season, Bertha had a one-year-old daughter and was living in Laredo, Texas, where her husband,

Jim, had recently been stationed as an Army Air Corps mechanic. As isolated as she felt in Laredo, a dusty town on the Mexican border, the idea of traveling around with a team and living out of a suitcase had even less appeal. What she craved, above all, was stability.

The United States had been at war for more than two years by then. Hundreds of thousands of American soldiers had lost their lives, and an even larger number had been seriously wounded. Every day, newspapers published lists of men who had been killed or were missing in action. Food was still being rationed, and advertisements for products as diverse as socks and tea implored consumers to keep buying war bonds.

There were signs that the war would soon be over, though. The famous D-day invasion of German-occupied France occurred in early June that summer, and a month later US forces took control of Saipan, in the Mariana Islands, which put them within striking distance of Japan. Americans were becoming more optimistic as the summer progressed, but it was still a time of tragedy for many families. That August, Bertha found out that her older brother Sam, who had driven her down to Orange when she first joined the Lionettes, had died in a German prisoner-of-war camp. He had been captured during a US army operation in Italy earlier that winter and had died a few weeks later. Other than that, details were scant, as they so often were in such cases. Some families never received word about what had happened to their loved ones after they had been reported missing or captured.

Bertha coped with her grief by focusing on the things she could control, such as taking care of Janice and maintaining their small house in Laredo. She kept that house spotless—she found that as an adult she had become obsessed with cleanliness just as her mother had been—and she made an effort to get to know her neighbors. One of the women who lived nearby had a son about Janice's age, and sometimes they would drive into Mexico together to go shopping. Mostly, though, Bertha kept Janice close and dreamed of the day when they would be able to move back to California.

When the Jax Maids arrived at the 1944 national tournament that September, they were once again the favorites to win. They had beaten the Phoenix Ramblers by a decisive 7–0 in the final game of the '43 tournament. Now they were hoping to become the first team to win three national titles in a row. They took a train to the host city, which was Cleveland that year, and got there a few days early as they always did. They had spent the summer playing against the best men's and women's teams they could find and felt as prepared as they could be. Then they lost their first game.

The game was close, and against a good team—the Erin Brews from Cleveland—but people were still shocked by the loss. It didn't eliminate the Jax from the tournament, though. The competition format had changed during the war to reduce costs and comply with government travel restrictions. Instead of a single-elimination contest with ninety-plus participating teams, it was now a double-elimination event with thirty teams, fifteen men's and fifteen women's, each of which were the winners of regional tournaments. The change made the field of competitors tougher, but it also gave teams a chance to come back from a loss. Only after losing twice did they have to go home.

Unfortunately for the Jax, their second game at the '44 tournament was against the Phoenix Ramblers. The Ramblers' sponsor, a local school-and-office-supplies store, wasn't rich, but the team always found a way to go to the national tournament, even if it meant traveling by car and staying at the cheapest motels. Many of the players had had offers to join teams in Chicago and elsewhere, but they all stayed loyal to the Ramblers. They were from the area, and they liked their coach, a schoolteacher named

Ford Hoffman. Some of the players had been with the team since it first formed in the early 1930s. They always had talented pitchers, and Dot Wilkinson, their catcher, was on par with the Savona sisters when it came to hitting. They were the one team that the Jax could never seem to beat consistently.

Korgan didn't pitch the Jax's game against the Ramblers at the '44 tournament, which was probably a mistake. Lottie Jackson, who pitched the game instead, only gave up two hits, but one of them brought in the winning run. With the Jax gone, the Ramblers became the new favorites to win the tournament, but a few days later they, too, were heading home disappointed, after losing the final game to the Portland Florists, or the Lind-Pomeroys, as they were known at the time. That was the cruel reality of the national tournament: a previously unknown team, such as the Higgins Midgets or the Florists, who were making their tournament debut in 1944, could always come in and take the title away from the veterans. No team, even a well-prepared one, could go into the competition assuming it would win.

The odds of success were better in the professional leagues. There were significantly fewer teams, and those teams played each other all season, which meant surprises were rare. Yet, Korgan and the Savona sisters never considered leaving the Jax. Freda was reportedly offered as much as $325 a week to play in Wrigley's league, but she turned it down, saying that she was "fairly well fixed" working at the Jax brewery. Korgan remained with the team her entire athletic career, and she kept working for the brewery as a bookkeeper long after she had retired from softball. She may have moved to New Orleans just to play sports, but the city and the brewery had become her home.

On September 2, 1945, Japan officially surrendered, bringing an end to World War II. Germany had surrendered months earlier, and American troops had steadily been returning home all summer. Some food items, including sugar, were still being rationed, but most of the restrictions on gasoline and train travel had been lifted. The war continued to be the main topic of conversation, but the tone in which it was discussed had changed. Now that the fighting was over, people could be reflective rather than fearful. Soldiers began to speak more openly about the horrors they had experienced overseas, and the willingness to acknowledge domestic injustices, such as the internment of Japanese Americans, increased. Slowly, people began allowing themselves to turn their attention back to mundane concerns, such as neighborhood gossip and home repairs, and to make plans for the future.

The national softball tournament, held in Cleveland later that month, still hadn't returned to its prewar size, but public interest in the event seemed to be increasing. Attendance for the opening game swelled to eighty-five hundred, more than a thousand higher than it had been the previous year. The Jax were a major attraction, as always, and this time they cruised to an easy victory. The Florists and the Erin Brews were eliminated early, and the Ramblers weren't there at all, having lost their regional tournament to the Denton Tire Queens, a different Phoenix team. Instead, the Jax played a team from Toronto, Canada, in the finals, and won by five runs. The entire week had been like that for them: they had won all five of their games without going into extra innings or even giving up a single run. The only obstacle they had faced was a cold fall rainstorm that drenched the field and delayed one of their games.

That year the tense, hard-fought contests were on the men's side of the tournament. The final came down to two Midwestern teams that had been battling each other all summer: the Zollner Pistons from Fort Wayne, Indiana, and M&S Orange from Flint, Michigan. Like the Ramblers and the Jax Maids, they were evenly matched, with neither team able to consistently defeat the other. The final turned into a doubleheader, with M&S taking the first game, 1–0, and the Pistons winning the second, also by 1–0, which netted them the title because M&S had lost a game earlier in the tournament.

Even with the travel restrictions and players being called to military service, men's fastpitch had thrived during the war. Many of the existing company teams, such as the Pistons and the Briggs Bombers in Detroit, remained intact, and all sorts of new teams appeared, including several from US military bases. In fact, the 1943 and 1944 national men's titles had been won by a team from the Hammer Field air base in Fresno, California. They might have won in 1945, too, but their unit was sent overseas earlier that year and didn't get back in time for the tournament.

Fastpitch appealed to American soldiers, both domestically and abroad, for the same reasons that it had become popular with city dwellers in the 1920s: it was fast paced, didn't require much space, and could be played on a variety of surfaces. "In every corner of the globe, wherever there was a lull in the action, men brought out bats and softballs, staked off a diamond, and the game was on," recalled Arthur Noren in *Softball with Official Rules*.

Men who wanted to keep playing fastpitch after the war had plenty of options. The United States was entering an era of unprecedented economic prosperity. People had more leisure time, and finding businesses and civic groups to sponsor sports teams wasn't difficult. Every region of the country had fastpitch teams backed by local hotels, breweries, and Elks and Lions clubs. The Midwest was also full of teams sponsored by automotive companies, and the West Coast had teams sponsored by aviation firms, such as Boeing and Lockheed Martin. Meanwhile, the Southeast had so many teams sponsored by soft-drink companies that it wasn't unusual to find two Coca-Cola or Dr Pepper teams playing each other, sometimes even in the same state.

As more men's teams formed, more women's ones did, too. An equal number of spots for men's and women's teams were available at the national tournament, and towns were more than happy to cheer for their women's teams, especially if they were winning and the men's teams weren't. By the mid-1940s, the Amateur Softball Association was reporting that 250,000 men's and women's teams were competing for spots in the national tournament each year, and a national survey estimated that softball games drew 125 million spectators each year, making them the most widely attended sports events in the country.

Female softball players also still had the option of joining one of the two professional leagues. Wrigley was no longer involved with his league—he sold it to his advertising executive, Arthur Meyerhoff, in 1944 after the second season ended—but the six teams he had founded were still going. In fact, Meyerhoff planned to add two more teams for the 1946 season. The league was also gradually transitioning away from softball and starting to more closely resemble baseball, with a smaller ball and overhand pitching.

The National Girls league in Chicago had expanded, too, from four to six teams, and it continued to attract players from California and other states. They came for the salaries and for a taste of big-city life. Next to New York, Chicago was the largest, most developed city in the country. It had twice as many people as Los Angeles and was about four times larger than Cleveland or St. Louis. It also had skyscrapers, an extensive public transit system, and was busy enough that a young woman was afforded a certain amount of independence, most likely more than she would be allowed in her hometown.

The professional leagues were small and regional, though. The national tournament had twice as many teams, and they were from all over North America, including, most recently, Mexico and Puerto Rico. The crowds at the games were usually larger, too, and the trophies, which Coca-Cola began furnishing in 1944, had already gotten so tall that they were almost the same height as the players. There was also talk of getting softball into the Summer Olympics, possibly in time for the 1952 Games. With the war over, anything seemed possible.

CHAPTER 6

Playing softball detracts nothing from femininity and good looks, and marriage and babies detract nothing from softball playing ability.

—*The Softball Story*

. . .

Bertha had been away from softball for the better part of three years, but by March of 1946, she was back in Orange and was reuniting with the Lionettes. She also had a new part-time job as a youth-sports coordinator for the Parks Department (at twenty-four, she felt she was a little old to go back to working as a lifeguard) and had her in-laws to help with child care. The remote existence she had been living in Texas soon seemed like a distant memory.

Bertha didn't like to be separated from Janice for too long, though. She had gotten used to its being just the two of them in Laredo, and it felt strange to be apart. One night, she agreed to take her two sisters-in-law to a play—they were still in high school and weren't allowed to go out without an adult—but by intermission she missed Janice so much that she insisted they go home, much to the girls' disappointment. One of the main reasons she accepted the job at the park was because she could bring Janice to work with her.

She was thrilled to be playing softball again. She hadn't realized how much she had missed pulling her orange uniform out of the closet every weekend and walking onto the field with her teammates. It was a therapeutic return to normalcy for her after all that she'd been through during the war. The teams that the Lionettes faced were different because none of their former Southern California rivals had re-formed after the war, but the feel of the games—the excitement and the intense focus—that part hadn't changed.

Even though Orange and the Los Angeles area, in general, were in the midst of a major population boom—the metropolitan area's population increased from about 3 million to 5 million during the 1940s, and Orange County's population had nearly doubled—the town hadn't lost its charm. Kids and adults still gathered around the fountain in the central plaza on weekends, and a long list of town events brought the community together. Bertha's favorite was the May Festival, which was held every spring and featured carnival rides and a parade with big colorful floats.

Everyone still came out to see the Lionettes play, too. The town had a men's softball team, the Cubs, but they weren't nearly as successful as Bertha and her teammates. The Lionettes won the 1946 Southern California championship, then in 1947 won it again. They still hadn't gone to the national softball tournament, though, so Bertha never got to find out how her team might have fared against Nina Korgan and the Jax Maids, who stopped competing in the tournament after 1947, when they won their fifth title. That disappointed Bertha, who was eager to test her skills against the best players in the country. Before the war, the best players in Southern California generally *were* the best players in the country, but that no longer appeared to be the case.

· · ·

Bertha wasn't the oldest player on the team, but she was no longer the precocious rookie, either. The memories of Lois Terry and the other Los Angeles pitching stars from the 1930s had faded, and now Bertha was the city's best-known softball pitcher. Any concerns that taking time off from the game during the war and having a child would weaken her athletic skills were misplaced. If anything, she seemed to have come back from the war a stronger pitcher. She had finally gotten over her nerves, and she didn't struggle with accuracy the way she had when she was younger.

It was only logical that she would be the pitcher chosen to work with Lana Turner on *Cass Timberlane*, an adaptation of a Sinclair Lewis novel of the same title. The film was a modest success when it came out, but it's mostly forgotten today. It tells the story of an upper-crust judge, played by Spencer Tracy, who falls in love with a "tomboy from the wrong side of the tracks," played by Turner. Tracy's character umpires a game that Turner's character is pitching in (the director apparently wasn't much for subtlety: Tracy literally has to step across railroad tracks to get to the field where the game is taking place). It's supposed to be a baseball game, but the ball and pitching style employed—Bertha's figure-eight delivery—are unmistakably from softball.

Before the war Bertha had heard of softball players getting to be in movies. Several of the Los Angeles players she'd played against when she first joined the Lionettes had been cast as extras in the 1937 film *Girls Can Play*, a softball-themed murder mystery starring Rita Hayworth. Some reportedly even had ongoing contracts with major studios. But this was the first time Bertha had been asked to work on a film. She couldn't wait to meet Turner, who was one of Hollywood's biggest stars. Once Bertha got on set, though, she found the actress to be aloof. Turner didn't talk much and seemed to spend most of her time in her trailer.

Turner may have resented Bertha's presence. The actress had played softball growing up, and she might have felt that she didn't need any coaching. Later, when she was promoting the film, Turner told newspapers that she'd only had to "brush up" on her softball skills to prepare for the role because she "hadn't forgotten any of the plays" from when she'd played in high school. Tracy was friendly, however, and Bertha enjoyed working with him. "I wish all the umpires were as much fun," she told people afterward.

The next summer, in 1948, Bertha had an encounter with another movie star, Carole Landis. The actress, best known for comedies, such as *Topper Returns* and *Moon Over Miami*, attended one of Bertha's softball games, and afterward they posed for a photo together. It was the last picture taken of Landis; two days later, she was found dead, at twenty-nine, of an apparent drug overdose. When Bertha heard the news, she couldn't believe it.

Bertha wasn't playing with the Lionettes that season. The team had gone on hiatus again, this time for personal reasons. A local newspaper article had suggested that Bertha thought she would be better off playing with a different team. She hadn't actually said that, but the damage had been done: egos were bruised, feelings were hurt, and before Bertha knew it, the team had disbanded. She wasn't living in Orange anymore, either. Jim had gotten a job working on fishing boats in Balboa, a tiny coastal community near Newport Beach. It wasn't that far from Orange, but it felt like a big change. They had found a cute two-bedroom house there, and it was the closest to the ocean that she had ever lived. She even had a little paddleboard-type contraption that she used to take Janice around the bay.

Balboa didn't have a softball team, but Bertha wasn't about to let that keep her from playing. She joined a newly formed team called the Red Gals in Monrovia, a town northeast of Los Angeles, even though it took her at least an hour to drive there. She missed playing with the Lionettes, but with the Monrovia team she got to play in a league that included the Phoenix Ramblers, the Portland Florists, and the Salt Lake City Shamrocks, among other competitive teams. It also meant that she would finally have a chance to play in the national tournament, which was to be hosted by Portland that year.

The 1948 tournament marked an important turning point for the national tournament, which in its fifteen-year existence had never before been held west of Chicago. At long last, teams from the West Coast would have an advantage instead of having to travel across the country on limited funds. Portland officials celebrated the occasion by building a brand-new sixty-two-hundred-seat stadium that was hailed in the press as the most modern softball field in the country. It included an announcer's booth and a press box and was in a picturesque setting surrounded by trees. The land around the new field, known as Normandale Park, would later be expanded into a community park with playgrounds and picnic areas, much like the one in Orange.

Bertha got to play five games at the tournament before her team was eliminated. The women's final came down to the Ramblers and the Florists, as most fans had expected it would. Although the Ramblers ultimately won the title, Betty Evans, the pitcher for the Florists, was the star of the tournament. At twenty-two, Evans, whose nickname was Bullet Betty, was already a veteran player, having been with the Florists since she was fourteen.

Like Bertha, Evans was adept at fooling batters. One of her signature moves was the "double windmill," in which she circled both arms around twice before throwing the ball so that the batter couldn't tell when or from where it was released (that pitch was later outlawed by the rule books). The next spring, Evans moved to Chicago to join the National Girls professional league.

Bertha, meanwhile, moved back to Orange and reunited with

the Lionettes. They settled their differences and joined the league that the Monrovia team played in. That September, they competed in the national tournament for the first time. The competition was held in Portland again, and many of the same teams participated. The main difference from the previous year's event was that the men's teams weren't there. Instead, they were competing in a separate tournament in Little Rock, Arkansas. The lack of male competitors meant little to the Portland crowd, though. They were there to see the Florists, who, with their 1944 national title and second-place finish in 1948, had become one of the most successful sports teams in Oregon history. It didn't hurt that the Beavers, Portland's minor league baseball team and the city's only professional sports team at the time, hadn't had a winning season in two years.

It seemed fitting that a city nicknamed the Rose City would have a softball team named the Florists, and Erv Lind, the team's coach and sponsor, did in fact sell flowers for a living. Supposedly, Lind had no interest in women's softball at first. He gave the players who started the team some money to be nice and only got involved as coach when he learned that they'd lost their first game 28–1. He was merely protecting his investment, he said. By the mid-1940s, though, Lind was fully committed to the team. He couldn't offer his players high-paying jobs and luxurious travel accommodations the way the Jax brewery and other large sponsors could, but he made sure that they had high-quality uniforms and equipment, and he was the driving force behind bringing the tournament to Portland.

Losing Evans to the Chicago league weakened the Florists, but they were still a formidable team. Their offensive lineup was particularly powerful and could usually bring in enough runs to win games even if their pitcher gave up a few. Like the Ramblers, the players were local. Several were from logging families, and all had grown up playing outdoors. Portland wasn't as liberal then as it is today, but the city appreciated strong women. In 1948, it became one of the first cities in the United States to elect a female mayor, and its parks director was a woman, too. Residents respected the Florists for what they were: entertaining but also tough, hardworking, and self-assured.

Bertha pitched well at the '49 tournament—she was described as "near perfect" against a team from Baton Rouge, Louisiana—but the Lionettes were outmatched by the Caterpillar Tractor Dieselettes from Peoria, Illinois. The Lionettes faced the Dieselettes twice and lost both times, which eliminated them from the tournament. For the second year in a row, Bertha watched the final from the stands instead of getting to play in it herself. Once again, it came down to the Florists versus the Ramblers, and once again the Ramblers won.

Bertha still left Portland with a trophy, albeit a somewhat silly one. She had been crowned Miss Softball, an award the Amateur Softball Association started giving out during the war (needless to say, there was no "Mr. Softball" award). She was flattered, but she hoped that the next year she and the Lionettes would be able to bring home the prize that mattered: the national championship trophy.

Bertha felt she was entering a new athletic phase now that she was in her late twenties. She no longer had to work to maintain her pitching persona. After years of practice, it had become second nature to her, as had the pitching itself. She knew exactly where she wanted the ball to go and what she needed to do to get it there. It still required effort, but it was no longer a struggle. It had become innate, like achieving fluency in a language. She had been talented before, but now she was truly an expert.

She had also decided to embark on a new career path: secretarial work. Had she played for a team with a company sponsor, she would probably have been given a clerical job no questions asked. As a Lionette, however, she needed to find her own work opportunities, which meant she needed training. She enrolled in a secretarial school in Anaheim, where she learned typing, shorthand, bookkeeping, and all of the other skills that a modern office worker was expected to possess.

Bertha was one of many women transitioning into secretarial jobs in the late 1940s and early 1950s. World War II had brought American women into offices in addition to factories. The US Civil Service Commission had even put out posters urging women to apply for stenographer positions. "Victory Waits on *Your* Fingers," one said above a picture of a woman sitting at a typewriter giving a military salute. When the war ended, most women lost their factory positions, but they got to keep the clerical ones, in large part because men no longer wanted those jobs. And more of them were available thanks to the economic growth that followed the war. The number of clerical jobs in the United States nearly doubled between 1940 and 1950, and they continued to increase rapidly.

Being a secretary in the 1950s had an element of prestige. It meant dressing up for work and often using new, complicated machines, such as photocopiers, which were just starting to come out. A secretarial textbook from the period felt compelled to caution readers against viewing the profession as a "rose-hued dream picture," adding that "people who admire a successful secretary often forget, or are unaware, that she has attained this enviable stage in her career only through a courageous struggle."

After Bertha finished her secretarial training, she became a clerk for the Orange Water Department. Her main responsibility was stamping addresses on customer bills with a desk-size machine called an addressograph. These machines, which first grew popular in the early twentieth century, revolutionized the way utility companies billed customers. Previously, electric and water bills were delivered and collected in person, but the addressograph allowed billing by mail, making it much less labor-intensive and time-consuming.

At first, addressographs were so large that they took up an entire room, but as with most machines, they became smaller and easier to use over time. The model that Bertha worked with was fairly simple to operate. She inserted the envelopes, lined them up with the metal plates on which the customer addresses were engraved, then pushed a button to stamp the addresses onto the paper.

Bertha liked working in an office. It made her feel professional and sophisticated, although she wasn't one to put on airs; she would have hated for anyone to think she was a snob. Softball was her passion, though, and it always came first. Fortunately, her supervisors at the Water Department understood this and were happy to give her time off whenever the softball schedule required it. Like most Orange residents, they were fans of the Lionettes, and they knew how important Bertha was to the team's success.

In March of 1950, it was announced that both the men's and women's national softball tournaments would be held in Texas that fall. The men's competition would take place in Austin, then the women's would be held in San Antonio the following week. It was an odd arrangement, especially for the women. All of the past tournament hosts—Chicago, Detroit, Cleveland, and Portland—had had strong teams, but no competitive women's teams had come out of San Antonio. Still, Bertha and her teammates were excited to go.

To get there, they chartered a Greyhound bus and rode across unpopulated desert landscapes for an exhausting three days. They passed the time by taking naps and playing cards. Mostly, though, they discussed the upcoming tournament. They wondered what the field would be like and which of the fifteen other participating teams they would face first (the pairings were always decided by a random drawing the day before the tournament). Bertha resolved to beat the teams that she had struggled with in the past: the Peoria Dieselettes, the Portland Florists, and, most of all, the Phoenix Ramblers.

The tournament's being in San Antonio would eliminate rain delays, which were so common in Portland and Cleveland. But on the downside, it would be extremely hot, which made afternoon games almost unbearable. The weather gave teams an incentive to win games quickly. Even though the tournament schedule had been extended in recent years to give the men's and women's competitions a full week each, teams could still expect to play two games on some days. The longer those games lasted, the greater a team's risk for fatigue and dehydration.

The Lionettes' first game was against a Denver team that they had defeated previously and had no trouble beating again. In their second game, they faced a team they hadn't played before and didn't know much about: the Raybestos Brakettes from Connecticut. Bertha was always apprehensive about playing unknown teams, but the Lionettes won the game easily. They scored five runs, while none of the Brakettes could even get a hit off Bertha.

Next, the Lionettes played the Dieselettes. The Peoria team, led by a veteran pitcher named Marie Wadlow, had won its game against the Fargo, North Dakota, Twinettes the day before by an intimidating fifteen runs. But Bertha didn't allow any of the Dieselettes batters to score a run against her, and the Lionettes won the game, 4–0.

The Florists had been eliminated early in the tournament, so the Lionettes didn't have to play them. They did have to go up against the Ramblers, though. Bertha knew that they would be a challenge. They had two amazing pitchers—Margie Law and Amy

Peralta—and Dot Wilkinson, the team's catcher, seemed to get a hit every time she went up to bat.

The Lionettes prevailed in the teams' first matchup at the tournament. Then, two nights later, they faced each other again in the finals. As the undefeated team going into the game, the Lionettes had the advantage: if they won, they would be the new national champions. Instead, they lost in a grueling eleven-inning battle, during which a line drive hit Bertha in the stomach so hard that she collapsed. She was glad that Janice wasn't there to see her get injured, especially because she had only twenty minutes to recover before she had to be back on the field for the final game.

As the night air in San Antonio finally began to cool, the Lionettes and the Ramblers faced each other one last time to determine which team would win the national title. At fifteen innings, this game went on even longer than the first one had. With the two games, Bertha had been pitching for twenty-six innings and about five hours straight. Finally, the Lionettes caught a break and won, 3–1. To some, their victory may have seemed like a fluke: this was only their second time competing in the tournament, and they hadn't done that well the first time. Bertha knew better, though. The capability had been there for years—it was just a matter of the timing and opportunity.

The next morning, she and her teammates loaded their giant gold trophy onto the Greyhound bus and headed back to Orange, singing the 1920s song "California, Here I Come" as they rode. When they arrived home a few days later, Bertha and her teammates found themselves surrounded by thousands of cheering fans. The bus driver took them on a slow victory lap around the town plaza, and people ran up to touch the players' hands through the windows.

It was a proud moment for the whole team, but it had special significance for Bertha and the handful of other players who had been with the Lionettes since before the war. They had known each other for more than a decade; a few of them had even grown up together. They had watched each other get married and have children and had endured being separated from one another during the war years. Later, after they got off the bus and were walking through the crowd, Bertha looked behind her to see Ruth Sears, the first baseman, wiping tears from her eyes.

The Lionettes already had a devoted following in Orange, but winning the national title made them heroes. Their float at the annual May Festival parade became more prominent and ornate, and Bertha was a star. She wasn't about to quit her day job, but she got recognized regularly, not just in Orange but all over the West Coast, and she had been featured in enough newspaper articles to fill a room. Sometimes people would save the articles and bring them by the house for her to sign. Bertha rarely held on to such mementos for herself, however. She preferred to focus on what was coming next and had little interest in looking back.

There were still close games, especially against tough teams such as the Ramblers, but the 1950 championship started a winning streak for the Lionettes. They won the national tournament again in 1951. Then, in 1952, they won it a third time. Bertha continued to pitch all of the team's games. By that year, she was closing in on the 100th hitless game of her career and had thrown more than 4,000 strikeouts. She was clearly destined for the record books, and she began receiving national newspaper coverage regularly.

Janice was getting used to spending weekends at her grandparents' house and watching her mother from the bleachers alongside the other fans. She never minded having to share her mom with the town. She had known from a young age that Bertha was special. At the beach, she would watch in awe as her mom walked past the sunbathers, dug her feet in the sand, and ran until she got tired. Janice wanted the Lionettes to win as much as Bertha did, maybe even more so. When she got old enough, she learned to play catcher so she could help her mom practice pitching in the backyard. She knew better than anyone else how much work went into Bertha's athletic achievements.

In 1954, Orange hosted the women's national tournament. It was the first time that the event had been held in California, and one of the only times that it hadn't taken place in a major city. The town went out of its way to make the eighteen teams feel welcome. A big barbecue was held at the park on the first day of the tournament, and an estimated eight thousand people, nearly the entire town, turned out to watch the final game. The Lionettes didn't win the trophy that year. They lost in the final to the Fresno Rockets, one of the other teams from the West Coast league that the Lionettes, Ramblers, and Florists played in during the regular season. Bertha still had a good year, though. Earlier that summer, she was featured in the *Ripley's Believe It or Not!* comic for having passed the one hundred no-hitter mark, and that fall she had another brush with Hollywood when she was invited to appear on *You Bet Your Life*, the popular game show hosted by Groucho Marx.

You Bet Your Life was nominally a trivia show, but Groucho's comical interactions with the contestants were the main attraction. The two-person contestant teams featured a man and a woman, who were usually noteworthy in some way. The other teams on Bertha's episode included a rocket scientist, an elderly Southern lady, and a man who claimed not to know where he was born. Bertha was paired with Red Sanders, the UCLA football coach. Bertha looked every bit the girl Friday with her fitted jacket and skirt and her shoulder-length hair pinned back behind her ears. She was hardly diminutive, though; she stood tall and, in her heels, was shoulder to shoulder with Sanders.

During the opening banter before the trivia questions, Groucho asked Bertha if the Lionettes were any good. "I think we're the best," she replied matter-of-factly. He then asked her what position she played and, when she said pitcher, what her stats were like. "I have the world's record for 106 no-hitters, 11 perfect games, and 143 scoreless innings," she said. Groucho waited a few seconds for the audience applause to die down, then delivered his punch line: "Bertha," he said, although his New York accent made it sound more like *Boytha*, "with a record like that, Philadelphia's crazy if they don't sign you first thing tomorrow morning."

The trivia portion didn't go as well for Bertha. She and Sanders got saddled with a tricky music category and only answered one of the questions correctly (the Southern lady and the man who didn't know his birthplace won). But Bertha hadn't gone on the show to win the game. Anyone living in the United States during the 1950s could see that television was the future of the entertainment industry, and Bertha wanted to be part of it. She wasn't pursuing an acting career, but she was open to whatever opportunities might come her way. She did live in Los Angeles, after all, and a lot of people watched *You Bet Your Life*. At the very least, it was good on-camera experience, which top athletes were increasingly expected to have.

Bertha was now widely regarded as one of the best softball pitchers in history, an all-time great. She appreciated the accolades, but it was a strange time to be a female athlete. Women had more opportunities to play sports than ever before, with more teams to join and more events to compete in at the Olympics, but they were also being told to put their interests aside and focus on being wives and mothers.

The Rosie the Riveter "We Can Do It!" posters that had encouraged women to enter the workforce during the war years were gone, and in their place were advertisements championing domestic life. "Her title may be just plain Mrs. Homemaker, but when it comes to proper feeding of her family, she's a specialist," read a 1950s ad for cookware. A 1954 home economics textbook instructed future wives to have dinner ready when their husbands got home from work and not to complain if they arrived late. "Count this as minor compared to what he might have gone through that day," it advised.

The press coverage of female softball players focused on domestic skills so much that it made the publicity campaigns for Wrigley's All-American Girls league seem subtle. Newspaper articles about Bertha reported that she stayed fit by dusting the house and that she darned her husband's socks in the dugout. Other reporters seemed amazed that women could have any interests beyond cooking and sewing. "No spinning wheel for this granny," cracked the *Fresno Bee* in an article about Fresno Rockets pitcher Vera Miller, who was forty-two at the time. A Florida newspaper article advised men that "if the little woman fails to prepare your meals several nights in the week, there is only one solution. You'd better join a softball team yourself. The hot diamond can outdraw the hot stove any day."

In 1955, presidential candidate Adlai Stevenson told women graduating from Smith College that their main job going forward would be to ensure that their husbands stayed purposeful. "This assignment for you, as wives and mothers, has great advantages," he said, adding that it could be done "in the living room with a baby on your lap or in the kitchen with a can opener in your hand." The magazine *Woman's Home Companion* published Stevenson's speech in September of that year, around the same time that Bertha and the Lionettes were in Portland winning their fourth national championship. Mamie Eisenhower, the first lady of the United States for most of the fifties, was touted as a model housewife who "turned the lamb chops" while her husband, Ike, ran the country.

Americans weren't completely sold on the idea that women shouldn't have ambitions of their own, however. When Gallup conducted its annual Most Admired Women poll during the fifties, Eleanor Roosevelt, the outspoken feminist wife of FDR, usually topped the list, not Mrs. Eisenhower. Other Most Admired Women of the decade included Helen Keller; Margaret Chase Smith, one of the first female senators; and Marian Anderson, a celebrated singer who, in 1955, became the first African American to perform with the Metropolitan Opera.

Babe Didrikson Zaharias, the Olympian-turned-golfer, often made the Most Admired list, too. When she died of cancer in 1956, her family received flowers and telegrams from all over the country. "I think that every one of us feels sad that finally she had to lose this last one of all her battles," President Eisenhower said at a news conference the day her death was announced.

None of these admired women could be described as a typical housewife. Indeed, some of them never married at all. Like Bertha, they were exceptional, and they were respected for it. Being exceptional could be stressful and lonely, but women in the fifties who wanted a career didn't have many other options. For them, it was the top level or nothing—there weren't many opportunities in between.

CHAPTER 7

Some few attempts have been made to professionalize
the sport, but it is today exactly what it was in the early
1900s: a game played by amateurs for their own enjoy-
ment.

—*Softball with Official Rules*

.   .   .

The Amateur Softball Association and the national tournament
were more than twenty years old by the 1950s. Softball had
become established. It had been added to the Merriam-Webster
dictionary and was a fixture of newspaper sports sections. It was
also still growing: the number of men's and women's teams competing for spots in the national tournament had doubled since the
mid-1940s, from 250,000 to 500,000. Not everyone was happy
with the way the sport was evolving, however. Tensions were
building, and fractures had already occurred.

Fred Zollner, the wealthy sponsor of Fort Wayne, Indiana's
Zollner Pistons team, was one of the most prominent dissenters.
Like the Jax brewery, Zollner attracted the best players to his
team by offering them high-paying jobs at his company, Zollner Machine Works. And like the Jax Maids, the Zollner Pistons
flourished during the war and got even stronger afterward. They
won the men's national title three years in a row, but Zollner

was increasingly frustrated with the ASA. He wanted fastpitch to become more competitive, but the ASA seemed to be more interested in holding successful teams such as his back.

The organization instituted stricter player residence rules to make it harder for teams to bring in players from other towns, and it began to crack down harder on what it deemed professional activity. At the 1947 national tournament, one of Zollner's players got disqualified for having played professional basketball even though he had been considered eligible during the regular softball season. The Pistons won the '47 title anyway, but Zollner was so annoyed with the ASA that he left the organization and decided to start his own softball league.

A similar development was taking place in Arizona. A group of team sponsors who were fed up with the ASA formed a rival amateur league called the National Softball Congress and started hosting their own state and national tournaments. The NSC wasn't as large as the ASA, but its more relaxed rules on player eligibility and practice of awarding prize money to cover travel expenses appealed to many top teams.

The Jax Maids joined the NSC in 1948. They had even more reason to be upset with the ASA than the Zollner Pistons did. The year before, they had been stripped of their national title after announcing plans to play against a team from the National Girls league later that week. The ASA decided that playing a professional team would make the Jax professionals and, therefore, ineligible to have competed at the national tournament even though they were amateurs at the time. The ASA later reversed its decision, but the damage had been done: the Jax never came back to the ASA, which the organization seemed to welcome. "We'll have a lot easier time getting teams to enter the tournament now that the Jax are out," Michael Pauley, the ASA's executive secretary, said after their title was revoked.

By the early fifties, the Portland Florists, Cleveland Erin Brews, and Salt Lake City Shamrocks had switched to the National Softball Congress, too, as had several men's teams. The ASA was not pleased and contended that awarding prize money at tournaments, even though it came from ticket sales and was meant to defray teams' travel costs, made the NSC a professional league. "To us, softball is a recreation and not a profession," an ASA official said.

In its defense, the ASA was merely following guidelines drafted by the Amateur Athletic Union, the governing body of amateur sports in the United States. Still, the organization often seemed more concerned with maintaining amateurism in appearance than in spirit. It imposed tight restrictions on the amount of money players could receive for travel expenses, but then allowed sponsors to pay players indirectly in the form of company jobs. Players were strictly forbidden to earn any money from sports, yet professional athletes, including former professional players, were permitted to join ASA teams as long as they had been retired for at least a year. Also, all professional experience was treated equally: it didn't matter if an athlete had earned $5 or $5,000 or had played professionally for ten days or a decade—the yearlong waiting period before he or she could rejoin the ASA was the same.

The problem wasn't unique to softball. Many athletes straddled the line between amateur and professional in the fifties. All Olympic events were amateurs-only, as were all of the major tennis competitions, and it didn't take much to get ousted for being a pro. In 1957, Lee Calhoun, a two-time Olympic gold medalist in hurdles, had his amateur status revoked for accepting modest wedding presents, such as a vacuum cleaner, on the TV show *Bride and Groom*. Sometimes just the rumor that an athlete had received an appearance fee was enough to get him or her suspended. It was as if athletes were supposed to pretend that money didn't exist in amateur sports when, in fact, it was everywhere. It was no coincidence that the teams with the richest sponsors usually won the national softball tournament, just as the richest countries tended to win the most medals at the Olympics.

Some amateur athletes grew so tired of living in poverty that they quit their sport prematurely. Althea Gibson had just won back-to-back Wimbledon and US Open titles when she announced that she was retiring from competitive tennis in 1958. She was a world champion at the height of her abilities, but she had no way to support herself financially. Tennis took up all of her time, but as an amateur athlete she wasn't allowed to earn any money from it. "I may be the Queen of Tennis right now, but I reign over an empty bank account," she said.

Zollner hoped that his men's softball league would eventually become professional like the National Basketball Association, the league he had helped create for his company's men's basketball team, also called the Pistons (they later became the Detroit Pistons). He hired a press relations person to promote his team and spent the equivalent of $1 million building a palatial softball stadium in Fort Wayne. His hopes that other large softball sponsors, such as Dow Chemical and State Farm Insurance, would follow his lead were misplaced, however. Those companies spent a lot of money on their teams, but they weren't willing to commit the colossal sums required to sustain a professional league. They also weren't ready to leave the ASA and its lavish national tournament. In 1954, Zollner decided that he'd had enough of fastpitch. He dissolved his team and sold the softball stadium he had built to a local high school.

The Jax Maids didn't survive the 1950s, either. Nina Korgan retired from pitching, and after playing in the National Softball Congress for a few years, the Savona sisters finally decided to turn professional and joined the National Girls league in Chicago. They played for a team called the Match Corp. Queens, and before long they had the highest batting averages in the league. Freda scored more than 85 runs during her first season, setting a new league record. She also developed a reputation as a "colorful character" who got into scraps with officials and other players. One time she even got charged with assault and battery after allegedly punching an umpire in the face. Her hitting and fielding skills were what fans came to see, though. Both she and Olympia were incredible athletes, and they seemed destined to become sports legends.

Then in the mid-1950s the National Girls league folded, as did the All-American Girls league. Both leagues had been struggling financially for several years. The novelty had worn off, and attendance dwindled. Many of the players returned to amateur softball. Betty Evans, who had gotten married and was now Betty Grayson, rejoined the Portland Florists. Virginia "Ginny" Busick, another pitcher from the National Girls league, went back to the Fresno Rockets. Others found places on new teams. They had to sit out a season first to comply with the ASA's rules on professionals, but they had few other options if they wanted to keep playing. The National Softball Congress still existed, but it was falling apart. It was just too small to compete with the ASA, and it probably didn't help that it held its national tournament in sweltering Phoenix almost every year.

Any hopes that the women from the All-American Girls league might have had of joining men's baseball teams had been dashed a few years earlier, when Major League Baseball officially banned female players in 1952. The move was supposedly to protect women from being exploited, but that motive seemed suspect. A far more likely explanation was that male baseball administrators wanted to shut down the notion that women could play their sport.

The All-American Girls league may have been small and gimmicky, but it had shown that women could play baseball (by the fifties, the league had fully transitioned away from softball). The higher-ups in the major leagues seemed eager to reestablish their sport as males-only, and when a minor league team in Harrisburg, Pennsylvania, announced that it had signed a female shortstop that June, they had the perfect excuse.

Even if it was partly a publicity stunt, the shortstop, a stenographer named Eleanor Engle, was, by all accounts, a serious athlete, and she wanted to play. But male officials didn't want her on the Harrisburg team. An umpire threatened to quit if she played, and one of the team's coaches assured reporters that he wasn't going to let her stay on the roster. "This is no-woman's land and believe me, I mean it," he said. The ban on women joining professional men's baseball teams went into effect the next day, and Engle's contract was ruled void before she ever got a chance to play in a game. The decision had a ripple effect that would keep women and girls out of baseball for decades to come.

Athletes who wanted to go professional but didn't have a professional league to join had one other alternative: the entertainment circuit. After she left competitive tennis, Althea Gibson spent a year as the Harlem Globetrotters' opening act (she and another player would string a net across the gym and hit balls back and forth). It wasn't an easy way to make a living—the travel was relentless, for one thing—but it enabled athletes to earn money from playing sports, and some found that they liked being performers.

There were several different entertainment fastpitch teams, each with its own angle. Joe Louis had a team called the Punchers, which traded on his celebrity as a boxer. Football star Jim Thorpe briefly owned a women's team called the Thunderbirds, which Faye Dancer, from the All-American Girls league, played on for a while (Thorpe would go onto the field and kick footballs in between innings). An African American team from Iowa called the Sioux City Ghosts was one of the oldest entertainment teams, having been around since the 1930s. But by far the most successful of these traveling softball acts was Eddie Feigner's King and His Court team.

Feigner was a pitcher from Walla Walla, Washington. Like Bertha, he grew up in a poor farming community during the Great Depression. Unlike her, though, he wasn't interested in the respectability that came with playing on a company-sponsored fastpitch team. He wanted money and autonomy, and he figured the best way to have both playing softball was to start his own entertainment team and give himself the starring role.

Feigner and his "court," a rotating cast of three other players who served as the catcher and infielders, began touring the country in the late 1940s, but the 1950s was when they really hit their stride. The main draw was Feigner's pitching tricks, which included throwing strikes from between his legs, from second base, and, perhaps most impressively, while wearing a blindfold. In true vaudeville fashion, he would also sprinkle a few jokes throughout each game, such as telling the audience not to worry about the score because it had already been "taken care of."

Feigner and his teammates would play against full teams of nine, and they usually won. Not surprisingly, the ASA prohibited its members from playing against him, but he still managed to organize five months' worth of games each season. He claimed that he was earning hundreds of thousands of dollars a year by the late fifties, which was much more than most professional baseball players were making at the time. He also appeared on several TV shows, such as CBS *Sports Spectacular*. Later, in the 1960s, he took his blindfolded softball delivery to the next level when he used it to knock a cigar out of Johnny Carson's mouth on the *Tonight* show.

Feigner's act won him legions of fans and was so popular that it inspired copycats, such as an all-female version called the Queen and Her Maids and a six-man group led by Canadian pitcher Metro Szeryk called the Silver Six. Ultimately, though, most softball players didn't want to be entertainers. They wanted to play on regular teams and participate in serious competitions, and that meant staying with the ASA despite the financial hardships that often entailed.

Softball games may have been America's most widely attended sporting events, but that didn't mean they were profitable. One of the main reasons that spectators liked going to them was that they were cheap. The only way to make money from it was through volume, which was why Eddie Feigner played some two hundred games per year, but amateur teams made up of players with full-time paying jobs couldn't maintain that kind of schedule. Meanwhile, as the national tournament grew larger, it was getting more expensive for teams to attend. The teams with rich sponsors could afford to go without much difficulty, but most others had to pass the hat at games and sell newspapers and other items door-to-door to cover the travel costs. Sometimes teams weren't able to raise enough money and had to stay home.

Severely cash-strapped teams generally didn't do well at the national level, but there were always exceptions, as the J. J. Kriegs team from Alameda had proved in the late 1930s. The Fresno Rockets were sort of a 1950s version of the J. J. Kriegs. Their manager, Bernice Amaral, had even played for the team when she was younger. Like the Kriegs, they faced numerous financial challenges, but they still made it to the national tournament nearly every year, and they won it three times.

The team was founded by two players from the Hammer Field men's team that won two national titles during the war, but that and their name were where their connection to the aerospace industry ended. Their sponsors were always changing—one year it was a car dealership, another year it was a hotel, and still another year it was a grape juice company—and the players' travel budget was so small that even Greyhound was out of the question. Instead, they would pile into two station wagons that belonged to a teammate who owned a pet shop and drive through the night, six to a car, only occasionally staying at motels. The players often drove to a faraway city such as Phoenix or Portland on a Friday, played softball all weekend, and then drove back to Fresno Sunday night. Sometimes they didn't arrive home until six thirty or seven on Monday morning, leaving them just an hour or so to get ready for work.

In 1953, when the Rockets won their first national title, the players had to unpack and rearrange the station wagons to make room for the trophies. Even then, there wasn't enough space, and some of the trophies wound up strapped to the roof racks (fortunately, they came in protective boxes). That year's tournament was held in Toronto, a long drive that was made even longer when one of the station wagons got a flat tire. The players had to unpack the car again to reach the spare. Then, they had to unpack it a third time when they got to the next town and bought a new tire. Finally, Jeanne Contel, the team's third baseman, drew a diagram of the back of the car so that they could remember where everything went.

Poorer teams had the smallest travel budgets, but, in a cruel twist, they were usually on the road the most because they didn't have the money or infrastructure to host tournaments themselves. The Rockets didn't even have a regular field to play on—like their sponsors, it changed frequently—and the closest they came to being the home team at the national tournament was when it was held in Portland or another West Coast location. It meant that they were often tired and sometimes hungry, although they usually found ways to eat well when they were traveling—for example, pooling their money together for a grocery trip instead of dining out at restaurants.

Not being the home team also meant that they didn't have the advantage of being cheered on by a home crowd. It was difficult to always be the outsiders, but the Rockets had ways of persuading fans to root for them. Their determination and athleticism could usually be counted on to win over some spectators, and when that failed, they threw raisins. The Raisin Advisory Board, which was based in Fresno, used to give the players free samples to take with them when they traveled. They would keep the little boxes in their shorts pockets during games, then toss them into the crowd whenever they wanted to drum up support. The tactic worked particularly well out East, where raisins cost twice as much as they did in California.

Another challenge that came with playing for a team such as the Rockets was finding an accommodating employer. Many players became schoolteachers so that they could have the summers off, but that was only a partial solution given that the softball season started in May and sometimes lasted until mid-September or later. Pat Richmond, one of the Rockets' best hitters, became a serial job-leaver. She would get hired somewhere, work there through winter, then quit when the inevitable schedule conflicts arose in springtime. She never once considered missing a softball game to keep a job. Playing on the Rockets meant more to her than any job ever could.

Amateur athletes were supposed to be glorified hobbyists. They were portrayed by the press as factory workers and housewives first and athletes second, but it was almost always the other way around. The teams that won the national softball tournament were not made up of recreational players any more than Olympic track teams were made up of casual runners. It took serious time and effort to succeed at the highest level. The top company sponsors understood this, which was why they gave their best players jobs with flexible schedules. Of the many advantages to playing on a company-sponsored team, arguably the biggest was the freedom to focus on sports without having to worry about getting time off from work.

The Rockets won their third and final national championship in 1957. This tournament was memorable for several reasons, but chief among them was that the competition was held in Buena Park, California, and all the players got to stay for free at the newly opened Disneyland Hotel in nearby Anaheim. (Disneyland itself was new, having just opened two years earlier.) The hotel was a short shuttle ride away from the theme park, which the players could visit free of charge. Some of the women brought their families and turned the trip into a vacation.

For Bertha, it was almost like having the tournament in Orange again. Buena Park was close enough to drive to from her house, and she invited a few of her Brakettes teammates to stay with her there. Of course, it felt strange to be staying in Orange but putting on her red-and-white Brakettes uniform instead of her orange-and-white Lionettes one. It was even stranger once the tournament began and she had to pitch against her former team.

They faced each other near the end of the tournament, after both teams had fallen into the losers' bracket. The Brakettes had lost to the Buena Park Lynx for the second year in a row, while the Lionettes had unexpectedly lost to a team from Denver. Both teams were eager to make it into the finals. The Lionettes, as the defending champions, wanted to prove that they were still the best. For the Brakettes, getting into the finals would signify that they belonged in the upper ranks of women's softball. They had Bertha, but until they had achieved a first- or second-place finish at the tournament, they couldn't be considered a top team.

Bertha had been pitching well all week. A few days earlier, she had pitched two hitless games in a row, boosting her career no-hitter total to 125. In one of the games, she struck out 17 batters. She knew that she wouldn't be able to strike out that many Lionettes players, though. Their batters were too skilled to not get on base at least a few times. The best Bertha could hope for was to avoid extra-base hits so that runners wouldn't get a chance to score. She succeeded and only gave up singles. Unfortunately, fielding errors allowed one of those singles to turn into a run, which cost the Brakettes the game and eliminated them from the tournament.

Always a gracious loser, Bertha immediately walked over to the opposing dugout to congratulate her former teammates. Still, she couldn't help but be disappointed. Bill Simpson had brought her to Connecticut to lead the Brakettes to a national championship, and she wanted to accomplish that goal badly. Now she would have to wait another year. The next night, she watched her longtime foes the Phoenix Ramblers take on the Rockets in the final game. As the best fastpitch matchups so often were, it was a pitchers' duel. Ginny Busick, the Rockets pitcher, only gave up two hits, and they were both singles. Margie Law, the Ramblers pitcher, didn't allow many batters to get on base, either, but a walk followed by a bunt and a single brought in a run for the Rockets in the fifth inning, and that wound up winning them the game.

Afterward, Bertha flew back to Connecticut with her teammates, while Janice stayed in Orange so that she could start ninth grade. Normally, Bertha would have stayed in California, too, now that the softball season was over, but playing for the Brakettes had presented her with opportunities in New York City that she didn't want to miss. Later that week, she represented softball at a festival organized by *Sports Illustrated*. The magazine transported her and the other participating athletes, which included Olympic medalists and a Mr. Universe winner, from Manhattan to Yonkers, where the festival was being held, in a caravan of twenty-two sports cars.

Then that October, Bertha traveled into Manhattan again to appear on the game show *To Tell the Truth*. The show was filmed in CBS's Studio 52, which was right below Central Park and was later the site of the infamous Studio 54 nightclub. The show, which was only a year old, was a huge hit. Every episode, three identically dressed contestants—one real and two impostors— would go before the show's rotating cast of celebrity panelists. As with *You Bet Your Life*, the contestants were always unusual in some way. They either had atypical occupations, such as zoo-keeper or military pilot, or had accomplished a noteworthy feat, such as winning a bubble-gum bubble-blowing contest. The pan-elists would ask the contestants questions about themselves, then try to guess which one was telling the truth. If the panelists got it wrong, the contestants won money.

Bertha and her impostors, both of whom were secretaries, all wore Brakettes uniforms. "My name is Bertha Ragan," each said before taking a seat in front of the panel. None of the four panel-ists seemed to know much about softball. Most of their questions concerned baseball, although one asked about the dimensions of a softball diamond. Kitty Carlisle, a former Broadway actress, asked Bertha if women played softball because it was less dan-gerous than baseball. "No," Bertha said with raised eyebrows, as if she were taken aback by the question. The panel's ignorance about fastpitch wasn't that surprising, though. Despite the sport's massive growth during the past two decades, its popularity was in pockets of the United States rather than evenly distributed. It still wasn't universally known the way that baseball and other major sports were.

None of the panelists guessed that Bertha was the softball player. They seemed to base their answers on superficial notions about female athletes. Three of the four chose the woman with the lowest voice and the most masculine facial features. Carlisle said she picked her because she had the most "athletic stance." The panel's failure meant that Bertha and her impostors each won $333, about $2,800 in today's dollars, courtesy of Geritol, the ubiquitous 1950s game-show sponsor. Bertha gave the money away to a charity. She had to, to maintain her amateur-athlete status, but she also enjoyed working with charities, such as the Shriners children's hospitals. To her, it was part of being a successful athlete.

The next winter, it was announced that the 1958 national women's softball tournament would be held in Stratford. The town had hosted the men's tournament a few years earlier, but the women's competition had never been held there, or in any other Northeastern city. Much had been made in the press about the West Coast's domination of women's softball in recent years. No team outside the Pacific Coast women's league had made it into the tournament finals since 1947, when the Jax Maids were still participating in the event. Simpson hoped that bringing the tournament East might help reverse that trend and give the Brakettes the advantage.

Hosting the tournament was also a chance to give Stratford, and Connecticut in general, a prominent place in the softball world. The timing couldn't have been better. The recent exits of Fred Zollner and the Jackson brewery had created a vacancy at the top of the softball hierarchy. Money, commitment to the sport, and a willingness to step in were all it would take to fill it, and Simpson had all three of those things in spades. With him in charge, the 1958 tournament promised to be memorable. By April, the *Bridgeport Telegram* was already predicting that it would be the "greatest sports spectacle conducted in the state" that year.

Bertha was excited when she heard the news, although she was a little apprehensive about being the host team. She remembered how much it had stung when the Lionettes lost in 1954, when the tournament was held in Orange. She knew that the fan support in Stratford would be great, though, and sometimes that was enough to propel a team to victory. She was also encouraged by the team's performance at the 1957 tournament. Both of their losses had been against strong teams, and they had been close games.

Two other former Lionettes were also still with her on the team—infielder Beverly Connors being the latest recruit—which was reassuring. In fact, Jo An Kammeyer, Bertha's former Lionettes catcher, had been living in Connecticut more or less permanently since joining the Brakettes with Bertha two years earlier. She had finished her teaching degree at a local college and had gotten engaged to a man she'd met there. Bertha didn't return to Stratford until June, when Janice was done with school, but she arrived ready. Within days of getting set up at the beach house where she and Janice would be spending the summer, she was pitching in the Brakettes' first home game of the season. Then the next night, she was back on the field, playing against a team from New Jersey called the Debs.

The Brakettes won both games. Without question they were the best women's team in the Northeast, although their opponents were steadily improving. What remained to be seen was how they would perform in September, when, for the first time, they competed in the national tournament with the entire town watching. Bertha hoped that it would be a positive experience.

CHAPTER 8

Control is the most important thing a pitcher can have,
and by control we decidedly *do not* mean the ability to
put the ball over the middle of the plate but rather the
ability to put it across the corners and to vary the speed
and curves which are put on it. Next in importance
to control is deception, or the ability of the pitcher to
conceal what she intends to do.

—*Softball for Girls*

.   .   .

B ill Simpson had pulled out all the stops to ensure that the
1958 tournament would be a resounding success. The eighteen visiting teams were being put up at the Hotel Barnum, a
luxurious art deco hotel in Bridgeport, and were treated to a series of luncheons and picnics. At the opening ceremonies, a drum
and bugle corps played as the four hundred players lined up on
the field waving their state flags, and the governor of Connecticut
was on hand to swing at the first pitch. The field, scoreboard, and
dugouts were also in perfect condition, which went a long way
toward making the visiting players feel appreciated. They had put
up with shoddy fields and half-empty stands plenty of times, but
it was dispiriting. The Raybestos field, conversely, seemed to bring
out the best in every team. Everything about it was first-class.

The Brakettes got through the early rounds of the tournament easily, but they had reason to worry as the week progressed and the field of competing teams narrowed. A few days before the tournament began, they had played against the Lionettes in a friendly preview game, and they had lost, 3–2. The Brakettes had gotten more hits, but once again fielding mistakes had been their undoing. The mistakes were minor—a missed catch at first base and a dropped fly ball that should have been an easy out—but in fastpitch those kinds of errors were often what won and lost games.

Bertha knew that the Brakettes would likely have to face the Lionettes during the tournament, and sure enough, the two teams wound up playing on the fifth night. The game dragged on for fourteen scoreless innings. In time one of the teams would slip up and give up a run, and this time the Lionettes made the costly errors. First, a wild throw by the Lionettes third baseman allowed Brakettes center fielder Edna Fraser to get on base in the fifteenth inning. Then Bertha bunted, and the Lionettes pitcher, trying to get Fraser out at second, threw the ball into center field, enabling both Bertha and Fraser to reach their bases safely. Another bunt and a single later, and Fraser was crossing home plate. She was so happy that she leaped about four feet in the air afterward.

The loss sent the Lionettes into the losers' bracket, and it meant that for the first time ever the Brakettes would get to play for a spot in the finals. It wasn't going to be an easy game: their opponents would be the Fresno Rockets. Some maintained that the Rockets had the strongest lineup in the country that season. They had Ginny Busick pitching plus a group of almost flawless infielders who were also among the nation's best hitters. The Brakettes were still adrenalized from beating the Lionettes the night before, though, and felt ready to take on any challenge.

More than twelve thousand fans turned out to watch the game, which took place on a Thursday night. Once again, the Brakettes found themselves in an extra-innings game. Bertha pitched for the duration and didn't give up any hits past the third inning. Then she helped her own cause when, in the tenth inning with two outs, she hit a triple that brought in the winning run. "Bertha Ragan Ace in Thrilling Game," read the headline of an article in the next morning's *Bridgeport Telegram*.

The Brakettes had secured a place in the finals. All they had to do next was wait to see which team would make it out of the losers' bracket the following afternoon. Then that night they would play that team for the national title. The deciding losers' bracket game came down to the Rockets and the Lionettes, and to no one's surprise, the Rockets won. The Brakettes would have to defeat them a second night in a row. On the plus side, the Brakettes were going into the game as the undefeated team, which meant that they only had to beat the Rockets once to win the tournament, whereas the Rockets would have to beat the Brakettes twice. It was little consolation, though: the Rockets were tenacious and more than capable of beating the Brakettes in a doubleheader. The Brakettes would be far better off if they could win the first game and get the tournament over with sooner rather than later.

It had been warmer than usual in Stratford that week, with temperatures in the eighties some days, but by the night of the finals it was starting to feel more like September. A noticeable crispness was in the air as the sun set and fans took their seats in the bleachers. Some of the California players may have found it chilly, but to the New England crowd it was perfect. Attendance was well beyond capacity that night. So many people bought standing-room-only tickets after the regular bleacher seats sold out that the tournament organizers decided to take down the canvas covering the outfield fence so that people could stand behind it. Attendance was said to be as high as fifteen thousand, one of the biggest turnouts in the history of the tournament.

The Rockets knew they had no chance of winning the crowd over with raisins. That didn't keep them from playing well, though. They were the first team to put a runner in scoring position, and Busick's pitching was as consistent as ever. The Brakettes were holding their own, however. They were getting runners on base, and their fielding had been solid so far. Then in the third inning, the unthinkable happened: Bertha went to field a bunt and strained a muscle in her hip so badly that she had to be taken to the hospital. The pain was horrendous, but having to leave the game early upset her more. She had worked so hard to get her team into the finals, and now when they were so close to winning, she was powerless to help.

Everyone at the field was stunned. No one wanted to see an athlete get taken out by injury, especially at such a critical juncture, but the game had to go on. Joan Joyce, who had been playing first base that night, took over as pitcher. She had just turned eighteen and had only recently started pitching seriously. Until that week, she had never even played in a national tournament. She was a natural athlete, though, and nerves didn't seem to be an issue for her. If she could silence the Rockets bats for the next four innings, the Brakettes might still win the game.

As the game resumed, the Brakettes seemed to come alive offensively. They were hitting the ball more and consistently getting runners on base. Meanwhile, Joan had struck out several of the Rockets batters and had yet to give up a hit. The game was still scoreless going into the final inning, and another extra-innings battle seemed imminent. Then, with two strikes against her, Brakettes outfielder Mary Hartman hit the ball deep into the corner of right field for an inside-the-park home run. As she rounded the bases, the crowd erupted into a deafening roar.

The game wasn't over yet, though. The Rockets were playing

as the home team, which meant they got to bat last. And the batters due up next were the toughest on the team: first baseman Gloria May, third baseman Jeanne Contel, and Kay Rich, an all-around athlete who could play any position and who many believed could have been an Olympic track-and-field star if she'd wanted to be. None of them could get a hit off Joan, though. Rich struck out, and May and Contel were easily thrown out at first. The Brakettes had won the game and the tournament.

At the hospital, Bertha breathed a sigh of relief as she listened to the game on the radio. Her mission to bring the national title to Stratford was complete, even if the ending hadn't exactly gone as she'd planned. Janice, who was then fifteen, was driven back to the stadium to accept her mom's trophy and take her place in the team photo. When Janice walked out onto the field, the crowd showered her with applause. Joan Joyce and Mary Hartman were the heroes of the game, but that didn't make the town any less appreciative of Bertha. They knew that she was the main reason that the Brakettes had become national champions. That the team had won the final game on their own was a tribute to her and a testament to how much she had influenced them.

Two weeks later, the Cardinals, the Raybestos men's fastpitch team, captured their second national championship. It was the first time since the World's Fair tournament that both the men's and women's title winners came from the same town, and it was the only time that both teams had the same sponsor. Congratulatory telegrams from state politicians poured in, and the town celebrated with a huge parade and an awards ceremony at town hall. Several players described it as one of the happiest moments of their lives.

Clearly, Simpson would no longer have to recruit players for the Brakettes. Softball players who hadn't before been familiar with Stratford or Raybestos certainly were now. The same could be said of Joan Joyce. She had made quite an impression—it was hard to top a tournament-winning clutch performance as an athletic debut—and fans couldn't wait to see her pitch the next season.

Joan was from Waterbury, Connecticut, an industrial town north of Stratford that was nicknamed Brass City for the brass buttons and clock parts manufactured there. She had always been a strong athlete. As a teenager, she was winning bowling competitions against adults, and was also a standout volleyball and basketball player. She picked up softball from her father, Joe, who played for various fastpitch teams around the region. An older classmate, Beverly Mulonet, convinced her to try out for the Brakettes. She made the team when she was only fourteen. Her mother wasn't keen on her traveling around at that age with an adult sports team, but she relented after Mulonet, who played shortstop for the Brakettes, agreed to drive her to practice and look after her.

Pitching had appealed to Joan from the beginning, but it took her several years to find a delivery style that worked for her. She couldn't get any speed on the ball when she tried Bertha's figure-eight delivery, and the windmill windup made her throw wild, so much so that the other players on the team stopped letting her pitch to them at practice (they were tired of getting hit with the ball).

Then, when Joan was about seventeen, "Cannonball" Baker, the pitcher who struck out Babe Ruth in 1937, taught her the slingshot delivery, in which the throwing arm was held up high, elbow bent, before the ball was slung forward from hip level. The technique clicked with her right away, and she practiced it at home obsessively. When she couldn't find someone to catch for her, she threw the ball against the outside of her parents' house, and when her mother forbade her from doing that anymore, she made a makeshift target of chicken wire strung between two trees.

Eventually, she got comfortable enough with the delivery to start adding curves and drops, and by the summer of 1958 she had started pitching for the Brakettes occasionally. She may have continued on like that, pitching a few games here and there, had it not been for Bertha's injury at the '58 tournament. Joan's performance against Fresno in the final game earned her a more prominent place on the roster, though. By the '59 season, she and Bertha were sharing pitching duties—the local press dubbed her the Waterbury Whiz Kid while Bertha was the California Comet—although Bertha still pitched the most important games. When Joan wasn't pitching, she played first base, and she had one of the highest batting averages on the team, too.

Joan and Bertha were a study in contrasts in many ways. Bertha was the methodical veteran, cool and calculating, who had become a top pitcher through sheer force of will. Joan, conversely, was the fiery young upstart who overwhelmed batters with power and strength, and she seemed to be born for the job. She had large hands, long legs, and she didn't get nervous. She was naturally intimidating, even at a young age, so she didn't have to cultivate a pitching persona the way Bertha had. She called to mind Nina Korgan, of the Jax Maids.

Bertha, although she felt welcomed in Stratford, would always be the California import, whereas Joan was the local girl, born and raised in Connecticut. And, while Bertha was never without makeup or a comb, Joan preferred a more natural look. She had high cheekbones and striking blue eyes, but she eschewed makeup and usually kept her light brown hair short and unstyled. At their core, though, the two women were more alike than different. They were both dedicated, ambitious athletes above all else.

Joan's idol growing up was Mickey Mantle, the famous slugger for the New York Yankees, and aside from a summer during which she helped build a house and contemplated a career in carpentry, sports were her sole focus. After she graduated from high school, she juggled three different jobs, all of which were sports-related. In the fall and winter, she worked for a bowling alley and refereed high school basketball games. She also worked briefly for Raybestos, although her job mainly consisted of helping to organize and promote the various softball tournaments the company hosted.

Joan had no intention of becoming a long-term Raybestos employee the way Bertha had. Her parents had worked at the same factories for most of their lives, but she wasn't ready to make that sort of commitment. She was young and unattached, and she wanted to see where her athletic talents might take her before she settled into a full-time job.

Meanwhile, Stratford was fast becoming the capital of women's softball. The town hosted the 1959 and 1960 national tournaments, both of which the Brakettes won. In addition to her numerous pitching records, Bertha was now the first fastpitch player to have won three consecutive national titles with two different teams. She was as big a celebrity in Stratford as she had been in Orange, and she and the Brakettes had started to get national media coverage. For example, in 1959 the *Saturday Evening Post*, famous for its Norman Rockwell illustrations, devoted a two-page photo spread to Brakettes outfielder Mary Hartman, who had hit the home run that won the 1958 title (it probably helped that she and her twin sister, Madeline, who had also played on the team, looked like 1920s film stars, with their large, long-lashed eyes and chic pageboy haircuts).

Bertha was still splitting her time between Connecticut and California, and every now and then she brought a new West Coast player with her when she returned to Stratford in June. Most of the transplants returned to California after a year or two, but a few decided to stay longer. Playing for the Brakettes came with perks the way that playing for the Jax Maids once had. There was the beach house on Long Island Sound and the cushy office jobs at Raybestos. Then there were the deluxe travel arrangements, which included getting to use the company's test cars to drive to regional games, flying whenever the team played outside the Northeast, and ordering whatever they wanted at restaurants. For women who were accustomed to driving for days in hot cars and buses, subsisting on cheap roadside hamburgers and using damp shirts and rolled-down windows to simulate air-conditioning, it was the height of luxury.

There were always events for the team in town, too—banquets and so on—and sometimes there were bonus trips. In 1960, the team got to go on a monthlong tour of the Caribbean after the softball season ended. Bertha and her teammates traveled from island to island, including Cuba, playing exhibition games against servicemen stationed at the various US military bases there. Such tours had become common due to softball's popularity with the military. The Jax Maids spent much of World War II playing military teams, and West Coast teams were frequently invited to play in the South Pacific. Bertha was supposed to go on a six-week armed forces tour of Japan and other Pacific islands with the Portland Florists team in the fall of 1959, but she wound up dropping out so that a different pitcher could go.

Touring military bases presented softball players with incredible travel opportunities, but playing against military teams wasn't always pleasant. Even though the games were supposed to be just for fun, the men didn't like to lose and sometimes played rough. The same year that the Brakettes went to the Caribbean, the Lionettes went on a South Pacific tour that saw them getting spiked in the leg with cleats and hit in the head with pitches. One base runner was tagged so hard by an infielder's glove that she got a black eye. Some of the injuries were unintentional, but others seemed to come from a more hostile place, perhaps the by-product of what one player called "the ego thing" that so often lurked in the background when men played against women.

Fortunately, the only injuries the Brakettes incurred during their Caribbean tour were minor and self-inflicted, the result of a fender bender when some of the players rented scooters. The tour marked the first overseas trip for most of the players, and they tried to cram in as many experiences as possible. On their down-time, they went swimming and rode horses. The crash put an end to the scooter adventure, however. There weren't chaperones per se, but Bill Simpson and his longtime secretary at the Raybestos plant usually accompanied the team on big trips to make sure that everyone stayed safe and, ideally, uninjured. When the team arrived back in Connecticut from the Caribbean, hundreds of people turned up to meet them at the airport. The players knew that a crowd would be waiting and had prepared an entertaining greeting: after they descended from the plane, they lined up on the runway and performed a Spanish-language cheer they had learned in Cuba.

Simpson told the Brakettes that he would take them on an even bigger trip if they won the 1961 national tournament. A fourth victory would mean a new record—no team, male or female, had ever won four in a row. Alas, it was not to be. The tournament was held in Portland that year, and being a visiting team, after having had the home-field advantage for the past three years, seemed to diminish the Brakettes' confidence somewhat. They still made it to the finals, but it was by way of the losers' bracket, which they had been sent into by the Reading, Pennsylvania, Crystalettes, a team they played all the time during the regular season and almost always beat.

In the finals, the Brakettes faced the Whittier Gold Sox, a relatively new team from the Los Angeles area that was mostly made up of students. Youth and inexperience had made the Gold Sox bold. They didn't seem to know enough to be intimidated by the more established teams. They had gotten to the tournament by defeating the Lionettes in the Southern California regionals. Then, upon arriving in Portland, they took out the Phoenix Ramblers, the Pekin Lettes, who were the latest incarnation of the Peoria Dieselettes, and a strong Toronto team called the Filtro-Perks.

The Brakettes managed to win their first game against the Gold Sox, 2–0. One more win, and they would have had the trophy. In the second game, though, the Gold Sox were able to eke out a win with gutsy baserunning tactics. The game had turned into an extra-innings marathon that seemed as if it would never end. Finally, in the bottom of the nineteenth inning, one of the Gold Sox players stole second after getting on base with two outs. Then she stole third base and ran home on a squeeze bunt. It was the kind of brazen plan that sounded ridiculous and almost never worked, but it won the Gold Sox the national title.

Joan, who pitched more than 33 innings that day, during which she threw 67 strikeouts, was named the tournament's most valuable player. She had emerged as a major pitching talent, and she was only twenty-one years old, which meant that she would likely continue to improve. Softball pitchers generally didn't reach their prime until they were in their mid- to late twenties. Plus, she had only recently grown into her lanky frame and started to develop some muscles in her legs and arms.

It never felt good to lose, but the Brakettes were in a good place going into the 1962 softball season. Their lineup was probably the strongest it had ever been, and Stratford would be hosting the national tournament in September, which meant the team would have the home-field advantage again. The team also had a new manager, Vincent "Wee" Devitt, who had previously coached the

Raybestos Cardinals and had a reputation as an expert softball strategist. The national tournament was also continuing to grow, with more participating teams (as many as twenty some years), more games, larger crowds, and the trophies were now more than six feet tall.

Bertha was starting the summer with a completely new look. She had gotten rid of her shoulder-length dark curls, or "flowing raven tresses," as one reporter once called them, and now had a platinum-blond bob like Doris Day's. Millie Dixon, one of the West Coast players Bertha had persuaded to move East, had helped her dye it. The '62 season marked their third summer living together, and they had become close friends. Both women were about forty years old, but when it came to hair and makeup, they were like teenagers. They loved trying out the latest products and styles.

Millie came from a farming background just as Bertha did—Millie had even won a cow-milking contest when she was in high school—and she and her five siblings all grew up playing sports. Her younger sister, Margie Law, became a star pitcher for the Phoenix Ramblers. Millie had started out with the Ramblers, too, but her daughter had asthma, and a doctor recommended they move to California. She chose Orange because she knew they had a good softball team. Then, after her daughter was older, she went back to the Ramblers for a few seasons. She played second base, but her real strength was as a batter. At games, fans would hold signs that said MILLIE HIT A DILLY.

After three summers together, Bertha and Millie had settled into an easy routine. In the mornings, they would drive to the Raybestos plant for work. Then in the evenings, Millie would fix dinner—she could always whip up something delicious no matter how meager the ingredient supply—while Bertha would tidy up the house. Throw in softball and sunbathing at the small beach on Long Island Sound, and it was quite a full summer.

A Chicago "indoor baseball" team from 1897.

Unidentified female softball pitcher, circa 1920.

Orange Lionettes after winning the 1940 Southern California championship (Bertha is bottom row, far left).

Bertha with Janice in 1945.

Bertha with one of the many trophies she received once she returned to softball after World War II.

5

6

Orange Lionettes in 1949 (Bertha is in the middle row, second from the left).

Bertha with Margie Law from the Phoenix Ramblers (left) and other players around 1950.

7

8

Fresno Rockets after winning the 1953 national tournament.

Fresno Rockets players loading up one of the two station wagons they used for long-distance trips in the 1950s.

9

Pitcher Billie Harris after joining the Phoenix Ramblers in the 1950s.

11

The Raybestos Brakettes in 1956 (Bertha is bottom row, center; Joan Joyce is top row, far left).

12

Bertha and her impostors on the set of *To Tell the Truth*, 1957 (others pictured, left to right: actress/panelist Joan Caulfield, actor/panelist Ralph Bellamy, host Bud Collyer, reporter/panelist Hy Gardner, and actress/panelist Kitty Carlisle).

Joan prepares to cross home plate after hitting a home run at the 1962 national tournament. Bertha stands waiting to congratulate her.

Bertha in 1967, which was supposed to be her last season.

Joan demonstrating her slingshot pitching style while playing for the Connecticut Falcons in the 1970s.

15

16

Joan and the Falcons during their historic trip to China in 1979.

Janice didn't come out to Connecticut that much anymore. She had graduated from high school the previous year and had recently announced that she was going to be married in the fall. Her life was in California: her friends and family were there as was her soon-to-be husband. Bertha was increasingly spending most of the year in Connecticut. She had started arriving earlier in the spring and leaving later in the fall. She would never be a full-fledged New Englander, but she was getting close. She was even starting to get used to the snow. Her bond with her daughter remained strong, however. They spoke to each other by phone regularly, and she was helping Janice plan her wedding. Though it was to be a small affair, Bertha wanted at least to make sure that all the guests got enough to eat and that Janice and her bridesmaids had nice dresses.

Softball was Bertha's main focus that summer, though. She was going into her seventh season with the Brakettes. Some considered her to be the matriarch of the team, but her pitching was as formidable as ever. She wouldn't have kept playing if it weren't. She always said that she would retire as soon as her skills started to go. She had no interest in playing if she couldn't be among the best.

The Brakettes had a successful regular season. They won nearly all of their regional games, as usual, and they beat the Florists, the Ramblers, and the Lionettes during a pretournament West Coast tour that the team went on that July. Soon enough, it was time for the national tournament. Stratford was hosting both the women's and the men's championships, which made the buildup to the event even more frenzied than normal. Most of the premium seats had been sold out since April, and extra bleachers had to be installed to increase the Raybestos field's seating capacity.

Stratford wasn't the easiest location to get to, especially for the West Coast teams, but the players were getting used to making the trip, and the town always treated them well. In addition to being put up at a nice hotel for free, the players got special discounts at local stores and restaurants, and the crowds at their games were always large and enthusiastic. The softball tournament had become the biggest event in town, even more popular than the American Shakespeare Festival that took place at a nearby theater and often featured big-name actors, such as Christopher Plummer and Katharine Hepburn.

The Brakettes were the favorites to win the title, but the level of competition at the '62 tournament was particularly high. Three teams were from California: the Fresno Rockets, the Orange Lionettes, and the Whittier Gold Sox, who, as the defending champions, were automatically guaranteed a spot in the tournament. Other tournament regulars, such as the Florists, the Ramblers, the Orlando Rebels, and the Pekin Lettes, were also there. And several teams had exceptional pitchers, such as the Toronto Filtro-Perks, who were sponsored by a coffee-percolator company, and the Ohse Meats from Topeka, Kansas.

The team spectators were most excited to see at the tournament, however, was the Takashimaya Department Store team from Osaka, Japan. It was the first time a team from outside North America had competed in the event, and everyone seemed curious about them. "Osaka Girls Add Orient's Spice to Softball Tourney," read the headline of a local newspaper story about the team. Most of their players were in their early twenties (the oldest was only twenty-four), and they all worked for their department-store sponsor in the tradition of the Jax Maids.

Before arriving in Stratford, the Japanese players took a tour of the United States, playing exhibition games along the way. They prepared for the trip by spending two months eating bread instead of rice to help them get used to the American diet. They started in California, where they played the Fresno Rockets and a Bay Area team called the Redwood City Jets. Then they made their way to Illinois, where they faced the Pekin Lettes and were treated to a town picnic. New York City was their final stop before the tournament, which gave them a chance to visit the store their employer had recently opened on Fifth Avenue, just two blocks from the Tiffany store. Through an interpreter, the players told reporters they were impressed by how big everything was in America and professed their love of hamburgers and bouffant hairdos.

The Takashimaya team didn't advance far in the tournament, but they at least won two of the four games they played, defeating teams from Tennessee and Massachusetts. The Brakettes fared better, but their week still ended in disappointment. After winning their first four games, they got sent into the losers' bracket by the Gold Sox. Then they lost to the Lionettes, which knocked them out of the tournament.

The final came down to the Gold Sox and the Lionettes. This exciting game was full of expert fielding and daring baserunning. The Lionettes won, but the Gold Sox showed that their victory the year before hadn't been a fluke. They appeared to be the latest in what was turning out to be a long line of scrappy California teams that managed to win at the national level despite having little to no financial resources.

Bertha's hip injury from the 1958 tournament had started bothering her again, and sometimes she struggled to pitch an entire game. She didn't want to quit after such a disappointing tournament, though. She decided that she would pitch the next season if she could. Then, if the Brakettes won that year's championship, maybe she would consider retiring.

CHAPTER 9

They've had some great pitchers in women's softball.
Some could make many a Class A men's team bite the
dust.

—*The Softball Story*

. . .

J oan seemed to be becoming more famous by the day as the
summer of 1963 progressed. She and Bertha still split the
regular-season games—one of the Bridgeport newspapers had
started calling them the Big Two—but Joan now pitched the most
important ones. Her marathon performance in the nineteen-
inning final against the Gold Sox at the 1961 tournament, parts
of which had aired on CBS *Sports Spectacular*, had also made her
a favorite of sportswriters across the country.

Then in August of 1963, Joan won over even more fans when
she pitched against legendary Boston Red Sox player Ted Williams. In many ways, it was a reprise of her mentor Cannonball
Baker's face-off with Babe Ruth in New York twenty-six years
earlier. Joan was in her twenties, as Baker had been, while Williams, like Ruth, was in his forties and had recently retired from
professional baseball. Williams also took the challenge seriously,
just as Ruth had, even though the setting was a charity event. He
went up to bat against Joan fully intending to get a hit.

She pitched to Williams for about ten minutes. He fouled off three and swung and missed at most of the others. Eventually, he got so frustrated that he threw down his bat. Joan felt bad afterward—she wondered if maybe she should have let him get a hit; it was a charity event, after all—but the crowd loved it. Everyone in Connecticut seemed to know who she was after that.

A few weeks later, she led the Brakettes to victory at the national tournament, which was held in Stratford again. She threw 14 strikeouts in the final game against the Portland Florists and was named most valuable player for the second time in her softball career. Then, immediately after winning the championship, Joan shocked everyone by announcing that she was moving to California to play for the Lionettes. California players moved East to join the Brakettes all the time. The team had acquired two former Lionettes players, Shirley Topley and Laura Malesh, just that year. The exchange had never flowed in the other direction, however.

What surprised people most about Joan's decision was the timing: At twenty-three years old, she seemed poised to become New England's next big sports star. An article in the Bridgeport newspaper went so far as to suggest that some sort of conspiracy might have been involved, saying, "Officials and others connected with the administration of Raybestos softball are dubious about the ostensible reasons given by Miss Joyce for her switch and feel there is something peculiar about it."

In reality, though, Joan just wanted to go someplace new. She had decided that she wanted to go back to school full-time, and she didn't want to do it in Connecticut. For the past few years, she had been taking night classes in physical education while working unofficially as a gym teacher and coach at various local schools. To get a more legitimate teaching job, she needed to finish her degree, but she dreaded having to sit in classes with students who knew her as a coach or referee from their high school basketball games. She wanted a fresh start, and she figured if she was going to leave town anyway, she might as well go all the way to the West Coast. Aside from the Brakettes, all the best teams were there. The Lionettes were her first choice—she didn't have much interest in dealing with the rain in Portland or the heat in Phoenix—and they indicated they'd love to have her.

Within days of announcing her decision to leave Connecticut, Joan was driving across the country with a suitcase full of clothes and a plan to enroll at Chapman College, the main four-year school in Orange. Bill Simpson tried to persuade her not to go, but she rarely changed her mind once it was made up. Perhaps realizing this, he wished her well and told her that she was welcome to rejoin the Brakettes anytime.

With Joan gone, Bertha knew that she would have to pitch for the Brakettes at least one more season, and that suited her fine. She felt much better physically than she had the previous year and had turned in several strong performances over the summer. One Saturday that July, she pitched two shutouts in a row, allowing only three hits in both games combined. A local sportswriter called it "another remarkable demonstration of her softball skill." Then at the national tournament, she pitched two more shutouts, first against Topeka's Ohse Meats and then against a Minneapolis team, to help the Brakettes advance to the finals.

She had also, understandably, grown attached to the team. She had known many of the players for eight years. A few had gotten married: Micki Macchietto, who at age eighteen had become Bertha's catcher after Jo An Kammeyer broke her ankle, was now Micki Stratton, and Beverly Mulonet, the shortstop who had recruited Joan Joyce, was now Beverly Danaher. Others had jobs in different parts of the state. Yet, no matter what was going on in their lives, most kept coming back to the team year after year. It had become a family.

Bertha was looking forward to reestablishing herself as a top pitcher—she was ready to test herself against the best teams again—but first she had a different type of challenge to overcome. In July 1963, she had filed for divorce from Jim, her husband of twenty-one years, and in November she would have to drive to Bridgeport, the closest city, and plead her case in court. There was no such thing as a no-fault divorce in the United States in 1963. In most states, the only way to get a divorce was to go before a judge and present evidence of adultery, desertion, or cruelty. Even then, there were no guarantees because the decision depended on how the assigned judge interpreted the state divorce laws, which were often arcane and oddly worded. For example, Illinois's divorce law defined cruelty as multiple incidents—a single cruel act, even if it was severe, was insufficient. In Connecticut, a spouse petitioning for divorce on the grounds of cruelty had to demonstrate "intolerable cruelty" that made the marriage "unbearable."

Many violent acts, including rape, were not considered cruel behavior under most state divorce laws in the 1960s. As a paper published in a 1965 law journal put it, "A reasonable or even somewhat forceful request for normal marital relations is generally held not to constitute cruelty . . . as long as the requesting spouse does not intentionally impair the health or endanger the safety of the other spouse." Abusive language didn't usually qualify as cruelty, either, unless it conveyed specific threats of physical harm.

On November 20, 1963, two days before President Kennedy was assassinated in Dallas, Bertha argued her case for intolerable marital cruelty before a Bridgeport judge. She described her marriage as a "long series of separations and reconciliations" and testified that her husband had physically abused her on several occasions. She recounted one incident in California when he threatened her with a gun and another when he hit her in the face multiple times. Frances Spellman, the mother of one of Bertha's

Brakettes teammates, and her husband, William, testified that they had seen Jim slap Bertha and push her into a chair. Frances told the court that such incidents always occurred after Jim had been drinking and that Bertha was "always high-strung when her husband was around."

No financial matters were discussed at the hearing. Bertha didn't request alimony, saying that she received a "substantial salary" working as a secretary for Raybestos. Jim didn't contest the divorce and didn't attend the hearing, as Bertha suspected he wouldn't. By the end of the day, the humiliating ordeal was behind her, and Bertha was free: her divorce had been granted. She didn't tell many people about it, but a local newspaper picked up the story. "Girl Softball Ace Strikes Out Mate," read the headline next to a giant photo of her in her Brakettes uniform.

The following spring, Joan took the field with the Lionettes for the first time, wearing the orange-and-white uniform that Bertha had helped make famous. Some Brakettes fans were still upset by Joan's move. A few spectators even booed her when she came back to Stratford to pitch in the annual all-star game that summer. Joan didn't let it bother her. She knew that her supporters vastly outnumbered her detractors, and she had plenty to keep her busy in California. In addition to her schoolwork, she had a part-time job as a substitute teacher, and in the winters she played and coached basketball.

She was also attending classes in a school surrounded by palm trees and living in a climate that allowed her to wear flip-flops every day if she wanted. She had her own apartment and was a short drive away from the Pacific Ocean. Southern California was expensive, though. She wasn't sure how long she would be able to stay there living on a teacher's salary.

Meanwhile, the Brakettes had assembled a particularly

offense-heavy lineup for the 1964 season. They still had Shirley Topley and Laura Malesh from the Lionettes, and they had
recently acquired Pat Harrison, an outfielder from the Portland
Florists who had one of the highest batting averages during the
last national tournament. Then they had a long list of veteran hitters, including Micki Stratton, Edna Fraser, and Millie Dixon, who
had remarried and was now Millie Dubord. Added to that was
seventeen-year-old Donna Lopiano, who was learning to pitch
but could also play at first or second base and was known for her
hitting.

Coaches didn't have to look too hard to find talented women's
fastpitch players in the early 1960s—they seemed to be everywhere. Men were starting to leave the sport, however. Playing
sports professionally was no longer looked down on the way that
it had been in the thirties and forties, and competitive male athletes were increasingly drawn to careers in professional baseball,
football, and basketball, all of which were expanding. The life of
the quasi-amateur who played on company softball and basketball
teams in return for a steady job had lost its appeal.

Meanwhile, men who preferred to play softball recreationally
began switching to slowpitch, the old-fashioned version of softball, which had heretofore been reserved for children and seniors.
In slowpitch, the pitcher was more friend than enemy: strikeouts
were rare, and home runs were so common that scores frequently
went into double digits. It was a sport that paired well with beer
and picnics.

Women, on the other hand, still had hardly any opportunities
to play competitive sports. Most school programs were of the
"play for play's sake" variety. Some sports, such as football and
baseball, were completely off-limits to women, while others were
severely watered-down—for example, women's basketball players were still stuck with the six-player version of the game from
the 1930s that restricted running and dribbling.

Athletic scholarships for women were essentially nonexistent. Women and girls who wanted to play sports at school often had to organize games themselves and wear their own clothes as uniforms. Just practicing could be a challenge because at many schools women could only access fields and gymnasiums when male students weren't using them. Women were also banned from using the swimming pools on some campuses so that male students could swim in the nude.

As for professional sports, women basically had no options besides golf and bowling, neither of which offered much in the way of money or publicity, especially when compared to what their male contemporaries were earning. The Summer Olympics remained the largest showcase for female athletes, but those opportunities were also limited. While male athletes had three Olympic team sports to compete in, women had none until 1964, when women's volleyball was added. There were also fewer women's track-and-field events in the 1960s: no pole vault, only one hurdles event, and the longest distance they were allowed to run was 800 meters, or two laps around the track (the men's distances went up to 10,000 meters). Cycling, rowing, shooting, weight lifting, sailing, boxing, and wrestling offered no women's events at all. Of the roughly sixteen thousand athletes that participated in the three Summer Olympics held during that decade, fewer than twenty-one hundred, or about 13 percent, were women.

Men may not have needed company- and community-sponsored sports anymore, but women still did, desperately. When a good women's fastpitch team folded, players scrambled to find new ones to join even if it meant moving to other cities or other states. Many of the adult teams also gave rise to youth teams—for instance, the Brakettes, Lionettes, and Ramblers had youth counterparts called the Robins, Cubettes, and Dudettes, respectively—which were often the only opportunities for girls to play team sports in town. Softball gave female athletes an open window in a room full of closed doors. It was the main reason why so many women played fastpitch in the United States in the sixties and why no shortage of them was likely anytime soon.

Australia had decided to host the first international women's softball tournament, which would, fittingly, also be the first international softball competition of any kind (the first men's event wasn't held until the following year). The Brakettes were going to represent the United States, and true to form, Bill Simpson was making the most of the occasion, using it as an excuse to take the team on an extravagant world tour, with stops throughout Asia and Europe. The trip was a once-in-a-lifetime travel opportunity for the players and also raised hopes that it would serve as the first step toward getting softball into the Olympics.

The main impetus for the tournament came from Australia, however. Softball had been popular there since the 1940s, when American soldiers introduced it to the country during World War II. Australian women had become particularly enamored with the sport, but geographical and financial constraints had kept them from competing in the ASA tournament. Hosting an international competition was a chance for them to play against top teams from other countries without having to travel. In 1962, three Australian women's softball officials had visited Stratford during the national tournament to promote the idea of an international event, and before long concrete plans were being made.

The tournament was scheduled for mid-February 1965, to coincide with Australia's summer, but the Brakettes' preparations for the trip began long before then. Because their world tour was going to include India, the players had to get multiple rounds of vaccinations for yellow fever, which they dutifully received from the Raybestos factory physician, starting in early December. Then in January, they began a regimen of indoor practice sessions at a local high school gym since it was too cold to play outside.

Routine matters also had to be addressed before the women went away for five weeks. Those with jobs outside Raybestos had to make arrangements to be away from work, and those with young children had to make sure relatives would be on hand to help take care of the kids. The players knew that all the extra work and planning would be worth it, though. They had had many adventures playing for the Brakettes, but this trip was clearly going to be the greatest one by far.

Bertha couldn't wait for the journey to begin even though flying still gave her motion sickness. She felt that she had been waiting her whole life to go on such a trip, and the thought that it could help make softball an Olympic sport filled her with pride. She had dreamed of being an Olympian since 1932, when the Olympics were held in Los Angeles and Babe Didrikson Zaharias won the three track-and-field medals that made her famous. More than that, though, Bertha wanted her sport to continue to grow, and she knew that getting it into the Olympics was one of the best ways to achieve that.

She still had blond hair and still worked at Raybestos, but her life had also undergone some major changes. Within the span of a year, she had become a grandmother (Janice had given birth to a daughter, Jennifer, the previous spring), and she had gotten married again. Ed Tickey, her new husband, was a Connecticut native and had been a catcher for the Raybestos Cardinals fast-pitch team. They had met years before, when Bertha first joined the Brakettes. There had probably always been a spark between them, but they were married to other people. By the end of 1963, though, they were both divorced and could be together.

Ed sometimes helped coach the Brakettes and so was able to accompany Bertha on the world tour. Micki Stratton's mother was coming along, too, but otherwise the players were leaving their loved ones behind. On the day of departure, they gathered at the Raybestos factory, dressed in the matching white skirts and jackets that they always wore on major team trips. It was early on a cold, cloudy Saturday morning, but a crowd of fans and family members still turned out to watch the team drive off together. Their first stop was New York's Kennedy Airport, from where they would fly to Los Angeles and then on to Honolulu. In Hawaii, they were treated to a luau and a hula performance. They were supposed to play a softball game there, too, but it rained. Then they were off to Melbourne for the tournament. The players had no idea what to expect, but they were excited.

Five countries were participating in the tournament: Japan, Australia, New Zealand, New Guinea, and the United States. It was assumed that the Brakettes would win the title easily. They wound up losing two games to Australia, however, leaving them in second place. The umpires officiating the games made some questionable calls, and the field, a converted cricket field, was significantly different from the ones used in the United States: the outfield was much larger, and the backstop behind the catcher was so far away that a wild pitch was almost guaranteed to bring in a run. The Australians also played well, though. Bertha and her teammates left the tournament disappointed but impressed.

Next came the international tour. The bulk of the trip would be spent promoting softball through classes and exhibition games, but Simpson made sure there would be plenty of opportunities for sightseeing, too. They made quick stops in Hong Kong, Taipei, Bangkok, and Manila, after which they flew to India for a week. Hundreds of women came to the softball demonstrations the team gave there. Some of them had traveled long distances to attend, and they took up the sport eagerly, even though most were dressed in constricting saris. Later, the team got to see the

Taj Mahal at sunset, but the memory from India that stayed with Bertha the most was seeing the local women hit and throw the ball with so much enthusiasm.

From India, the team traveled to Europe, where they toured Amsterdam's canals by boat and visited 10 Downing Street in London. Bertha particularly liked how clean Amsterdam was. She always checked the hotel rooms she stayed in for dust and stains—she couldn't help it—and she decided that her room in Amsterdam was one of the cleanest she'd ever seen; even the windows were completely spotless. They also made stops in Paris and Rome, but the bus ride that the team took into East Berlin was probably the most memorable part of the European tour. The Berlin Wall had been up for only about three and a half years. American tourists could go through the heavily guarded Checkpoint Charlie entrance, but they weren't allowed to leave their vehicles once they got into the Communist side of the city. As they drove around, the players were struck by how eerily quiet and stark East Berlin was. It almost looked deserted, as if no people were living there. Many of the players were haunted by the experience for months, even years, afterward.

A few months later, it was summer and time to prepare for another national tournament. The event was back in Stratford, after being held in Orlando the previous year. Bertha knew that she would probably have to pitch against Joan, and she did, in the last winners' bracket game. It was a tense night. The Brakettes had faced the Lionettes at the 1964 tournament, too, but this time they were in Stratford, and the stakes were higher: the winner would advance to the finals, while the loser would get sent into the losers' bracket. As thousands of fans looked on, a classic pitchers' duel ensued, with Bertha and Joan trading strikeouts back and forth until the game went into extra innings. Finally, the

Lionettes scored a run in the eighth inning, driven in by a bunt from Joan, giving them the win.

The next day, the Brakettes beat the Pekin Lettes to make it into the tournament finals, which meant they would play the Lionettes again that night. Bertha had pitched the afternoon game, so Donna Lopiano pitched for the Brakettes in the final. It was another close game that went into extra innings, but the Lionettes ultimately won, with Joan scoring the winning run. It was a tough loss for Bertha and her teammates. They hated to disappoint the Stratford fans. Plus, it was their third major defeat in a row. Before losing in Australia, they had come in second at the 1964 national tournament, which was won by the Portland Florists and was televised, making matters worse. (Why was it that every time the Brakettes were featured on TV they lost? fans wondered. It had happened in '61, '64, and then most recently at the Australian tournament.) Perhaps it was unrealistic to expect victory every time, but the players couldn't help it: the Brakettes were supposed to be the best, especially at home. Still, they weren't bitter as they watched Joan and her new teammates collect their trophies on the field that night. They just wished that she would come back to Connecticut and rejoin their team.

They wouldn't have to wait long. Joan had almost completed her degree, and she had secured a teaching job back in Connecticut, where she felt she'd be able to live more comfortably. Before she returned, though, she wanted to win one last championship with her California teammates. The national tournament was back in Orlando in 1966, which meant that neither the Lionettes nor the Brakettes would have the home-field advantage, although the Lionettes were used to that (Orange had only hosted the tournament once, in 1954, and the event hadn't been held in California since 1957).

In a repeat of the previous year's tournament, the Lionettes sent the Brakettes into the losers' bracket, then faced them again in the finals. This time, however, the Brakettes wound up winning, even though, as the losers' bracket team, they had to beat the Lionettes twice to take the title. Lopiano pitched the first game that night. She delivered a nearly flawless performance and also hit the single that brought in the Brakettes' winning run. Bertha similarly dominated when she pitched the second game. The Lionettes had several star hitters that season, including two former Gold Sox players and Shirley Topley, who had recently rejoined the team after spending two years with the Brakettes. Bertha had studied them all, though, and knew their weaknesses. She only gave up three hits, none of which scored a run. Meanwhile, the Brakettes scored three runs, although that didn't happen until Joan hurt her knee in the fifth inning and had to be replaced by a different pitcher. Still, a win was a win, and neither game had even gone into extra innings.

The night after the Brakettes arrived back in Stratford, they found nearly five hundred people waiting to congratulate them at the Raybestos field even though it was a Sunday and it had been raining. The '66 title marked the team's fifth national title and was the first they'd won outside Stratford, proving, in case there was any doubt, that they didn't have to be the home team to win.

Later that fall, Bertha made her third game-show appearance when she and Ed went on *I've Got a Secret* (she pitched to the show's host, Steve Allen, while Ed served as her catcher). She also announced that the 1967 softball season would be her last. Wee Devitt, the Brakettes coach, told reporters that he knew Bertha had to retire eventually but that it was still difficult news to accept.

A few weeks after that, Bertha was the featured speaker at a luncheon given by the Stratford Exchange Club, a local civic group. Her athletic career may have been winding down, but she was still a public figure. She told the audience about her upbringing on a farm, where, she said, "the nearest girl was ten miles away," and about how Bill Simpson had brought her to Connecticut and allowed her to change the Brakettes' uniforms from pants to shorts. Simpson was women's softball's "biggest asset," she told them, and she meant it. He had also given her the financial freedom to make her life better and for that she would always be grateful.

CHAPTER 10

Some object to having girls play the game because they
are afraid they will ape the men's game, with its hurling
of everything from the vilest of epithets to the hardest
of pop bottles, but their fears are not necessarily justified
for girls can be just as ladylike on the diamond as they
are on the tennis court or at the bridge table.

—Softball for Girls

. . .

It is difficult to overstate the impact that Bertha and other
female athletes had when they appeared on television. The
message that they conveyed—that women who played sports
were real people who could speak and laugh and dress in regular
clothes—was vital at a time when female athletes were usually
regarded as anomalies, if they were thought about at all; most of
the time, they were ignored as if they were invisible.

That a woman could be serious about sports shouldn't have
been news in the 1960s, yet the media continued to treat female
athletes as novelties. It was hard to find an article about women's
sports that didn't involve at least a little "gee whiz" spin. "The girls
on the U.S. track team not only run like startled gazelles, they are
as lithe and graceful," the Associated Press stated incredulously in

an article about the 1964 Olympics. A woman's athletic achievements were rarely discussed without also mentioning her marital status and whether she had children.

Her physical appearance would usually be noted as well. Joan's height, weight, and hair color were often listed alongside her pitching stats. In her more than twenty-five-year-long softball career, Bertha had been described all kinds of ways, from "little" to "big," "modest" to "glamorous," and "chunky" to "shapely." A 1967 *Sports Illustrated* article referred to her as a "plump grandmother" with "hair that swirls into a blond pile like whipped cream."

That same year, a middle-aged official named Jock Semple tried to shove twenty-year-old Kathrine Switzer off the course of the Boston Marathon, yelling, "Get the hell out of my race!" At the time, the Boston Marathon was males-only, as were most long-distance races. In the press coverage that followed the incident, Switzer was described as having dark blond hair and big brown eyes. "What is a girl, a former beauty contestant, doing in a marathon?" asked the *New York Times*.

The implication of such questions was clear: sports were masculine, and therefore any woman interested in them was supposed to be masculine, too. In reality, female athletes had always been a diverse lot in appearance, going back to the days of the Bloomer Girls. Glamour queens played alongside farm girls and everything in between. And looks could be deceiving. Dot Wilkinson, the longtime catcher for the Phoenix Ramblers, could come across as a prim office worker off the field, but she was one of the toughest, most outspoken players in the league. She argued with umpires, and she once chased an announcer out of a ballpark with a bat after he made what she felt was an inappropriate comment about the pitcher's legs.

The criteria for being considered an attractive woman in the 1960s were also extremely narrow. Qualities that were desirable in an athlete, such as strength and height, were deemed negatives in a woman's appearance. Being tall was thought to be such a social hardship for women that it was accepted practice for pediatricians to treat adolescent girls with estrogen to stunt their growth (in the 1960s, a predicted height of five feet nine inches was considered tall enough to warrant the treatment, which was later linked to cancer and fertility problems). Likewise, teenage girls were encouraged to diet, regardless of their size, and doctors readily prescribed amphetamines and other drugs to aid them in this.

Smiling was also essential if a woman wanted to be considered attractive. A serious facial expression could get a man labeled as pensive or determined, but on a woman it was just a scowl—ladies were supposed to be pleasant, not serious. Curry Kirkpatrick, the author of the 1967 *Sports Illustrated* article on the Brakettes, described Joan and the other players on the team as having a "hard-visaged, baby-I've-been-around" look. An instructional book published by *Seventeen* magazine that year advised girls that a smile and a gentle speaking tone were more important than the words they said.

Few young women got into athletics without encouragement. Wider public acceptance was possible once they became skilled athletes, but most needed someone, such as a parent or sibling (an inordinate number of female athletes from this period grew up with brothers) to help them get started. Some women had such encouraging families that they didn't realize that it was unusual for a girl to grow up playing competitive sports. By the time they figured it out, it was too late: they were hooked, and being an athlete had become part of their identities.

Joan's parents, especially her father, had always nurtured her athletic talent. Beverly Mulonet, Joan's high school classmate and Brakettes teammate, also had supportive parents. They followed all of her games, attending as many as they could in person, and, when possible, listening to the long-distance ones on the radio. One night, they drove around for hours, with Beverly's young brother in tow, to listen to a game the Brakettes were playing on the West Coast (they couldn't get a good radio signal at home). The game didn't finish until 2:30 a.m. Pacific time, which was 5:30 a.m. in Connecticut. A police officer approached their car to see what they were up to. "Our daughter's playing in the national softball tournament," they explained.

Finding a husband who supported his wife's athletic endeavors unconditionally was more challenging. Many of the female athletes who came of age in the fifties and sixties never married. Some had no interest in men whatsoever. For others, staying single was more a matter of preserving their personal freedom. They knew that if they got married, they would be expected to defer to their husband, that his job and schedule would take precedence over theirs. There were exceptions, of course. It helped to marry a fellow athlete, someone who could appreciate his wife's talent and share her passion for sports. Some fastpitch players even got their husbands involved with their teams as assistant coaches. It didn't always work out, but it usually converted the men into fans if they weren't already.

Having children tended to take women away from softball, at least for a year or two, although it wasn't unheard of for players to rejoin their teams shortly after giving birth. Kids usually made great supporters, too. Many got involved with their moms' teams directly by becoming batboys or bat girls, while others were content to cheer from the stands. Gloria May, from the Fresno Rockets, frequently brought her daughter Jamie along on the team's road trips. Like Janice, Jamie was her mom's biggest fan. She was also her good-luck charm: at games, she would kiss her mom's bat in the hopes that it would bring her a hit. Dixie Turley, who pitched for teams in Arizona and Georgia, had four children to root for her at games.

· · ·

Support at home could only get athletes so far, though. To succeed at the highest level, they needed competitive teams to play on, and not everyone had access to the same opportunities. The Amateur Softball Association didn't have any rules barring racial minorities, but the teams that played in the league were still overwhelmingly white. Many of the companies that sponsored fastpitch teams in the 1930s through the 1960s didn't hire minorities. And if you couldn't get a job at the company, there probably wasn't a place for you on its softball team, either. Tiby Eisen, an outfielder who played in the All-American Girls league and later joined the Lionettes, was turned away by the Los Angeles Bank of America team in the 1940s because she was Jewish. Similarly, the automotive-industry teams that dominated the Midwestern men's fastpitch scene in the forties and fifties were closed off to most African Americans.

Many minority groups formed their own teams. In 1944, a group of African American women who worked at the Boeing plant in Seattle started a team called the Challengers when they weren't allowed to join the regular company team. True to their name, they challenged the company team to a game and, according to an African American newspaper article, "whipped the white team soundly." Orange had a Mexican American women's team called Los Tomboys, although the Lionettes also had Mexican American players, most notably Margaret Villa, who later joined the All-American Girls league.

Indeed, Mexican American, African American, and Japanese American fastpitch teams could be found throughout the country. Most were small, neighborhood outfits sponsored by churches and local businesses, but that didn't mean that they weren't competitive. They had their own championships, and they provided crucial outlets for athletes who might not have been able to join a fastpitch team otherwise. They also served as springboards for players who wanted to join larger teams. Nancy Ito, the main catcher for the Lionettes in the 1960s, got her start playing for a Japanese American team in Colorado. A coach who saw her play invited her to join a Denver company–sponsored team, which then led to a spot on one of the National Girls professional teams in Chicago. Mary "Toots" Edmonds and her two sisters played for their town's Native American teams before getting recruited by an Oklahoma City squad that competed at the 1963 national tournament.

Minorities who joined ASA teams often faced discrimination, though, especially while traveling. When the men's national tournament was held in Little Rock, Arkansas, in 1949, pitcher Charlie Justice and two other African American players on the Tip Top Tailors team from Toronto weren't allowed to stay in the same hotel as the other competitors. Justice and his teammates wound up winning the tournament in an eighteen-inning thriller against the Clearwater Bombers from Florida, but the locals still treated them coldly. The host city usually held a banquet for the tournament winners, but the Tip Top Tailors had to throw their own celebration at their hotel on the black side of town.

The situation hadn't improved much when Billie Harris became the Phoenix Ramblers' first African American pitcher in the 1950s. Harris lived in Tucson, and at first the Ramblers only brought her up to pitch when they played against the Ebonettes, an all-black women's team from Los Angeles. She would take the bus up to Phoenix by herself, then find a black family to stay with if she needed to spend the night there; hotels weren't an option nor were her white teammates' houses.

Eventually, Harris moved to Phoenix and became a full-time member of the Ramblers, but she always felt distant from the other players. Sometimes the team would stop in Las Vegas on the way back from road trips to California, but Harris would have to wait in the car because blacks weren't allowed inside the casinos. On more than one occasion, the team had to leave a restaurant because the owner refused to let her eat there. When it was announced that the 1956 national tournament would be held in Florida, the Ramblers coach decided that it would probably be best if Harris stayed home. After her teammates came back from the tournament, they told her that an African American player on a different team had gotten hurt during a game and that no one would go out to help her. They said she just lay there on the field for what seemed like an hour or more.

Racial tensions were still high the next time the national women's tournament was held in Florida, in 1964. A few months before the teams arrived in Orlando, a hotel manager in nearby St. Augustine made national headlines when he refused to let Martin Luther King eat at his restaurant and then dumped acid into his whites-only pool because black protesters were swimming in it. Harris decided to compete in the tournament with the Ramblers anyway, and she didn't experience any problems. She led the Ramblers to one of their more successful tournament performances of that decade, as they defeated the Pekin Lettes and the Salt Lake City Shamrocks before getting edged out by the Lionettes on the last day.

Two years later, the Ramblers folded after struggling financially for several years. Several of the top women's teams were facing this predicament in the mid-1960s; their existence depended on the generosity and leadership of one person, and when something happened to that person, the team began to dissolve. For the Ramblers, the difficulties began when Ford Hoffman, their founder and manager, pulled away from the team in 1958. The school-and-office-supplies store that he had gotten to sponsor the team in the 1940s continued to provide equipment and uniforms, but travel costs and other expenses still had to be covered. Dot Wilkinson, the team's catcher, took over as manager and kept the team going for as long as she could, but eventually it became too much.

The Portland Florists were dealt an even more serious blow in 1964, when Erv Lind, their coach and sponsor, died after suffering a stroke. The team had won their second national title that fall, just a few months before Lind passed away, but with their benefactor gone, they were only able to play for one more season before disbanding. The Atlanta Lorelei Ladies, one of the first nationally successful women's fastpitch teams to come out of the South, found themselves in a similar situation in 1966 when their longtime sponsor, Hollie Lough, passed away. They were fortunate to get rescued by a different sponsor: a local business-woman, Bobbie Bailey, who had been friends with Lough. On his deathbed, Lough made Bailey promise that she would keep the Lorelei Ladies going after he died. She agreed and kept her word, even though the money he'd set aside for the team turned out to be squandered and she wound up having to foot the costs herself. As popular as fastpitch was, it remained a labor of love, for both the players and the sponsors.

After the Ramblers called it quits, Billie Harris moved to Yakima, Washington, to pitch for the Webb Cats, a team sponsored by a logging company. She'd never lived outside the Southwest before, and it was also her first opportunity to work for a team sponsor (in Phoenix, she'd supported herself by working various retail and maintenance jobs). The logging company asked her if she wanted to work inside or outside, and she chose outside. She worked ten-hour days, driving trucks around the woods. Then she spent her nights and weekends pitching against other Pacific Northwest softball teams with names such as the Gold Nuggets, the Chainsaws, and the Lumberjills. She could stay in hotels when the team traveled, and she was no longer barred from entering the Las Vegas casinos, but she still felt separate. No matter what part of the country the team went to, she was usually the only African American there, either on the field or in the stands.

. . .

In 1967, Harris and the Webb Cats traveled to Stratford for the national tournament. Everything was bigger and brighter to celebrate the tournament's thirty-fifth anniversary and Bertha's last season. The opening ceremonies featured a costumed drum and bugle corps called the Trumbull Troubadours, and each of the nineteen participating teams was escorted onto the field by marines in dress blue uniforms. The tournament also included a special guest team from the Netherlands, which, like Australia, had picked up softball from US servicemen during World War II.

The press coverage of the Netherlands team focused mostly on the players' appearance. One reporter described a pitcher on the team as a "freshly-scrubbed, apple-checked" blonde with a "little girl's face" and compared the other players' movements to a swan drinking water, writing, "After a few short jerky strokes, its head dips into the water and its derriere pops up into the air awkwardly. Swans are so awkward when they drink, but then again they are so graceful and beautiful, who cares how they drink."

Bertha was already on a high going into the tournament. A month earlier, the Brakettes had gone on a two-week tour of the West and Midwest that culminated in an appearance at the Pan American Games, which were held in Winnipeg, Canada, that year. Softball was only in the competition as a demonstration sport, so there was no tournament as there had been in Australia. Instead, the Brakettes played a three-game series against the reigning Canadian national champions, which the Brakettes won easily. Still, the gold medals that she and her teammates received afterward mattered to Bertha. She knew that it was the closest she would ever come to winning an Olympic gold medal.

That the Brakettes would win the national tournament was clear almost from the start. They won their first game, against a New Jersey team, by seven runs. Then the next night, they beat a

South Dakota team by six runs. Joan was back with the team, plus Bertha and Donna Lopiano were still pitching well, too. Meanwhile, the Lionettes were eliminated from the tournament early, after losing to the Webb Cats and the Salt Lake City Shamrocks. By the end of the week, the Brakettes hadn't lost a game or even given up a run. They won the last game that Bertha pitched by ten runs, three of which she helped score. Afterward, the crowd gave her a standing ovation that lasted several minutes, and it was announced that the 1968 tournament would open with a Bertha Tickey Night celebration (West Haven, the town where she and Ed lived, had already held its own Bertha Tickey Day earlier that summer).

Joan pitched the Brakettes' final game of the '67 tournament, against the Redwood City Jets from California, and the Brakettes won in another blowout, 6–0. They seemed to have achieved a playing level that the other teams hadn't caught up to yet. The Lionettes appeared to be the only team left that was capable of beating them. The others had to settle for the glory of winning state and regional tournaments and the possibility of making it into the national finals as the Redwood City team had done.

Many teams had also started competing in a smaller national tournament that was held in Houston, Texas, each July. Neither the Brakettes nor Lionettes ever entered, so it gave second-tier teams, such as the Pekin Lettes, the Shamrocks, the Lorelei Ladies, and the Orlando Rebels a chance to shine. They all had talented players, but the Brakettes and the Lionettes had pulled so far away from the rest of the pack that the other teams seemed deficient in comparison.

Bertha knew that she would miss playing with the Brakettes, but she was also ready to take a break from softball. She had never fully recovered from the hip injury that she had suffered in 1958, and more recently she'd been plagued by nerve spasms in her back. She also hadn't had a summer to herself since the war, and those years weren't exactly full of vacations. She and Ed liked to play golf and travel to warm destinations such as Puerto Rico. She was also looking forward to spending more time with Janice and her two granddaughters.

Then that spring, she received a frantic call from the Brakettes coach. Donna Hebert, a pitcher who had been with the team a few years, was having shoulder surgery and would be out for most of the season. With Donna Lopiano starting graduate school, that left Joan as the only full-time pitcher. Not to worry, Bertha told him. She had kept her throwing arm in shape during the off-season just in case and was available to play whenever he needed her. The leisurely summer she had been planning would have to wait.

By the time Stratford's Bertha Tickey Night rolled around, Bertha had pitched more than twenty games and was preparing to play in the national tournament. In fact, she was scheduled to pitch in an exhibition game against the Lionettes later that night. Four thousand people attended the ceremony honoring her, which took place on the Raybestos field. Bill Simpson and several others gave speeches, and local business owners presented her with various gifts and awards, including plaques, a massive bouquet of roses, and two Super Bowl tickets for her and Ed.

By far the best part, though, was the appearance of Bertha's family members from California, whom Simpson had secretly flown in for the occasion. One by one, they walked out onto the field: her four surviving brothers, three of her sisters-in-law, and, finally, Janice, along with her husband, Mike, and their two daughters. Bertha was touched, but she didn't allow herself to get emotional. She still had a game to pitch, after all.

CHAPTER 11

There are several definable reasons why softball has forged ahead of its parent (baseball) in public esteem and participation. One is that it is more readily available to the average person because of the lesser cost of equipment.

—The Softball Story

.   .   .

As Bertha's athletic career was winding down, Bernice Sandler, an academic from Maryland, and Edith Green, a congresswoman from Oregon, had begun drafting a piece of legislation that would revolutionize women's sports in the United States. Neither Sandler nor Green was an athlete, and they didn't have sports in mind when they put together Title IX, one of several amendments to an education bill. Their focus was on academic opportunities for female students and faculty. Sandler struggled to find a faculty position after completing her doctorate and was later told that it was because she came on "too strong" for a woman. She and Green aimed to rid college campuses of such blatant sexism.

The crux of the Title IX amendment is a single thirty-seven-word sentence that builds off the 1964 Civil Rights Act and is quite general. It reads, "No person in the United States shall, on the basis of sex, be excluded from participation in, be denied the benefits of, or be subject to discrimination under any education program or activity receiving Federal financial assistance." At the time, the number of women in the United States with college degrees was nearly half that of men, and women accounted for fewer than 20 percent of university faculty positions. Several fields, including criminology, were completely closed off to women, while others, such as medicine and law, had strict quotas for female students, often admitting only one or two per class.

The women's rights movement had been growing steadily since the 1960s, and calls for gender equality in schools and the workplace were getting louder and more numerous. Title IX garnered the support of several influential male politicians, including Senator Birch Bayh from Indiana, who cosponsored the legislation. The amendments passed in the House and the Senate by a wide margin, and on June 23, 1972, President Richard Nixon signed them into law. From that day forward, schools that received federal money would be legally required to provide male and female students with the same opportunities.

Nixon didn't mention athletics in his statement that accompanied the bill's signing. He didn't mention women, either, instead using the moment to express his displeasure with a different amendment that concerned public-school busing practices. Title IX's significance for female athletes was immediately apparent to women with sports education backgrounds, though. They knew that it would force schools, for the first time, to offer women's sports and award athletic scholarships to female students. They also suspected that the National Collegiate Athletic Association (NCAA), college sports' main governing body, would resist the amendment, and they were right.

Schools were given several years to comply with the Title IX amendment, and the NCAA used that time to fight the legislation, even going so far as to sue the US government in 1976. The

amendment stood, though, and colleges gradually began develop-
ing women's athletic programs, complete with full-time coaches
and real competitions instead of glorified field days. Some schools
already had women's softball teams (many had men's softball
teams, too, although they were on the decline). Others started
fresh, drawing on the vast network of players and coaches from
the ASA league to put the programs together. Suddenly, female
athletes had a multitude of opportunities in a place where previously they'd had close to none.

The company-sponsored softball scene was also changing. Several
of the top women's teams from the sixties had new names. The
defunct Portland Florists became the Dr. Bernard's for a few years,
named for the dentist who took over the team after Erv Lind passed
away. Then in 1972, the team name changed again to the Dave Lee
Nuggets when a sporting goods store owner became the sponsor.
The Phoenix Ramblers had been reborn as the Sun City Saints, and
Topeka's Ohse Meats had become the Teamsterettes after getting
sponsored by a local teamsters union. Other teams, such as the
Whittier Gold Sox and the Yakima Webb Cats, were gone for good.

The uniforms the players wore were noticeably different, too.
The shorts were still short, but the shiny "jockey satin" ensem-
bles began getting replaced by plain polyester outfits that were
cheaper and easier to maintain (the satin ones had required serious ironing). The Brakettes made the switch in 1974, bringing an
end to a nearly twenty-year-old tradition of players getting fitted
by a seamstress before the start of each season. Bertha, who still
lived in the area, thought it was a shame, but she recognized that
styles were changing. She had also recently taken on a new job
as the assistant director of the Barnum Festival, an annual celebration of Connecticut-native P. T. Barnum, which kept her busy
for most of the summer.

One thing that hadn't changed was the demand for strong women's fastpitch teams. Young women still flocked to towns such as Stratford and Orange in the hopes of spending their summers playing alongside legends such as Joan Joyce and Shirley Topley. The college teams that were forming in response to Title IX were competitive, but they were still nothing compared to the Brakettes or the Lionettes. The school teams had a steady source of funding, though, while the adult amateur teams were increasingly short on cash. Wealthy benefactors, such as Bill Simpson, were even scarcer than before, and the days of getting hired to play on a company softball team were essentially over.

One reason for this decline was slowpitch, which, by the seventies, had become the dominant form of softball played by men in the United States. Another was the increase in color television ownership, which meant that more people were watching sports at home instead of going out to their community ballparks. The main cause, though, was economic: the local businesses that had once sponsored men's and women's sports teams across the country—the breweries, factories, and retail stores—were disappearing, either by getting bought out or going bankrupt.

The Jackson brewery, which had so generously supported the Jax Maids team in New Orleans, closed in 1974, its grand building left abandoned for ten years before getting restored and converted into a shopping plaza. Morris "Munny" Sokol, who, through his local furniture-store chain, sponsored some of Alabama's best men's and women's softball teams during the 1950s, sold his business in 1969. The Fresno Rockets, who had gone through so many different sponsors over the years, finally folded in 1975, and the Salt Lake City Shamrocks, who had been sponsored by the same family-owned department store since the forties, weren't far behind.

Even the companies that had money had stopped funding teams. The relationship between employers and the communities they operated in was changing. Corporations, such as Dow Chemical, that had previously been at the center of town life—building parks and organizing parades—began turning inward. Employees could no longer expect the kind of job security that Nina Korgan had enjoyed at the Jackson brewery or that Harold "Shifty" Gears had gotten at Eastman Kodak (he started working for the company in the 1930s and didn't retire until 1973, a year before he died). Layoffs were becoming common, and the manufacturing jobs that were so abundant during the forties and fifties began moving overseas.

Raybestos remained steadfast in its support of fastpitch, however. The company continued to spend tens of thousands of dollars on the Brakettes each year in addition to hosting the national tournament most summers. While other teams were still getting around by car and bus, the Brakettes traveled in style. They flew all over North America, always staying in nice hotels, and also got to go on occasional international trips, such as a 1972 excursion to Italy to play in a small tournament there.

In 1974, Stratford hosted the third international women's softball tournament (Japan had hosted the second one in 1970), which featured more than three hundred players from fifteen visiting countries. It was like a mini-Olympics, with the Bridgeport Holiday Inn serving as the Olympic village. The players cooked and ate meals together in the hotel dining room and entertained one another by singing songs. It was the only international softball competition in existence. Softball officials were still campaigning to get fastpitch into the Olympics, but their efforts hadn't gotten far. The sport wasn't even in the Pan Am Games yet, even though it had been seven years since softball had appeared in the competition as a demonstration sport, and baseball had been part of the event since the 1950s. Hopes were that the situation would soon change. It needed to if fastpitch was ever going to have a chance of growing again.

Japan had won the 1970 championship, so it wasn't a surprise that it had one of the strongest teams in the international tournament. Australia, Canada, New Zealand, and the Philippines had good teams, too. None of them was a match for Joan, though. Oddly enough, it was her first time competing in the tournament: she had been with the Lionettes when the Brakettes represented the United States in 1965, and with the Brakettes when the Lionettes got to go in 1970.

Not one to waste an opportunity, she pitched all nine of the Brakettes' games that week, and she didn't give up a single run. In the final, the Japanese team tried to defuse her pitching by bunting, but it didn't work, and the Brakettes won the game, 3–0. The stands were packed as Joan and her teammates stood on the podium that had been brought out onto the field and accepted their first-place medals. It was a lot like the Olympics, but, of course, it wasn't the same.

Joan was approaching her midthirties, but her athletic abilities hadn't diminished. In fact, they seemed to be improving. Her only weakness was that she couldn't run fast anymore—she'd endured too many knee injuries—but that hardly mattered when you could hit home runs the way she could. The 1973 season, her nineteenth, had been among the Brakettes' best ever. One of the team's few losses that summer came at the second annual Old-Timers' game, where they played a squad of former Brakettes led by Bertha, but Joan didn't pitch that night.

At the 1973 national tournament, Joan had only allowed 1 run and threw 134 strikeouts, a new record. She also scored several runs and had the second-highest batting average of the tournament. Even veteran sportswriters were impressed. "I've seen eleven women's and three men's tournaments, but never a performance to match Joyce's in the 1973 event," wrote one. "It is so rare that one person so dominates a sport," wrote another.

The following spring, Joan became the first female recipient of the Connecticut Sports Writers' Alliance's Gold Key award. At the awards banquet, which drew a crowd of more than seven thousand, she accepted the key "on behalf of women athletes," adding that she hoped she wouldn't be the last female athlete honored (she wasn't; in fact, Bertha was the second female recipient).

By August 1974, when the international tournament took place, Joan's career win-loss record had reached an astounding 375–27, and that was only with the Brakettes; it didn't include the three seasons that she'd spent with the Lionettes. A week after winning the world title, she and the Brakettes flew down to Orlando for the national tournament, and they won that title, too, although the final game against the Sun City Saints lasted twenty-five innings. Micki Stratton, Joan's former catcher and whose husband, John, now helped coach the Brakettes, was there holding up a giant sign that said RAYBESTOS IS NUMBER ONE IN THE WORLD AND THE USA. It had already been the consensus for quite some time, but 1974 was the year that it became an actual fact. The Brakettes had also finally achieved their goal of becoming the first fastpitch team to win four consecutive national titles.

Joan was outstanding as an individual, but her team made her better. The same could be said of the Brakettes and Raybestos: the team would still have been great with an average sponsor, but the support of Raybestos allowed them to truly shine. A terrible secret lurked beneath the company's generosity, however. For decades, its manufacturing facility had knowingly exposed workers to harmful chemicals without telling them and had used

Memorial Field, where the Brakettes played and the company put on its annual Fourth of July fireworks show, as a dumping ground for toxic waste.

The first asbestos-related lawsuits against Raybestos were filed in the early 1970s, but they weren't widely reported in the media, and the company's reputation didn't suffer much. Then, later in the decade, it was revealed that Sumner Simpson, Bill Simpson's father, had known about the potential health hazards of asbestos exposure as early as the 1930s and had actively sought to conceal this information from the public. "I think the less said about asbestosis, the better off we are," Sumner wrote to a lawyer from another asbestos company in 1935. The lawyer wrote back, "I quite agree with you that our interests are best served by having asbestosis receive the minimum of publicity."

By the 1960s, several studies had linked asbestos, the main component of the brake linings that Raybestos manufactured, to cancers, such as mesothelioma. The extent to which workers at the Stratford plant were put at risk is unclear. In 1972, the company physician, the one who had given Bertha and other Brakettes their shots before the team's world tour, claimed that there had never been a case of mesothelioma at the factory. Subsequent studies have found the disease in former Raybestos workers, however, and other surveys indicated that rates of mesothelioma and other cancers were higher in Stratford in the 1960s, '70s, and '80s compared to other parts of Connecticut. Still, definitively connecting those cancers to the Raybestos plant has been difficult.

The pollution was a different story. The Environmental Protection Agency directly tied the Raybestos facility to potentially harmful levels of asbestos, lead, and polychlorinated biphenyls (PCBs) at several sites in Stratford, including a school and a public park. Memorial Field, the company's softball field, which was the setting for so many of the town's proud moments, was one of the most polluted areas. It would eventually be sealed away behind a tall metal fence, its once-admired scoreboard and bleachers left to rot under a canopy of weeds.

The Brakettes would later find new sponsors and a different field to play on, but their association with Raybestos would forever be tarnished. How could a company that seemed to do so much for its employees and the town of Stratford be simultaneously poisoning both? There is, perhaps, no satisfying explanation.

That said, environmental regulations were scarce before the 1970s—the EPA didn't even exist until 1970—and industrial pollution was rampant. Stratford is one of many towns in the United States struggling with toxic contaminants from decades past. The hazardous waste left behind by companies such as Eastman Kodak, Dow Chemical, and DuPont has caused health scares, lowered property values, and required cleanup efforts that cost hundreds of millions of dollars. "There are a lot of things we did then that we wouldn't do now, knowing what we know now," a DuPont spokesperson said, following a pollution-related legal settlement in the 1990s. No doubt, many of the people who lived in these towns and worked for these companies would say the same thing.

CHAPTER 12

It is true that each individual has certain limits beyond
which she cannot develop, but few indeed are those who
ever reach or even approach these upper limits.

—Softball for Girls

.   .   .

Joan was ready for the next stage in her athletic career. Several
of her former teammates had moved on to full-time coaching
jobs, but at thirty-four years old, Joan was still in her prime physically, and she wanted to keep competing. She couldn't help but
be a little envious of the fame and financial success that female
golf and tennis players were starting to attain. Billie Jean King,
the tennis player, had recently become the first female athlete to
earn $100,000 a year. Joan, meanwhile, shared a house with her
sister and ran a small travel agency to bring in extra income.

In September of 1974, she accepted an invitation to participate in the first Women's Superstars, a televised contest that
featured top athletes competing against each other in different
individual disciplines, such as swimming, bowling, and cycling.
King had helped organize the event. There had already been two
Men's Superstars competitions, and she thought there should be
one for female athletes, too. King had become a tireless promoter
of women's sports. She was leading the crusade for equal pay in

women's tennis, and earlier that year she had founded the Women's Sports Foundation, a nonprofit that aimed "to advance the lives of women and girls through sports and physical activity."

The Women's Superstars competition was an extension of those other efforts, and even though the premise was kind of silly, the broader purpose—to call attention to female athletes outside of tennis, golf, figure skating, and gymnastics—was serious. It was probably the most high-profile event that Joan had been involved with so far. She had received a fair amount of media coverage over the years, but it was sporadic and mostly regional. Outside of New England, few people knew who she was unless they were softball fans, and fewer of those were around as the 1970s progressed. The competition was also offering prize money: the winner stood to earn tens of thousands of dollars, which was a significant amount for most athletes at the time.

Thus Joan spent the weekend before Christmas that year at the Astrodome in Houston, running through an obstacle course, riding a bike, and shooting hoops alongside King and twenty-one other competitors. Each contestant competed in seven events, none of which could be her primary sport, which meant Joan was ineligible for the softball throw. She excelled in the basketball and bowling events, though, which won her some prize money and helped her secure one of the twelve spots in the finals, which were held in Florida a month later.

Joan didn't do as well in the finals. She aced the basketball and bowling portions again, but she faltered in the swimming, rowing, and tennis events. She finished in eighth place, earning a combined total of about $6,500, which she was allowed to keep, thanks to a recent Amateur Softball Association rule change that permitted players to earn money from sports as long as it didn't come from softball or baseball. Mary Jo Peppler, a volleyball player who had competed in the 1964 Olympics, won first place, which came with about $50,000. "I wouldn't even know what that much money looks like," Mary Jo said afterward. "The amount of money I've made up to now is just zilch."

That summer, Joan led the Brakettes to their fifth national title in a row. She didn't know it at the time, but it would be her last season with the team. After meeting Joan at the Superstars event, Billie Jean King had decided to start a professional women's softball league. She partnered with Dennis Murphy, a sports promoter she'd worked with on previous projects, and by fall they were putting the teams together. They decided that the Connecticut team, name to be determined, would be built around Joan.

King had been an elite tennis player since she was fifteen years old, but she spent most of her childhood playing softball. Baseball was her family's main sport. Her father had worked as a scout for the Milwaukee Brewers when he was younger, and her brother Randy became a pitcher for the San Francisco Giants and other teams. She also grew up in Southern California during the late 1940s and early '50s, when the Lionettes were at the height of their success. She and Bertha might have been teammates had her parents not encouraged her to quit softball and take up tennis instead.

Still, King's main motivation for starting a professional fast-pitch league was to create more opportunities for female athletes. Team sports dominated the American sports landscape in 1975, as they do today, but there were no major professional women's teams. There had never been any, aside from the National Girls and All-American Girls baseball leagues, which, despite their names, had never actually become national and weren't full-time—players had to find other jobs during the off-season. The professional women's softball league aimed to fill this void. The hope was that it would lead to the formation of women's leagues in other team sports, such as basketball and hockey, and bring gender equality to professional athletics the way that Title IX was starting to do at the college level.

Joan was excited about the idea of a professional softball league. She had long thought that fastpitch would get more respect if the word *amateur* weren't attached to it. She also wanted to remind the public what skilled softball looked like—slowpitch had become so pervasive that people were starting to forget—and to show everyone that many talented fastpitch players were out there, that it wasn't just her. "I think the players who haven't been getting any coverage will now," she said when she announced that she was joining the league.

Joan felt that, as the most famous player, it was up to her to make the league a success. In addition to serving her team directly as its coach, part owner, and top player, she used every connection she had to drum up publicity and secure sponsors. She knew that the league would probably never make much money, but she was convinced it could develop a following if enough people found out about it. After all, it hadn't been that long since she and the Brakettes had played before crowds of fifteen thousand or more, and the pro teams only needed audiences a fraction of that size to stay afloat.

There were skeptics, as there always are with new ventures, but overall, response to the softball league was positive. The mid-1970s was a time of sweeping cultural changes. More women were entering the workforce, and they were increasingly taking on fields that had previously been males-only, including engineering, law enforcement, and the military. The gay rights movement was also in full swing. Of course, there was opposition to these changes, but barriers seemed to be coming down. TV shows featured single, working women (*Alice*, *The Mary Tyler Moore Show*), divorced women (*Maude*), openly gay characters (*Soap*), and African American families (*Good Times*, *The Jeffersons*).

The 1970s were also an experimental period for professional sports. There were two different basketball and hockey leagues, and numerous attempts were made to launch new sports.

King and Murphy had recently launched World Team Tennis, a mixed-gender, team version of the sport. A professional surfing tour was starting up. There was also an indoor lacrosse league and a North American soccer league featuring Pelé and other international stars. A fledgling women's football league was even getting off the ground, and there was a new coed volleyball league, too. It didn't seem like much of a stretch to think that professional women's softball could survive, maybe even thrive, in such an environment.

The softball league's first season began in May of 1976, and it got off to a strong start. The historical significance of a professional women's team sport and the association with Billie Jean King garnered press attention. Each team received local newspaper coverage, and *Sports Illustrated* published a feature article on Joan and her new team, the Connecticut Falcons. Attendance was high at first, too. Many games drew crowds of five thousand or more, putting them on par with minor league baseball teams.

Of the ten teams, five were from the Midwest and the East Coast, and five were from the West, each with its own quirky mascot and color scheme, which usually involved orange or yellow, this being the 1970s. Most teams were variations of established amateur ones. The Santa Ana Lionettes were essentially the Orange Lionettes in different uniforms, and nearly all of the players on the Falcons were former Brakettes. The goal was to take the best of the existing women's fastpitch scene and enhance it with better fields and larger crowds, creating a sort of season-long version of the national tournament.

Player salaries wouldn't be much at first—average pay for the season was about $2,500 (roughly $10,000 in today's dollars)—but there was the promise of more money as the league grew. Many of the players were happy to be getting paid at all and to be able to call themselves professional athletes. Some quit their jobs; others, such as Nancy Ito and Donna Lopiano, came out of athletic retirement; and several relocated to other cities. They believed in the league, and like Joan, they wanted to do their part to help it succeed.

It didn't take long for problems to arise, though. Some of the team's owners had little-to-no experience with competitive softball, while others had softball experience but no business background. There were disagreements over money and management styles, and more than a few players and coaches quit or asked to be traded to different teams at the end of the season.

One of the biggest controversies concerned the Southern California Gems team that league cofounder Dennis Murphy had started. First, the league already had two Southern California teams: the Lionettes and the San Diego Sandpipers. Murphy had also decided to build the team around Rosie Beaird Black, the pitcher from the Queen and Her Maids act, and made her father, Royal Beaird, head coach.

Neither Rosie nor her father had much experience outside of the entertainment circuit, and bringing them into the professional league smacked of a publicity stunt. Rosie told reporters that pitching to women would be like a day off for her because the Queen and Her Maids usually played against men's teams. Meanwhile, her father developed a reputation for disruptive antics on the field, such as arguing with umpires and taunting players on the opposing teams. Murphy dismissed the theatrics as part of the show. "He's colorful, that's all," he told a reporter. "The fans will either love him or hate him. I think what many of the girls are going to have to realize is that we're trying to get people out."

By June of that year, the Gems had lost seventeen of the twenty games they'd played, and Rosie and Royal had left the team. Murphy's son, Dennis Murphy Jr., took over as head coach, and the Gems finished out the season. But four months later,

Murphy was looking to sell the team, and by the time the 1977 season rolled around, it had dissolved completely.

The Gems weren't the only team to not make it past the first season. By 1977, only four of the original ten teams were left. Some folded on their own, while others were forced to sell when they couldn't pay the league's franchise fees on time. The Falcons, which counted King, Martina Navratilova, and professional golfer Jane Blalock as owners, seemed to be the only financially healthy team left.

While it wasn't exactly the breakout debut that the players had hoped for, they had reasons to be positive going into the '77 season. Two new teams had formed to bring the league total to six, and the talent level on each roster was still staggeringly high. Joan had also taken on a more visible leadership role, replacing Murphy as the league's president. "I don't know what we'd do without Joan," one of the team owners said.

The press coverage the teams received was less encouraging. Newswire services, such as United Press International, which had always covered the amateur national tournaments, refused to write about the pro league until it was more established. Local newspaper coverage was also flagging now that the novelty of the first season had worn off. Some team owners resorted to stunts to attract media attention. The Santa Ana Lionettes brought in self-proclaimed male chauvinist Bobby Riggs, the tennis player King famously defeated in 1973, for a "Battle of the Sexes" event. Advertisements for their season opener also promised an appearance by "a real live lion."

The San Jose Sunbirds, the league's Northern California team, had started out as a professional version of the Santa Clara Laurels, who had become the Brakettes' main rival at the national tournament in recent years. By the start of the '77 season, though, their owner, a local architect, had brought in a manager with a baseball background to liven up games (he promised to "get more action into the game" by cutting down on the bunting and introducing trick plays) and began marketing the players as sex objects. Karen Ambler, a blond, nineteen-year-old infielder, was presented to the media as the face of the team even though she had one of their lowest batting averages that season. "She's not the best player in the league. Not by a long shot," one newswire article noted. An article in *California Today*, the Sunday magazine of the *San Jose Mercury News*, featured a full-page photo of Ambler kneeling in a white bikini with the headline "Who Is This Girl? (A) Model, (B) Actress, (C) Athlete, (D) None of the Above." "We're in the sports entertainment business," the owner explained in a different article. "We're trying to put a winning team on the field, players fans can relate to. If they're gorgeous in addition to that, that's a plus."

New decade, same old story. The notion that playing sports was unfeminine stubbornly would not die. Female athletes were often assumed to be lesbians—especially if they had short hair, as many softball players did—and some were, although not necessarily openly. Despite the gains that had been achieved by the gay rights movement, being openly gay during the 1970s was still potentially dangerous, both socially and physically, in many parts of the country. For women who worked as teachers or coaches, it could also mean losing their jobs.

Of course, lesbians had been in sports before the 1970s, but they were more hidden. Women generally didn't have to worry about anyone assuming they were gay—being gay was considered too socially unacceptable to even warrant discussion in most places. One of the reasons that softball emerged as a popular activity among lesbians in many communities was that it was one of the few ways they could socialize with each other without getting harassed. Going to gay bars was out of the question, especially in

Southern cities, such as Memphis and Atlanta, where such places were frequently raided by the police. At the town park, however, they could watch or play in a softball game without people paying much attention.

The women's and gay rights movements were helping to make society more accepting and open, but they also created new issues. Before, female athletes were either "single" or "married" and were rarely asked about their political affiliations, perhaps because they were presumed not to have any. By the late 1970s, though, the pendulum had swung so far in the other direction that women who played sports were almost treated as political activists and were constantly being asked about their opinions on lesbians and "women's lib."

The field was where softball players could truly be free. During a game, it didn't matter what you looked like or if you were gay or straight: all that counted was skill. There was comfort in the simplicity of it. If you were good and you enjoyed playing, it could feel as if you were doing what you were born to do. For many of the women who played in the professional league, that feeling was worth putting up with difficult owners and half-empty stands.

Several players did quit the league after the '77 season, though. Ten of the Sunbirds players went on strike, citing "numerous differences" with management. A Santa Ana Lionettes player left to join a French basketball team sponsored by the Michelin tire company. It was rumored that the league would be expanding in the spring—more than twenty cities had reportedly expressed interest in starting teams—but at the start of the 1978 season, the league was down to only four teams: the Falcons, the Sunbirds, the Buffalo Bisons, and the St. Louis Hummers.

The financial troubles had become too obvious to ignore, and even the younger players began having doubts about the league's future. Most of the money the teams brought in from ticket sales went toward travel expenses. Players took cuts in their already meager salaries so that everyone in the league could at least get paid something. The end seemed near, but nobody had gone into the league expecting instant success. From the outset, Murphy and King had said that it would take three to five years to get the league off the ground. "There will be tough times," King had said at a press conference that first year. "It's going to take a lot of hard work, a lot of money, and a lot of great softball. Keep an open mind and believe in us."

By 1979, players were allowing their optimism to return, albeit cautiously. Joan had helped broker a corporate sponsorship deal with Bic pens, and two new teams were supposed to join the league that summer: one from Philadelphia and one from Edmonton, Canada. The '79 season was also going to see a rebirth for the San Jose Sunbirds. They had a new name, the Rainbows, and new feminist owners who were bringing back the players who had quit the previous year.

Softball also wasn't the only professional women's team sport anymore. The Women's Professional Basketball League had formed earlier that winter, and it appeared to be doing well. And then, a month before the 1979 season started, Joan and the Falcons embarked on a historic ten-day goodwill tour of China (they were the first professional US sports team to visit the country). *People* magazine sent along a writer and photographer to cover the story, and many newspapers wrote about it as well. "I always wondered what it would feel like to play in front of fifty thousand people," one of the players was quoted as saying in the *People* article. "It's too bad we had to go to China to find out." The softball league and women's sports in general, it seemed, were finally garnering respect.

The players knew that the league was still a long ways from

stable, but they were willing to make sacrifices to keep it going. When the planned Philadelphia team fell through at the last minute, a group of players, most of whom were from California, agreed to move to Mount Vernon, New York, to play on a hastily formed replacement team. Little about that experience felt professional. The players were put up in an old house and then later in a college dormitory, their uniforms and team name didn't match (they were supposed to be the Golden Apples, but the shirts they were given to wear were blue and orange and said NEW YORK EXPLORERS on the front), and only twenty-five people showed up to watch their first home game.

It wasn't clear how much they would get paid, if at all, but the players decided to finish out the season anyway. They still got to travel, and they had some good games. Once, they even beat the Falcons by five runs. At night, they drank beer and played cards in the dorm kitchen. There were certainly worse ways to spend the summer.

No one was surprised when a review of the league's finances at the end of the year found that most of the teams were in bad shape. Then, in early 1980, Bic pens withdrew as a sponsor, and the league went "on hold" for the season. The younger players weren't quite sure what to do. They didn't want to take a year off from softball, which, as "professionals," they would have to do to join an Amateur Softball Association team. Most of them went into limbo, finding temporary jobs and doing what they could to stay in shape while they waited to see what happened with the pro league.

Players in the women's pro basketball league were facing a similar situation. After two seasons, only a few of the original eight teams remained. Even the New York Stars, the team that won the 1980 league championship, was on hiatus. And it wasn't just the women's leagues that were struggling. By the end of the decade, most of the sports experiments of the seventies were in trouble. The alternative basketball and hockey leagues had been swallowed up by the NBA and the NHL, respectively, the professional lacrosse league had folded, and the North American Soccer League had lost Pelé and was fading fast.

Each of these new leagues faced different challenges, but they all struggled with securing television contracts. Major TV network coverage was critical for a sport's survival in the 1970s, but getting airtime on the broadcast channels (cable TV barely existed) was notoriously difficult. New sports were relegated to odd time slots and given tape-delayed coverage instead of live. Then, when the ratings were inevitably low, the networks would drop them from the schedule. The best the softball league ever managed to achieve was a few games per season on local networks—hardly enough to build an audience. However, the Falcons did have the distinction of being one of the first teams featured on ESPN, which, like them, was based in Connecticut and just starting out.

Joan pitched in a Falcons exhibition game that July and suggested that she would play for the team if and when the pro league came back. Her former teammates were doubtful, though. They knew that only one sport had her full attention: golf. Joan had played golf recreationally for years, but she started training seriously after meeting top pro and Falcons co-owner Jane Blalock and had already competed in a few LPGA tournaments (she went through LPGA qualifying school with future star Nancy Lopez). At thirty-nine, Joan was outperforming women half her age who had been golfing their whole lives. The press couldn't seem to get enough of the story. Suddenly, the news reporters that had refused to cover the women's softball league until it got bigger were calling her up wanting to talk about golf. Thanks but no thanks, she told them.

Joan knew that she would never be as dominant in golf as she had been in softball, and she was at peace with that. She was driven to win, but she didn't set any expectations for herself. What she cared about was doing her best. Blalock marveled at the way Joan played in tournaments: so intensely but also with so much joy.

CHAPTER 13

Girls who play on the better teams—those which go to
the state and regional tournaments year after year—have
found softball the vehicle to make new friends and to
renew pleasant acquaintances.

—The Softball Story

. . .

The list of athletes who have attempted to switch to golf after
retiring from professional careers in other sports is long and
varied: tennis champion Ivan Lendl and former NFL quarterback
Dan Marino are just two of the more recent examples. The number who have successfully made the transition is much smaller,
however. That Joan was able to do so when she was in her forties
and in such a short time was remarkable. It put her in the rarefied
company of Babe Didrikson Zaharias and Althea Gibson, the only
other notable female athletes to have carved out second careers
in golf.

Joan's golf game was continuing to improve with each passing year. In the spring of 1981, she held the lead in an LPGA
tournament, a first for her, for eight holes before falling out of
contention. The next year, she set a record for the lowest number of putts needed in a single round of golf (seventeen, and the
record still stands).

When she wasn't touring, she stayed with friends in Florida. She had a sponsor to cover basic travel expenses, but she didn't have much in the way of actual income. Her tournament winnings were enough money to buy groceries and other essentials, but that was about it. She was having a great time, though. She loved playing on the pro tour, and she decided that she didn't care that much about money. She was doing what she wanted to be doing, and that was what mattered.

Meanwhile, fastpitch was now primarily a college sport. A few of the competitive adult teams from the 1970s were still around, such as the Brakettes and the Sun City Saints in Phoenix, but even they were mostly made up of students. The young women who had once sought out towns with strong company-sponsored fastpitch teams were now flocking to the places that had good college teams. The underlying goal was the same: to play on the most competitive team possible. Joining a college team was inherently a short-term plan, however. In the fifties and sixties, players often stayed with a fastpitch team for a decade or more, but college was over after four years.

The college softball tournaments were also decidedly less glamorous than the ones that Bertha and Joan had played in during their athletic careers. The NCAA didn't hold its first women's softball tournament until 1982, and it was a modest affair. It took place in Omaha, Nebraska, the same city where the NCAA baseball tournament was held, but at a different park and during a different week, so there wasn't any overlap. Attendance was in the low thousands at the most, and the games received hardly any media attention, although there was at least a small amount of television coverage.

The competition at the tournament was serious, though. Most of the teams' coaches had been top players themselves—a few had even played in the professional league with Joan—and they taught their students to play hard. They weren't going to put their teams through the punch-and-cookies-type sporting events that they'd been subjected to when they were young.

Without these coaches, it's doubtful that fastpitch would have been preserved as a competitive women's sport. The schools didn't have much interest in the game or in women's athletics, in general. For most schools, softball was a means to an end and not much more. Colleges had to offer women's team sports to comply with Title IX, and softball was a ready-made solution. That didn't mean that the teams would be nurtured or well funded, though.

It's a common misconception that Title IX required schools to spend the same amount of money on men's and women's sports. It didn't, and men's sports continued to receive the lion's share of college athletic funds as they still do today. All that the amendment stipulated was that colleges that received federal money had to offer female students the same athletic opportunities as their male counterparts. For example, if there was student interest in women's basketball, the school had to start a women's basketball team and give the players access to athletic scholarships. Other than that, the requirements were, and still are, quite vague.

It was largely up to the coaches to make college fastpitch teams competitive and worth joining. They stretched their teams' often minuscule budgets as far as they would go to get their players decent equipment and to take them on road trips. When that money ran out, they organized community fund-raising efforts and, frequently, dipped into their own pockets. They were as dedicated to the teams they coached as they had been to the ones they'd played on when they were younger.

Softball influenced other areas of women's college sports, too. Many of the women who were brought in to coach women's volleyball and basketball also had softball backgrounds, which made sense, given the sport's history as one of the few outlets for competitive female athletes. Billie Moore, UCLA's celebrated women's basketball coach, got her start on the Ohse Meats team in Kansas and later played on the Brakettes with Joan. Louise Albrecht, the volleyball coach and associate athletics director at Southern Connecticut State University, played for the Whittier Gold Sox and the Lionettes, among other teams. Perhaps the best-known former softball player in college sports was Donna Lopiano, who made history when she became the first women's athletics director at the University of Texas in 1975 and was also an outspoken defender of Title IX.

At first, when the NCAA was fighting Title IX and wanted nothing to do with women's sports, the female coaches put together their own tournaments, and not all of them welcomed being brought under the NCAA umbrella. As a result, two college softball championship tournaments were held in 1982: the NCAA one in Omaha and one sponsored by the Association for Intercollegiate Athletics for Women (AIAW) in Norman, Oklahoma. One school, Oklahoma State University, participated in both tournaments, but most teams took sides. By the next year, though, the AIAW was defunct, making the NCAA tournament the only option. There wouldn't have been talented teams to play in it, however, had it not been for the AIAW and the pioneering coaches who supported their players, finding them uniforms to wear and fields to play on when the schools were mostly indifferent.

Softball was already on the path to becoming a women's-only game in the 1970s, but its growth as a women's college sport in the early 1980s finished the job. Women were still largely barred from playing baseball. Little League was gradually starting to become more inclusive, amending its rules so that girls at least had the possibility of joining teams, but high school baseball was still males-only. The ban on women playing professional baseball was still in place, too, apparently just in case a female player managed to sidestep all the other barriers and tried to jump straight onto a minor league team.

Meanwhile, memories of men's fastpitch were starting to fade. However, one male fastpitch pitcher, Ty Stofflet, did become a minor celebrity in the 1970s. He had won numerous tournaments and set several pitching records while playing for small-town teams with names such as Sal's Lunch and Rising Sun Hotel. *Sports Illustrated* published a feature about him in 1979, declaring that he "would be famous were he not the modest Prince of the Front Porch." By the eighties, though, Stofflet had retired, and the few competitive men's fastpitch teams that remained in the United States had to import pitchers from other countries, such as New Zealand, where the sport was still popular among men.

Being a women's sport without a male counterpart made fastpitch unique but also marginalized. Many people wrongly assumed that softball was easier than baseball because women played it and not men; others confused fastpitch with slowpitch. The program cover for the '82 NCAA softball tournament seemed designed to combat these prejudices. On it, a young woman with her mouth open, as if shouting, and a glove in her hand jumps in the air beneath the tagline "It'll catch you by surprise!"

Initially, all the best college softball teams came from California. Each of the eight NCAA tournament finals played during the 1980s featured at least one school from the state. UCLA and Fresno State University were the top teams in 1982. The next year, Cal State–Fullerton, an Orange County school, made it to the finals (Fullerton also won the 1986 championship). Other strong teams included Long Beach State and Cal Poly Pomona, which was coached by two former Lionettes, Carol Spanks and Shirley Topley. Even Texas A&M, the only non-California school to win an NCAA softball title in the eighties, was mostly made up of California players.

The California college teams excelled for many of the same reasons that had made the state a softball powerhouse forty years earlier: the warm climate allowed for year-round practice, and the area's democratic attitude toward sports, which encouraged everyone to play regardless of gender or social status, created a large talent pool. Indeed, California schools did well in all women's college sports, but their dominance in softball was especially pronounced.

The UCLA team was probably the closest analog to the Orange Lionettes. By far the most successful college softball team in the country, it won five of the eight NCAA championships held in the 1980s. Sharron Backus, the team's head coach, was herself a former Lionette. Bertha was partial to the Fresno State team, though. She and Ed had moved to the Fresno area after she retired from the Barnum Festival in 1988, and sometimes she and her former rivals from the Fresno Rockets would go to the school's games together. The older players couldn't get over that young women could now get scholarships to play sports at four-year colleges; they thought it was wonderful.

Bertha enjoyed watching the college students play, although she couldn't help but size up the batters. She was pretty sure that she would be able to strike most of them out even though she was in her midsixties. After all, she had pitched at the Old-Timers' game back in Stratford just a few years before, and no one had got a hit off her.

Bertha knew that one of the reasons the younger players had struggled with her pitching was that her delivery was unfamiliar to them. Joan's would have been, too. The windmill style had become the standard, and techniques such as the figure eight and slingshot had all but disappeared. It wasn't a deliberate change so much as happenstance. The windmill delivery had long been the most popular, and eventually it became the only one that people taught.

Having all the pitchers use the same delivery style made it easier on batters and umpires, and aesthetically, there was perhaps no better way to differentiate fastpitch from baseball and slowpitch. The combination of the windmill's big circular arm motion and the dramatic step forward before the throw was so obviously different. It was also visually compelling, a dance that took on hypnotic qualities the more it was repeated, and it could consistently be counted on to draw in newcomers, which was important for a sport on the margins.

College fastpitch players didn't have the built-in audience that athletes in other established sports, such as basketball, did. Fastpitch had been around as long as those sports had, if not longer, but it needed to be reintroduced to fans. In this sense, the college players were a lot like the ones who had enticed passersby at the World's Fair fifty years earlier. They were ambassadors, and they were the sole representatives of their sport to most of the general public. The great players from the past—Bertha, Freda Savona, and even Joan—were already all but forgotten. They had been famous, but not quite famous enough to become household names. In the spring of 1982, the CBS show *60 Minutes* aired a segment about the Brakettes. "Hold on, sports fans," the host said in the introduction. "This is not the kind of softball played by the Playboy Bunnies in Central Park. We're talking about a hard, fast game played by top athletes." No matter how old fastpitch got, it was always being presented as new.

Many softball players were happy just to have the opportunity to get a college education. Young women who hadn't even considered attending college before suddenly had access to a whole range of new experiences and career options. It was a chance to travel and explore and to start to see themselves in a different light. It could be literally life-changing.

For the college players who were solely focused on sports, though, four years was a painfully short time. Often, they had to leave just when they were starting to feel comfortable with their teams. With the pro league gone, there weren't many places for them to go after they graduated. More coaching jobs than ever before were available, but coaching wasn't the same as playing. To have to quit a sport because of injury or lack of talent was one thing, but to have to quit when they were in their prime because there were no teams to join—that was a much harder fate to accept.

The one beacon of hope that kept players going was the possibility that softball would soon be in the Olympics. Softball players had been hoping for that for decades, and by the early eighties it was starting to seem likely, maybe even probable. Women's basketball had been added to the Summer Olympics program in 1976, and in 1979, fastpitch finally became an official event of the Pan American Games. The international softball tournament was still held every four years, too, and it was getting larger—more than twenty teams had competed in the 1982 women's championship in Taipei.

The Olympics also appeared to be expanding. Olympic organizers had steadily been adding new events to the summer program since the seventies, and baseball was going to be featured as a demonstration sport at the 1984 Olympics in Los Angeles. It seemed logical to assume that softball was next in line.

The Olympics continued to be the ultimate goal for most female athletes, especially those in team sports. Boys could fantasize about playing in the World Series or the Super Bowl, but for girls who dreamed of that kind of sports glory the Olympics were the only option. Women who played softball and basketball at the elite level in the fifties and sixties often said that not getting to compete in the Olympics was their greatest disappointment in life. There would clearly be a surplus of interested players if it came time to put a US Olympic softball team together. The question the college players from the 1980s had to ask themselves was how long they were willing to wait.

Spending a summer or two playing for an amateur team such as the Brakettes was easy enough, particularly as a student. From there, players could try to get on the US national team and maybe get some overseas playing experience. Neither of these options offered any sort of financial support, though. At the most, housing might be covered, which usually meant staying with a local family. Even if players found jobs that allowed them to take most of the summers off, the routine was difficult to maintain year after year. Then by the mid-1980s, it became apparent that softball wasn't going to be featured in the 1988 Olympics after all. Players in their midtwenties or older had to decide if they were willing to put their lives on hold for yet another four years. The hard part was not knowing if the dream they were so willing to make sacrifices for was even feasible. They were stuck in limbo, much like the young players in the pro league had been ten years earlier.

To even have a chance at making the national softball team, though, players needed fastpitch experience, and many towns and schools only offered slowpitch. The dearth of fastpitch teams was particularly noticeable in the Southeast. Aside from the occasional nostalgic newspaper article, it was as if people had forgotten the sport had ever existed there. Parents, mostly dads, sued the schools, arguing that not offering fastpitch was depriving their daughters of college scholarship opportunities. The parents won many of the cases, but the suits often dragged on for years—too long to benefit their daughters.

Some of the most contentious school lawsuits were in Florida, which, ironically, had more historical ties to fastpitch than any other state in the Southeast. It had hosted the national softball tournament numerous times over the years and was also home to one of the most successful women's fastpitch teams from the 1970s and 1980s, the Orlando Rebels, who had not only faced the Brakettes in the national finals several times but had beaten them in 1981, which earned them the right to represent the United States at the international tournament the next year. The Clearwater Bombers team had also dominated men's fastpitch at the national level for decades. Yet, the Florida high schools argued that they didn't have people who were qualified to coach the sport.

The Florida schools dragged their feet on the issue for years. Then in 1991, fastpitch was finally selected to be part of the Olympics, starting in 1996. The news further galvanized the crusading parents, and in 1993 Florida passed a law requiring public schools to offer fastpitch. Even then, some coaches refused to switch from slowpitch. "I won't sit and watch fifteen to eighteen strikeouts," one said. Meanwhile, the softball coaches at Florida universities had to recruit players from California because the local girls didn't have the right skills.

Similar scenes were playing out all over the South during the 1990s. Even though fastpitch was the only form of softball recognized by the NCAA, high school coaches throughout the region fought to keep slowpitch. Some claimed that switching to fastpitch would lead to decreased participation (because it was more difficult), while others worried that it would cause injuries (again because it was more difficult). "How much money are we going to waste defending something we shouldn't even be defending?" asked state legislator Anne Northup in 1994, when she introduced the bill that required Kentucky schools to offer fastpitch.

But not just Southern states were resistant to change, nor was it just softball coaches. High schools in Iowa and Oklahoma stuck with the six-player version of women's basketball until the mid-1990s, even though the nation's colleges had transitioned to the "men's rules" five-player format for women two decades earlier. As with softball, it took lawsuits to get the schools to change. Coaches who opposed the switch expressed concern that girls wouldn't be able to meet the athletic demands of running full court. Of course, girls were more than capable of playing regular five-player basketball, as high school teams in other parts of the country had already made abundantly clear.

Coaches in Florida, Oklahoma, and several other states also resisted having their girls' cross-country teams run longer distances. Like the coaches who fought to keep slowpitch, they argued that changing their programs to match the national standards would reduce participation. "The programs who have had girls coming out just for something to do or to get a letter will go under," one warned. They were wrong, though. States that made the transition found that girls had no problem running the same distances as the boys and that, if anything, lengthening the race distances seemed to increase participation.

Some critics saw the school lawsuits as a sign that people were taking high school sports too seriously. They waxed nostalgic about the days when playing on a high school team was about gaining experience and "learning the fundamentals" of a sport. College sports were becoming more competitive, though, and high school sports naturally followed suit. As the twentieth anniversary of Title IX came and went, young women were no longer content just to be able to play sports casually at school. They knew that to compete at a national or international level, they needed to start training seriously before they got to college and possibly even before they got to high school.

UCLA went into the 1990s as the fastpitch team that everyone admired and no one wanted to face. The school's coaches had no problem attracting talent, especially since most of the top high school players already lived in Southern California. The team's roster in the early 1990s was particularly impressive because it included Lisa Fernandez, who had won national awards for both pitching and batting.

Other West Coast schools were beginning to catch up, though. They were getting more funding and building their own stadiums, which was, in turn, making the regional youth teams more competitive. Fresno State University had become UCLA's main rival at the NCAA championships. The team, coached by Margie Wright, who pitched for the St. Louis Hummers in the 1970s professional softball league, didn't have a big budget and couldn't entice students with beaches the way the Southern California schools could. Thanks to the support of Jeanne Contel and other former Fresno Rockets players, though, they had a huge fan base and actually set a college softball attendance record one season. They had made it into the NCAA finals against UCLA several times, and although they hadn't yet won, they seemed destined for a victory soon.

Then in 1991, the University of Arizona showed that they were a team to be reckoned with when they upset UCLA in spectacular fashion to win their first national title. The game had been scoreless until the third inning, but then two walks and a fielding error allowed Arizona to load the bases. The next batter hit a triple, which brought in two runs (the runner from first base was thrown out). Then another batter brought in a third run to make the score 3–0. By the fourth inning, two more runs had scored, both on small hits. The game quieted down for the remaining three innings, but other than a solo home run hit by Fernandez, UCLA wasn't able to score. Arizona had strong pitchers, but the team's 1991 victory was largely due to its mastery of a relatively new batting style that, like bunting, capitalized on softball's small field dimensions.

This batting technique, called slap hitting, allowed the batter to get a running start while hitting the ball, usually for an infield single. The style first emerged in the 1980s, but Arizona was the first major college to build an offensive strategy around the tactic. It changed the pace of the game, making it even faster than it already was, and it posed a new challenge to teams' infielders, at least at first.

Being a good slapper was an art: the swing and the running head start needed to be precisely coordinated to be successful. The key component was speed. Nearly all slappers hit left-handed to get them closer to first base, and the fastest runners could get there in about two seconds. After Arizona showed how effective a slap-hitting-based offense could be, other schools began incorporating the technique more. Some teams were so committed to the strategy that they started recruiting fast runners from other sports, such as track and field, just to convert them into slappers.

Few schools could match the skill level of Arizona and UCLA, however. The Pacific-10 Conference, which both schools played in, had become the equivalent of the Pacific Coast softball league of the 1950s, and like the Lionettes and the Phoenix Ramblers, UCLA and Arizona became familiar foes who pushed each other throughout the regular season to get better. They faced each other in the NCAA finals the next two years in a row, with UCLA winning the title in 1992 only to have Arizona take it back in 1993.

In 1994, though, UCLA played and lost to Arizona in the semifinals, which meant that, for the first time in seven years, they wouldn't get a chance to compete for the national title. The next year, UCLA showed up at the NCAA championship with a twenty-three-year-old Australian pitcher named Tanya Harding (not to be confused with Tonya Harding, the figure skater), who had joined the team midway through the season. Once again, they faced Arizona in the tournament finals, and Harding, who had a 17–1 record going into the college tournament, led UCLA to a

4–2 victory, winning the MVP award. "No Mercy for Arizona," read the headline of a *Los Angeles Times* article about the game, a reference to several of Arizona's earlier tournament games that had ended early due to the "mercy rule," which called games after five innings if one team was ahead by eight or more runs.

A week later, Harding returned to Australia, taking incompletes in the courses she had enrolled in. She reportedly planned to complete her course work during the summer. Despite no obvious rules violations, the incident generated a lot of negative press. The *New York Times* called Harding "UCLA's ringer from down under," and *Sports Illustrated* wondered if "she ever really knew the name of the school . . . or the names of her teammates."

The bad publicity brought the UCLA team's recruiting practices under scrutiny, and not long afterward, the NCAA began an investigation that found the school's softball program had misused scholarships. The team was dealt a number of penalties, including having to forfeit the '95 title, and the school's entire athletic department was put on probation for three years. Sharron Backus, the head coach, retired.

Some fretted about what the UCLA case signified for women's sports. Even as support and funding for women's athletics increased, the prevailing public opinion was that women were only supposed to play sports recreationally and "for the love of the game." It was considered disappointing when a men's college team got embroiled in a cheating scandal, which, it should be noted, happened frequently. But people were shocked that a women's team could be associated with such behavior. "I thought that women's athletics wasn't like the men's win-at-all-costs, but I guess it is," one coach lamented to the *Los Angeles Times*.

It was all a bit hyperbolic. At the same time, a change had occurred. Female athletes were no longer pleasantly surprised to get college scholarships; they expected them. They also expected to be provided with high-quality uniforms and practice facilities and to have coaches who pushed them to compete. They took themselves seriously, and others were beginning to also. ESPN began covering women's college sports, particularly basketball, in prime time, and there was talk of starting up professional women's leagues again. For softball players, the biggest competition coming up was the final week of tryouts for the 1996 Olympic team. It was going to be an intense couple of days, and although the players might be friendly with each other, they would definitely be playing to win.

Around this time a school, Florida Atlantic University, was finally able to persuade Joan to take on a full-time coaching position. She had been playing on the LPGA tour continuously for more than fifteen years. The 1984 season, during which she turned forty-four years old, had been her most successful to date. She achieved her best score, a 66, that year and earned $31,483, about $72,000 in today's dollars, in prize money. Staying on the pro tour year after year wasn't always easy. She often finished in the middle of the pack at tournaments and had to play without a sponsor some years. To save money she sometimes stayed at friends' houses instead of hotels when she traveled.

She had moved to Boca Raton, Florida, pretty much permanently and had gotten a side job teaching golf at a local course to help cover her living expenses. Florida Atlantic University was small and didn't even have a softball team. Joan decided that she was ready for a new challenge, though, and true to form, she threw herself into her coaching job completely. Not only did she build a nationally ranked softball team from scratch, but she managed every aspect of it, from recruiting the athletes to painting the dugout to running the concession stand at games. Then, as if that weren't already enough, she became the school's women's golf coach, too.

Few of the athletes Joan coached were aware of her athletic accomplishments or how famous she had once been. The golfers cared about the celebrities of the moment, such as Annika Sörenstam, and the softball players idolized the members of the US national team, many of whom would soon be competing in the Olympics. One day Joan took her players to watch the national team practice in Orlando. Afterward, the students wanted to get the players' autographs, but before they had a chance to, the players from the national team crowded around Joan to get *her* autograph. They recognized her legendary status even if her own players didn't.

Joan understood. She knew that if she were her players' age, she would probably be fixated on the Olympics, too. Had she been born a decade later, she might have gotten an Olympic medal of her own. She was good enough to play on the national women's basketball team, and, indeed, she did for part of the 1960s (growing up in Connecticut, she had experience playing the more competitive five-player version of the game). But by 1976, when women's basketball first appeared in the Olympics, she was past her prime as a player and had her hands full with the professional softball league. She was still satisfied with what she had been able to achieve as an athlete, though. She had made the most of the opportunities available to her, and she encouraged the students she coached to do the same.

Most softball players in the United States wouldn't get to compete in the 1996 Olympics. The Olympic team had only fifteen spots, and they were highly sought after, not just by current college players, but by former stars, too. The average, or even above-average, college player didn't have much of a shot at making the team. Even some of the national team players whom Joan's students had met in Orlando might not make the cut.

The final tryouts took place in August of 1995 in Oklahoma City, which was the home of the Amateur Softball Association and was also where the NCAA softball championship had been held since 1990. Sixty-six players had been invited to try out. The group had already been whittled down from an original applicant pool of thousands. By the end of the week, it would be reduced again to fifteen players, five of whom would be pitchers.

As the players completed drills and played scrimmages against each other, a selection committee made up of former players, including a few former Brakettes, observed and took notes. The process was meant to be as merit-based as possible. It didn't matter how old the players were or how much experience they had. Determined players in their thirties who had been waiting for the opportunity to compete in the Olympics for more than a decade were given the same consideration as wide-eyed high school students who were surprised to be there at all.

The next Monday morning, the players gathered in their hotel lobby to find out who had made the team. The roster wound up being a mix of older and younger players: the majority were in their mid- to late twenties, but two were in their midthirties, several were in college, and one was still in high school. Those fifteen players and, to a slightly lesser extent, the five who had been chosen as alternates, were elated. But the other forty-six players, particularly the older ones who knew that they probably wouldn't have another chance to be in the Olympics, were crushed.

One of the most disappointed players was Debbie Doom, who, as a pitcher for UCLA in the early 1980s, was one of the first college softball players to get national attention. She set an NCAA record for strikeouts one year and led UCLA to three national championships. After graduation, she played for various amateur teams and also on the US national team (at the 1991 Pan American Games she pitched two perfect games in a row). At the Olympic tryouts, though, she was overshadowed by younger pitchers, such as Lisa Fernandez and Christa Williams, the high school student who made the team. Doom had had such an enviable college career—few college athletes win three national titles as she did—but she had been dreaming about competing in the Olympics since childhood. Having to put that dream aside after coming so close to achieving it was heartbreaking.

Many softball players, though, found it satisfying enough just to see their sport in the Olympics. Some of the older players were more excited about softball's being in the Olympics than they had ever been about any of their own games. For the younger players, having softball in the Olympics gave them a new goal to strive for, and it made fastpitch more visible. Soon, they hoped, the days of constantly having to explain their sport to people would be over.

CHAPTER 14

More and more, the girls are claiming the spotlight in the
major softball tournaments. And more and more thousands are enjoying this splendid game every year.

—*Softball with Official Rules*

.   .   .

The first Olympic softball game in history got off to an early
start—9:00 a.m. on a Sunday—but it also took place in Georgia in the middle of July, and it was so hot and muggy that officials raised a black flag to indicate potentially hazardous weather
conditions. "The black flag means danger is imminent. Danger is
imminent," an announcer repeated over the PA system. Bertha
and the approximately eighty-five hundred other fans in attendance were undeterred, however. They stayed in their seats for
the duration of the game, which the United States won easily,
10–0, over Puerto Rico.

Bertha was one of several former players who were invited to
witness softball's Olympic debut. Ed had died two years earlier,
so she traveled to Atlanta alone. She was surrounded by familiar
faces once she got there, however. She had been retired from softball for almost thirty years, but Bertha had a connection to nearly
every player on the US team: five were former Brakettes, four
had attended Fresno State University, and three of the pitchers

had won the ASA award named after her. She also knew two of the coaches. Ralph Raymond had been her coach back when she was still playing for the Brakettes in the late 1960s, and Margie Wright, the assistant coach, was from Fresno State.

Then, there were all the women Bertha knew in the bleachers, including Donna Lopiano, Shirley Topley and Carol Spanks from the Lionettes, and several former Fresno Rockets players. Joan was there, too, although she opted to sit in the enclosed staff area instead of out in the stands. Ostensibly, her job was to monitor attendance, but mostly she was there for the air-conditioning.

The field that the US team played on had no ties to softball before the Olympics (it was a converted minor league baseball stadium), but it would forever be linked to the sport's history going forward. It had taken more than thirty years of campaigning to get fastpitch into the Olympics. So many steps, so many meetings, and so many tournaments had to be put together before a sport could even be considered for the Olympic program. Even then, there was no guarantee of success. You could jump through all the hoops and still not get in, while other sports, such as table tennis and synchronized swimming, seemed to gain admission with much less effort.

The initial plan had been to get both men's and women's fastpitch into the Olympics, but when men's baseball was added to the Olympic program in 1992, men's fastpitch was seen as being too similar. Had women's baseball been more widespread, softball probably wouldn't have made it into the Olympics at all.

Fastpitch was already secure as a college sport, but getting it into the Olympics meant worldwide recognition. The Amateur Softball Association also had a chance to regain some of its former glory. The organization celebrated the occasion by taking the US team on a sweeping pre-Olympics national tour. Each of the tour's twenty-one stops offered glimpses into fastpitch's past. Former Jax Maids star Nina Korgan threw out the first pitch at the team's game in Tulsa, Oklahoma. In Illinois, the team played against the Pekin Lettes. Even the tour sponsor, Coca-Cola, was familiar, a reminder of the giant trophies the company used to supply for the national tournament.

Everyone expected the US team to win the 1996 softball gold medal. Out of the 111 games that the US national team had played internationally in the previous decade, they had only lost one. They did lose one of their Olympic games, though. Australia beat them, 2–1, near the end of the Olympic tournament. The United States rebounded quickly from the loss, however, and had no trouble securing a spot in the finals. They won the gold-medal game against China by two runs, and despite some close moments—for example, an attempt by China to steal home in the third inning that was called an out but that many felt should have counted as a run—few doubted that the Americans would win in the end. Even the loss against Australia was the result of a technicality: third baseman Dani Tyler hit a home run that would probably have won the United States the game, but she missed touching home plate as she rounded the bases, and so it didn't count.

In a way, though, winning the gold medal was somewhat beside the point. American women had an advantage in most events at the Summer Olympics. Title IX had expanded women's sports in the United States to a degree that few other countries could match, especially in the 1990s, when the end of the Cold War decimated the government-funded sports programs in Russia and Eastern Europe. During that decade, US women dominated in track and field, swimming, basketball, gymnastics, and women's soccer, which, like softball, made its first Olympic appearance in 1996.

Of course, winning Olympic medals matters to the individual

athletes and the nations they represent, but the true significance of the Games is their global reach. They are far and away the largest sporting event in the world and are hugely influential. In many countries, the Olympics determine what sports get funded. Adding new women's events to the Olympics program—and there were a lot to add, given the Olympics' long history of discriminating against female athletes—helped finance women's sports in countries that might not have invested in them otherwise. Female participation in the Summer Olympics increased by more than 60 percent between 1988 and 1996, in large part due to the incorporation of new women's events.

Softball alone counted for 120 additional female participants at the 1996 Olympics. While the eight countries that competed in the first Olympic softball tournament had all been playing the sport for decades, their appearance in the Games inspired other nations to form teams. By the end of the decade, more than one hundred countries were members of the International Softball Federation, the sport's global governing body.

The minimal space and equipment requirements made it easy to put a fastpitch team together. Plus, softball gave women their own game, particularly in countries that didn't play baseball. It made female athletes the focus, and it wasn't watered-down like other women's-only sports, such as netball, a no-dribble, no-contact women's basketball alternative from the early 1900s that's still played in many countries.

The 1996 Olympics boosted softball domestically, too, even though NBC, the TV network covering the Olympics that year, didn't broadcast any of the softball games (Dick Ebersol, who was president of NBC Sports at the time, later said it was his only regret about the '96 Olympics coverage). Afterward, youth softball teams began cropping up around the country, and the few remaining places that only offered slowpitch in schools—which, ironically, included parts of Georgia—finally transitioned to fastpitch.

A second attempt was also made to launch a professional softball league. This one, called Women's Pro Fastpitch, consisted of six teams, all of which were located in the Southeastern United States, presumably to capitalize on softball's increased popularity there during the Atlanta Olympics. The league's primary sponsor, AT&T Wireless Services, also insisted on it. Maybe the plan would have worked if some of the players from the US national team had joined the league. Professional athletes could compete in the Olympics by then, and the US women's national basketball team had no problem with its players participating in the newly formed WNBA league. The ASA wouldn't allow it, though, and players didn't want to risk losing their chance to compete in the 2000 Olympics.

The ASA changed its position before the pro league's third season got under way in 1999, but by then it was too late: attendance was abysmal and most of the teams were folding. The WNBA was struggling, too, and the National Soccer Alliance, a women's professional soccer league that was formed shortly after the '96 Olympics, was over before it started, dissolving four months before its first season was supposed to begin. For the athletes who had been involved with the 1970s women's sports leagues, it was a depressingly familiar scenario.

Everyone seemed to support women's sports during big competitions, such as the World Cup or the Olympics, but when the excitement from those events wore off, so did the publicity and investment dollars. For the athletes, the most disappointing part of losing the professional women's leagues wasn't missing out on fame or money, although those things would have been nice. Like their 1970s predecessors, they just wanted competitive teams to play with regularly. They'd had that in college, but after graduation they were cast adrift, with no opportunities to develop their skills apart from the occasional game with the national team. It was a bit like being a musician in the New York Philharmonic but only getting to play with the orchestra a few times a year. The players were good, but they knew that they would be even better if they had a chance to play at a high level full-time.

With the pro softball league near collapse, competition for the fifteen spots on the 2000 Olympic team grew even more intense than it had been before the Atlanta Olympics. Not only had the pool of young players increased, but most of the veterans from the 1996 squad wanted to keep their places on the team. When the final roster was announced, two players—one veteran and one newcomer—filed grievances, claiming that the selection process had been unfair. The newcomer was later given a spot as an alternate. Then, the alternate whom she'd replaced filed a grievance. Alternates didn't get to sit in the dugout or collect medals when the team won. Even this mostly honorary role, with no real chance of playing time, had become a coveted position.

The 2000 Olympics were going to be held in Australia, which meant that softball would again be a high-profile event. It had been thirty-five years since Australia had hosted and won the first international softball tournament, and the country's enthusiasm for the sport had only increased since then. NBC had also agreed to broadcast all of the US team's games. This was to be the year that softball came into its own as an Olympic sport. The pressure of the game's being new to the Olympics was gone, allowing softball players to worry less about proving that they belonged on the program and to concentrate more on the games themselves.

The early portion of the tournament was full of exciting moments. Several games went into extra innings, and the US team suffered three losses in a row—first to Japan, then to China, and finally to Australia, much to the crowd's delight. In fact, the Americans almost didn't make it past the first round, creating a sense that anything could happen. Eddie Feigner was also on hand to throw out the opening pitch at one of the games. In his seventies, he had to be pushed onto the field in a wheelchair. Once there, though, he was back to his vaudevillian tricks: he stood up and threw a perfect strike to the catcher from around his back.

Eventually, the United States secured the 2000 gold medal, but only after several close games; no one would describe it as a dominant performance. Fastpitch had become a global sport, with multiple countries vying for supremacy. China, Taiwan, Australia, Japan, Canada, and New Zealand all had strong teams, and the game was on the rise in Latin America, particularly in Cuba and Venezuela. It called to mind the 1960s, when Japan and other countries outside North America first started competing in the ASA national tournament and the international softball scene was beginning to blossom.

Yet, two years later, the Olympic Program Commission published a report recommending that softball be removed from the Olympics because it was only popular in "certain countries." Just as softball seemed to be finding its place in the Olympics, its future in the competition was suddenly in jeopardy.

CHAPTER 15

The only thing critics of softball have been able to say against it is that it is too much of a pitcher's game. It gets monotonous, they claim, to have the pitcher strike out 50 percent to 90 percent of the batters who come to the plate.

—*The Softball Story*

. . .

The 2000 Summer Olympics were a huge success—that much everyone seemed to agree on. The fans and the athletes were happy, and the television ratings were high. Juan Antonio Samaranch, the outgoing president of the International Olympic Committee, labeled them the "best Games ever." But they were also the largest Olympics ever with 300 medal events and more than 10,600 participating athletes, and some felt that they needed to be trimmed down.

Expanding the Olympics program during the 1980s and '90s had created more opportunities for women as well as for athletes from regions that had historically been underrepresented in the Games, such as Asia and Africa. But it was decided that no new sports would be added for the 2004 Summer Olympics in Athens, Greece, which had been plagued by serious budget issues. Olympic officials had also started suggesting that the only way new sports could be added in the future was if some existing sports were removed. "Somebody's got to get off the bus" became a common refrain at International Olympic Committee meetings.

Of course, none of the existing sports was going to volunteer to get off the bus. So it fell to the Olympic Program Commission to suggest a few candidates. In the fall of 2002, the commission presented a report suggesting that baseball, softball, and modern pentathlon, a sport with running, swimming, equestrian, fencing, and shooting events, be eliminated from the 2008 Olympics to make room for golf and rugby. The commission wanted to put the matter to a vote right away, but the proposal was met with such outrage from other IOC members that the vote was postponed until 2005 and all of the sports in the Summer Olympics were made subject to elimination, not just the three mentioned in the report.

While the IOC members squabbled, the players on the US softball team worked hard to prepare for the 2004 Games. They didn't want to risk getting eliminated in the first round, as the 2000 team almost had. The team composition had changed considerably since the 1996 and 2000 Olympics. The players were younger, and only a few had ties to historic amateur teams, such as the Brakettes. Instead, the team was largely a reflection of the country's top high school and college programs. Most of the players had attended either UCLA or the University of Arizona, and all but four of them had grown up in Southern California, which was still home to the country's best youth teams. There had been a coaching change, too: Ralph Raymond, the former Brakettes coach, was out, and Mike Candrea, from the University of Arizona, was in.

In the spring of 2004, the US team embarked on its traditional pre-Olympics national tour. What had started as a victory lap for the ASA in 1996 had become an integral part of the Olympics softball experience for US players. The 2004 tour, with thirty stops, was mostly about generating publicity, although it also helped the team members get used to playing with each other.

The tour had been going well: the players were getting along, and they had been winning all of their games, most of which were against college teams. Then, just before the last stop on the tour, which was Stratford, tragedy struck: Coach Candrea's forty-nine-year-old wife, Sue, who had been traveling with the team, collapsed suddenly at the airport from a brain aneurysm. She died two days later, about a week before the team was to depart for Athens.

Candrea considered staying home, but ultimately he decided that his wife would have wanted him to continue coaching the team. He flew to Athens with his two adult children, and he and the team began preparing for the tournament. The United States was already favored to win the gold medal, but the players' grief over Sue's death seemed to give them added incentive to do well. Their performance throughout the week was extraordinary. Not only did they win every game they played, but they only gave up one run during the entire tournament, and that didn't happen until the sixth inning of the final game. "Women's softball has never been played better, at least not since it became an Olympic sport," declared the Associated Press. After they won the gold medal, the players gathered around Candrea and lifted him above their shoulders. Later, he thanked them for giving him the greatest moment of his life.

The next week, *Sports Illustrated* put the players on the cover with the headline "The Real Dream Team," a dig at the US men's basketball team, who had barely come away with the bronze medal, despite having LeBron James and Dwyane Wade on the roster. Later that fall, the team received the Arete Courage in Sports award, along with swimmer Michael Phelps and cyclist

Lance Armstrong. Then that winter, the US Olympic Committee awarded Candrea the Olympic Shield, its most prestigious honor.

The 2004 Olympics also introduced the world to Jennie Finch, arguably the biggest celebrity to come out of softball. Like Joan Joyce and Lisa Fernandez, Finch was a pitcher who could hit. She was also a tall, outgoing blonde with a movie-star smile. She made *People*'s 50 Most Beautiful People list and appeared in several national ad campaigns. She revived the tradition of softball pitchers humbling professional baseball players, striking out Mike Piazza and Albert Pujols, among others. Finch did for softball what Mia Hamm did for women's soccer in the 1990s. Girls started wearing their hair like Finch's, and she was the main reason that the professional women's softball league, now called National Pro Fastpitch, was able to start back up and survive.

Finch made television networks care about softball, which in turn brought attention to the other stars of the '04 US team. They were a diverse group, as befitted a sport that caters to all different body types. Some were physically imposing, such as Crystl Bustos, a power hitter with tattoos on her large biceps. Others were tall and wiry such as shortstop Natasha Watley and pitcher Cat Osterman. The short players were mostly slap hitters, but some could hit home runs. The group was racially diverse, too. A wide range of girls could look at the team and find someone who looked like them, which mattered when it came to inspiring young women to play sports.

Bertha's dream of fastpitch becoming mainstream finally seemed to be within reach. In 2006, more television viewers watched the college softball championship than the first game of the National Hockey League's Stanley Cup. There were hundreds of college teams and thousands of youth teams. Girls often started playing the sport at age four.

But in the summer of 2005, softball was voted off the Olympic program. The sport's advocates had known the vote was coming for three years, but it was difficult to prepare for something completely unprecedented. For decades, getting added to the Olympic program had been like becoming a tenured professor at a university: it took a long time to achieve, but once granted, appointments were basically permanent. No sport had been eliminated from the Olympics since 1936, when polo was removed.

The 2005 vote was a compromise, designed to put all the Olympic sports on equal footing. The format was simple: IOC members would vote yes or no on each sport; those that received a majority of yes votes would stay on the Olympic program, and any that didn't would be off. Softball players knew their sport was in more danger than others, however. First, there was the power of suggestion. Broadening the vote to include all Olympic sports didn't change that softball, baseball, and modern pentathlon had been mentioned in the Program Commission's report. As a result, they were bound to stand out in voters' minds.

The Summer Olympic program was also organized in a way that made some sports more vulnerable than others. For example, all track-and-field events fell under the umbrella of athletics, which was considered a single sport. Similarly, diving, water polo, synchronized swimming, and all other swimming events were in the aquatics category, which was also treated as a single sport. Obviously, the likelihood of either athletics or aquatics getting voted out of the Olympics was pretty much zero, which meant that all of the events in those categories would be safe. Ironically, even though the point of the vote was to reduce the size of the Olympics, only the smaller sports, the ones that had just a few events, were at risk of being eliminated.

The US softball team's commanding performance at the 2004 Olympics had also led to criticism that fastpitch was an Americans-only game. That alone shouldn't have been grounds for elimination, though. Many Olympic sports were dominated by one or two countries, including table tennis, fencing, and beach volleyball. Plus, softball had only been in three Olympics. It seemed premature to criticize the United States for being too dominant in the sport, especially given how much the American team struggled at the 2000 Olympics.

What really put softball's Olympic status in peril, though, was its relationship with baseball. Even though they were categorized as two separate sports on the Olympic program, the common misconception was that softball was women's baseball. And baseball had fallen out of favor with the IOC. Unlike other professional leagues, such as the NBA and the NHL, Major League Baseball wouldn't let its players participate in the Olympics.

That wouldn't have mattered that much prior to the 1990s, but the Olympics had become increasingly professional since then. The best athletes from each sport were supposed to participate, and not having Major League Baseball players in Olympic baseball was seen as a major omission. The American team, made up of minor league players, hadn't even qualified for the 2004 Games. Doping was also a concern, although baseball was hardly the only Olympic sport with that problem.

The 2005 vote took place on a hot July day in Singapore, where the IOC held its summer meeting that year. Of the three sports that had been targeted by the Program Commission in 2002, modern pentathlon was the only one that survived. Baseball fell short by three votes. Softball received exactly 50 percent of the votes—just one more yes vote and it would have been spared from elimination. Worse yet, Jim Easton, a US IOC member, could have provided that additional yes vote, but he voluntarily recused himself from voting. Easton owned an athletic-equipment company, and although he wasn't required to, he refrained from voting on any of the sports that his company manufactured equipment for, which included softball, baseball, and archery. The 2002 Salt Lake City Winter Olympics ethics scandal was still fresh in many people's minds, and Easton said that he wanted to avoid even the hint of a financial conflict of interest.

When it was revealed how close the votes had been, the international baseball and softball federations requested a revote, and, six months later, the IOC leaders partially acquiesced: in classic bureaucratic fashion, they held a vote on whether to have a revote. This time, Easton participated in the vote, but it was no use. The revote measure didn't pass, which meant that softball would be out of the Olympics after 2008. The earliest that it could hope to get back onto the program was 2016, and that was only if another existing sport got ejected.

Finch and her teammates were devastated, not because of how the decision would affect them, but because of what it meant for younger players. The girls who had watched the United States win the gold medal in 2004 probably wouldn't get a chance to compete in the Olympics themselves, and they would inherit a sport that was losing funding and exposure instead of gaining it.

At the 2008 Olympics, in Beijing, Japan beat the United States to win the softball gold medal, proving once and for all that Americans didn't always dominate the sport. But without the Olympics to shoot for, many countries, including China, which had won the silver medal in the sport in 1996, began to dismantle their national softball programs. At the 2010 World Cup of Softball, only three countries were represented—Canada, the United States, and Japan—instead of the usual six. All of the growth that being in the Olympics had helped achieve was quickly slipping away.

· · ·

Softball and baseball were purportedly cut to make room for golf and rugby, but neither of those sports got enough votes to make it onto the 2012 Olympic program. They didn't even receive the most votes (squash and karate did). As a result, the London Olympics featured two fewer sports than had been budgeted for, and the park that organizers had set aside for the Olympic softball tournament went unused. Any financial savings were negligible. For all the hand-wringing over construction and maintenance costs, the most expensive aspects of the Olympics tend to come from areas that have little to do with sports, such as security, which reportedly cost upward of $1 billion at the London Games.

The only all-female sport on the Olympic program had been eliminated, yet the 2012 Olympics were touted in the press as the "women's Olympics." There was little evidence to justify this declaration, however. The addition of women's boxing meant that no sport in the Summer Olympics excluded women, but males-only events remained in track and field, rowing, canoeing, kayaking, shooting, and wrestling. The female boxers also only had three medal events compared to the men's ten, and whether the women should be required to wear skirts in the ring was debated (ultimately, a skirts-optional policy was adopted).

The other statistic used to support the women's Olympics claim was that the London Games marked the first time in Summer Olympics history that every participating nation had sent at least one female athlete. That this could be considered a major milestone in 2012 set the bar for progress pretty low, but it wasn't even true. While Saudi Arabia and two other nations did send female athletes to the Olympics for the first time in 2012, two other participating countries, Barbados and Nauru, didn't send any. And although the percentage of female competitors at the 2012 Olympics represented an all-time high, it was only a small increase over previous years and, at 44 percent, still fell short of the desired fifty-fifty split.

Golf and rugby did eventually make it onto the Olympic program and will appear in the 2016 Olympics in Rio de Janeiro, Brazil. Both sports will feature female athletes, but the women won't be the stars. Rugby sevens, the version of rugby that will be in the Olympics, didn't even offer a women's tournament until 2009, and golf's Olympics campaign was built around male athletes, mainly Tiger Woods. Jacques Rogge, the president of the IOC from 2001 to 2013, liked to point out that golf and rugby created a combined 204 spots for women, but had softball been added back onto the Olympic program instead of golf, that combined total would have been even higher, at 264. It would have been the obvious choice if maximizing the number of female-athlete spots were truly the priority.

In 2013, the IOC executive board caused another uproar when it dropped wrestling from the Olympic program. The goal had been to open up a spot for a new sport for the 2020 Olympics, but the public outcry over wrestling's removal was so strong that it was reinstated instead. The incident forced Olympic wrestling to add more women's events—with only four women's events to the men's fourteen, it was a long way from gender equality—and it spelled the end for the prohibitive "somebody has to get off the bus" approach to adding new sports. A year later, the IOC had a new president and a revised policy that allowed new sports to be added without having to eliminate existing ones (events will be removed or restructured instead).

The future of Olympic softball is uncertain. Thanks to the recent policy change, chances are good that it will be included in the 2020 Olympics, which will be held in Tokyo. If it is, it will be a marquee event: Japan is the biggest softball supporter besides the United States and is eager to defend its 2008 gold medal in the sport. Being in the 2020 Olympics wouldn't give softball a permanent place on the program, though. It would still have to campaign to get into the 2024 Games, which might not be held in a softball-friendly nation. Softball's Olympic fate is also officially tied to baseball now—they recently began campaigning as a single sport, with baseball as the men's event and softball as the women's—which could hurt it if Major League Baseball continues to clash with the IOC.

Competing in the NCAA championship is what today's young softball players dream about. The tournament receives the kind of television coverage that was once only reserved for football and men's basketball, and it continues to grow in popularity. It could be argued that fastpitch is bigger in the United States now than it ever was when the sport was in the Olympics. The caveat is that it's only big as a college sport. To actually make a living playing softball, most players have to go overseas.

CHAPTER 16

There seems to be no universal agreement as to which name is the most suitable. Some claim that "kitten ball" and "soft ball" are too effeminate.

—*Softball for Girls*

. . .

Female athletes have long been willing to travel far and wide for the opportunity to play sports at a high level. In the 1940s, they relocated to New Orleans to play for the Jax Maids. In the fifties and sixties, they moved to Connecticut to join the Brakettes. Today, fastpitch players go to Japan, which has a company-sponsored league that is similar to the one that used to exist in the United States and is almost as old.

Like their North American counterparts, Japanese companies began sponsoring sports teams to boost worker morale and strengthen community ties. Some teams date back to the early 1940s, but most arose during the country's postwar rebuilding period in the late 1940s and early 1950s. The companies sponsored all kinds of sports—baseball, softball, rugby, basketball, and even skiing—and before long the teams became so competitive that they started recruiting players from other parts of the country and, eventually, all over the world. League rules prevent the softball teams from having more than two foreign players, though.

Pitchers tend to get picked first, but a variety of American players have found success in the league.

Most of their Japanese teammates work for their teams' sponsors, which include Toyota and Hitachi. They work in the company offices in the mornings, usually from eight until noon, then practice with the team for the rest of the day. The Americans are among the few players who get paid just to play sports, and they typically only live in Japan for part of the year. They arrive at the start of the softball season, then return home after it's over, just as Bertha used to do when she first joined the Brakettes.

Michele Smith, a pitcher on the 1996 and 2000 US Olympic teams, was one of the first Americans to play in the Japanese league. She started playing for Toyota Shokki, one of two Toyota teams in the league, in the early 1990s and stayed there for the better part of sixteen years. Her success opened the door for other American players, particularly those with Olympic experience. Then, National Pro Fastpitch emerged in 2005, giving Americans two professional leagues to play in. Because the Japanese softball season is split between spring and fall, players can spend the summer in the United States playing for an NPF team, then go back to Japan to finish the season. The schedule can be grueling, but it allows players to compete nine months out of the year and get paid for it, which they wouldn't be able to do in the United States.

Playing in the Japanese softball league has other benefits. Team sponsors, in addition to providing salaries in the $60,000 range, put the American players up in nice apartments (the whole team is usually housed in the same building) and cover all of their travel expenses. It's also a chance to explore a new culture and learn different playing styles—for example, Japanese softball tends to be more defense-focused—which many players feel makes them better athletes.

Playing overseas for part of the year has become the norm for women in other team sports, too. The basketball players go to Russia and China, while the soccer players go to Western Europe. Money is the main motivator. Because American female athletes are in high demand overseas, US players on international teams often receive salaries that are tens of thousands, sometimes hundreds of thousands of dollars higher than what they could get playing domestically. Some also enjoy the experience of living abroad, but most would play in the United States full-time if they could. Living in another country half of the year has its challenges, such as long separations from family and language and cultural difficulties. Plus, the playing level is generally higher in the United States, especially in basketball.

What the American professional women's sports leagues lack is financial support, which restricts their size and limits how much impact they can have. For example, the National Women's Soccer League had nine teams in 2015, while the men's league, Major League Soccer, had twenty. The Women's National Basketball Association is slightly larger, with twelve teams, but it's still small compared to the NBA, which has thirty teams. The National Pro Fastpitch league is even smaller. In 2015, it had five teams, one of which was a year old and another of which was brand-new. (Major League Baseball, like the NBA, has thirty teams.) The Japanese women's softball league, conversely, boasts twelve teams, all of which are well funded.

A league with only four or five teams can exist, but it can't thrive. Even if the teams are the best in the world, and in the NPF league's case, they probably are, it's just too small. The same teams have to play each other over and over, and the fan base is inherently limited. It needs to grow to attract the media exposure and prominent playing venues that would help it become mainstream. Expanding costs money, though, and finding investors has been difficult. The corporate sponsors that support women's teams at the college and Olympic level seem to have little interest in the professional women's leagues. Russian oligarchs and Japanese companies have probably poured more money into professional women's sports than American investors have.

Some critics have argued that low profitability is what keeps people from investing in professional women's sports. Investors seem to have no qualms about losing money on men's sports, however. Several teams in the NBA reportedly operate at a loss, yet investors are willing to spend millions, even billions, on them. Many professional baseball and hockey teams similarly cost more than they earn. They're considered vanity investments—high on prestige, in part because of the astronomical purchase prices, but low on actual profits. Women's sports, meanwhile, are perceived as being less valuable and are treated as such. Even though the WNBA had higher television ratings, on average, in 2013 than Major League Soccer did, MLS secured a $75 million per year TV deal in 2014, while the WNBA's is only for $12 million per year.

Major League Soccer has investors who are committed to making it succeed no matter how much money it loses (and it lost hundreds of millions of dollars in its early years). Few, if any, professional women's sports in the United States have had that kind of long-term support, although that's starting to change. At the least, people are less willing to let women's leagues fail. When the Los Angeles Sparks women's basketball team abruptly went up for sale a few years ago, it not only found a buyer, but a high-profile buyer: former Lakers star Magic Johnson. Likewise, the US national soccer program stepped in to help the professional women's soccer league when it faced financial collapse in 2012.

National Pro Fastpitch has lost teams over the years, but the league itself is unlikely to fold. It hasn't missed a season since it began in 2005, and it has three firmly established teams—the

Akron Racers; the USSSA Pride in Kissimmee, Florida; and the Chicago Bandits, Jennie Finch's former team—each of which has its own field and loyal fans. The question isn't whether the league will last but whether it can grow.

Recently, the NPF has been expanding its presence in the South. In 2014, it moved its championship series from Chicago to Alabama, and its newest team is based in Dallas, Texas. The audience wasn't there when the league's predecessor tried to establish teams in the region after the 1996 Olympics, but it is now. Today, Southern states, such as Georgia and Florida, have not only transitioned away from slowpitch, but they have some of the best high school and college softball teams in the country. Eight of the last ten NCAA softball tournament finals have featured at least one school from the Southeastern Conference, and two Southern colleges—the University of Alabama and the University of Florida—have won the title.

Having softball back in the Olympics for 2020 would also be a boost for the NPF. For now, though, the league is an extension of the college game. Players get drafted by teams their senior year just as athletes in other professional sports do, and many accept. But unless they also plan to play in Japan, they have to find other jobs to support themselves for the rest of the year. Some, especially college-championship winners, can make a modest living from softball-equipment endorsements and giving private lessons, but most seek out something more permanent, such as an assistant coaching position. There isn't a straightforward path to follow. Instead, the players take it year by year, seeing what opportunities arise and figuring out what works best for them.

Coaching is probably the most stable career option in softball right now, but those jobs are more difficult to obtain than they used to be. In the early days of Title IX the vast majority of college softball coaches were women, but as the sport grew more popular and funding for the teams increased, more men began applying for the positions. Today, roughly 35 percent of college softball teams are coached by men.

Some players see this trend as encouraging. Women's sports are treated as a niche product, and for many players, male coaches represent mainstream acceptance. Some have even said that they prefer being coached by men. Bertha shared this view, although in her day male coaches were the norm. It's not a completely surprising stance, considering how many girls get introduced to sports by their fathers and look up to male athletes (a striking number of the US national softball team members' "favorite athletes" are men). Studies have also shown that athletes who grow up without female coaches are more likely to be biased against them later in life. The result is that many women don't pursue coaching at all, and those who do often find themselves limited to lower-level assistant-coach positions.

While men coaching women's team sports has increased in general, it's particularly noteworthy in softball because so few men have fastpitch backgrounds. Despite exceptions, such as the University of Oregon's Mike White, who grew up in New Zealand and was a pitcher for the country's national men's fastpitch team, most of the men coaching today's college softball teams have only ever played baseball. It's not that baseball players aren't capable of coaching softball—the two sports are related, after all—but they're an odd choice for head coach when so many women have direct softball experience. The situation would also be different if more women got hired to coach men's teams, but they hardly ever do: only about 3 percent of men's college teams have female coaches, and those tend to be in individual sports, such as swimming and tennis.

When softball players do go into coaching, they usually do so through their alma mater. Lisa Fernandez went back to UCLA as a coach shortly after competing in the 1996 Olympics and has been with the team in some capacity ever since. Others, such as Laura Berg, who played with Fernandez on the US Olympic team, start out at their alma mater—in her case, Fresno State University—then move on to different schools. Volunteer or assistant coaches more or less have summers off, allowing them to join teams in the NPF or play on the US national team. That flexibility starts to disappear as they move up to higher-level coaching positions, though. Summer is the main season for recruiting new students. Plus, coaches are often expected to run camps and skills clinics. It quickly becomes a full-time, twelve-months-a-year job.

Until recently, softball players commonly transitioned into careers in coaching or other fields by their midtwenties and retired from playing completely by their late twenties. The prospect of softball's being back in the Olympics for 2020 has changed that time line, though. Now, players are considering staying with the sport into their thirties just to have a chance at making the US Olympic team. It's reminiscent of the early 1990s, when softball was first added to the Olympics.

As much as they have learned to adjust their expectations, most of today's softball players still grew up dreaming of the Olympics. They had posters of Jennie Finch and Lisa Fernandez on their bedroom walls and fantasized about the day that they, too, would represent their country and compete before a worldwide audience. That dream seemed to vanish forever in 2013, when wrestling was selected as the "new" sport for the 2020 Games. But now that softball might be in the 2020 Olympics after all, they're allowing themselves to hope again.

If there is a 2020 US Olympic softball team, the number of players applying to try out for it will probably reach record levels. Like the players who went out for the 1996 Olympic team, they will put their lives on hold, delaying marriage or quitting jobs if necessary. No sacrifice is too large for what most female athletes still consider the opportunity of a lifetime.

Whether a girl who is ten years old today will ever have a chance to play softball in the Olympics remains to be seen. She will have the opportunity to play fastpitch in high school and college, though, in all fifty states. She may also choose to play baseball. Major League Baseball finally lifted its ban on female players in 1992, and some girls opt to play on boys' baseball teams up through college. There are also international women's baseball competitions. It would be wrong to assume that all women would rather play baseball, though. Such assumptions, which probably wouldn't exist at all if men still played fastpitch, are predicated on the belief that softball is easier to play than baseball. Both sports are difficult, however, as illustrated by the long list of legendary baseball players, such as Babe Ruth, Ted Williams, and Reggie Jackson, who have struck out against softball pitchers. For decades, men had the choice between fastpitch and baseball, and there were plenty of men who preferred fastpitch. It stands to reason that many women would also pick softball over baseball if given the choice—historically they just haven't had the option.

College softball, meanwhile, continues to grow. Television ratings for the college tournament have steadily climbed and are consistently higher than those of the college baseball championship. The number of schools offering the sport has also increased, with about 90 percent of colleges now fielding teams. The young players wear pants now, and their uniforms aren't shiny, although they often wear ribbons in their hair that are. At school, they have access to opportunities that female students from fifty years ago could scarcely have imagined: they play on beautifully maintained fields, travel to games by bus and plane, and, most crucially, can focus on sports more or less full-time rather than having to juggle their athletic pursuits alongside a regular job.

As adults, though, today's college players may find that they actually envy the 1960s players, who had numerous competitive adult teams to join and got to keep playing well into their thirties and sometimes forties. Even if softball gets back into the Olympics, playing on the national team isn't a career: it's a part-time situation at best, which means most players still won't get to devote themselves to the sport all year. Some of the pitching records set by Bertha and Joan will likely never be broken because no one today plays for as long as they did. Some say that players burn out faster now because they start playing at such young ages, but they also have few adult teams to play on. It's difficult to gauge the interest level when the playing opportunities just aren't there.

Young athletes don't usually spend a lot of time thinking about history. They don't necessarily think about the future that much, either. It's the luxury and, perhaps, pitfall of youth to be self-absorbed and live only for the here and now. Whether they realize it or not, though, today's young softball players are part of a family tree that spans across North America and goes back more than a hundred years. Some are connected by geography: Orange County youth teams, such as the national-championship-winning Batbusters, could be said to be descendants of the Lionettes and the Buena Park Lynx (one of the area's youth teams is even named after the Lionettes). Similarly, the Erv Lind Stadium in Portland, Oregon's Normandale Park links players to the Portland Florists. For others, the connection comes from their coaches and fans. There are even equipment connections—for example, the neon-yellow ball that most high school and college players use now originated in the 1970s pro league.

Most of all, it's the desire to be serious athletes that binds today's players to the women who developed their sport. In this sense, they are kindred spirits, regardless of how different their lives may appear to be otherwise. On the surface, the recipe for athletic success seems simple: train hard and develop your skills by competing against the best. But for women, being an athlete has never been simple, especially in team sports. They can be the best in the world and still be invisible, not to mention poor. Some always press on, though. They find teams to join and come up with ways to continue playing. They stay with it even when it becomes so impractical that it borders on ridiculous because there isn't an alternative. For them, playing isn't a choice: it's a vital part of who they are and, in many cases, what makes their lives worth living.

EPILOGUE

On January 24, 2009, Bertha's former high school in Dinuba, California, officially named its softball field after her. At the dedication ceremony, she threw a ceremonial pitch to Melitas Forster, her catcher from when she first joined the Lionettes in the 1930s. After catching the pitch, Forster, who was in her early nineties at the time, asked Bertha to throw her another one, but harder this time, and Bertha gladly obliged. She had already been inducted into numerous sports halls of fame, but she considered having a field named after her in Dinuba to be a particularly special honor.

Five years later, in 2014, Bertha passed away at her home at age ninety-two. She lives on in the memories of those who knew and loved her and also in the game of softball itself. It's not an exaggeration to say that women's softball would not exist as we know it today were it not for Bertha. As a 1968 article in the *Bridgeport Post* put it, she "has done more than any other player the game has ever known to increase the popularity of women's softball."

Joan continues to coach softball at Florida Atlantic University. In 2015, the team won 14 games in a row, one of which was Joan's 800th win as coach, and advanced to the NCAA regional tournament. Joan also coached the university's women's golf team until 2014, when her assistant coach took over. She still plays golf in her free time, what little of it she has. She's known in Boca Raton, where she has lived off and on since the 1980s, but she's a sports legend in Connecticut. The softball field at Municipal Stadium in Waterbury, where she struck out Ted Williams back in the 1960s, was recently named after her.

Sadly, other women's fastpitch players have spent their later years in almost complete obscurity. Freda and Olympia Savona eventually moved back to Ohio and are buried together at a cemetery in their hometown of Malvern (they even share a headstone). They were only rarely written about after the 1950s, and by the time Freda passed away in 1987, few people seemed to remember her. In 1998, Freda was finally posthumously inducted into the Amateur Softball Association Hall of Fame. Olympia still hasn't been added, though.

In Fresno, Jeanne Contel, Gloria May, and other former Fresno Rockets continue to root for the Fresno State Bulldogs softball team every spring. Women like them are scattered throughout the country: former players for teams, such as the Pekin Lettes, the Phoenix Ramblers, and the Atlanta Lorelei Ladies, who dutifully go out to support the young female athletes in their area. Pioneers in their day, they're now some of the most committed women's sports fans around.

Thanks in part to the efforts of these former players, girls who dream of playing team sports professionally no longer have to imagine themselves as men, as Joan and many of her Brakettes and Falcons teammates had to do when they were young. Still, the lack of professional opportunities for female athletes today is glaring, and media coverage of women who play sports continues to be poor. In fact, in some cases it has gotten worse: a recent study found that the percentage of *Sports Illustrated* covers featuring women, excluding the annual swimsuit issue, was higher from 1954 to 1965 than it was from 2000 to 2011.

Television coverage of women's sports, while less overtly sexist than in previous decades, remains appallingly sparse. For example, a 2015 report found that, in the fifteen years between 1999 and 2014, the percentage of ESPN's *SportsCenter* episodes devoted to women's sports never rose above 2.5 percent and often fell below 2 percent. Moreover, the study noted that when women's sports are featured on television, it's usually as a dull, obligatory aside, or, as the researchers described it, "the vegetables" in between the more exciting main course and dessert coverage.

Media outlets frequently cite low public interest as the reason they don't devote more coverage to women's sports. "I tend to point the finger at the fans," a *New York Times* reporter wrote in a recent article about the WNBA. According to this view, people (mainly women, because it's assumed that only females could care about women's sports) are somehow supposed to find out about teams that receive hardly any publicity and then go out of their way to attend games in what are often underwhelming, hard-to-reach venues. If they don't, it's their fault that the teams are struggling.

Many colleges made similar arguments before Title IX was passed. Lack of interest was what kept women out of fields, such as sports and medicine, not discrimination, they said. After Title IX, though, female participation in sports, medicine, and many other previously male-dominated fields not only increased, it skyrocketed. Today, women account for nearly 50 percent of medical school graduates, and more than 40 percent of high school athletes are girls, up from only 7 percent in 1971. The interest increased when the opportunities increased.

Similarly, women's sports attract large audiences when they're given the opportunity to be presented as high profile, as they are during special events, such as the Olympics and the Women's World Cup. Then, public interest inevitably fades after that opportunity and the prominent media coverage that comes with it disappears and women's sports are moved back into the shadows.

Tennis is often touted as an example of a women's sport that consistently gets good media coverage. It's presented as the mysterious exception to the rule, the one competitive (as opposed to artistic) women's sport that, for some reason, TV audiences are willing to watch regularly. What people tend to forget, though, is that television coverage of women's tennis was practically non-existent until Billie Jean King rose to fame in the late 1960s and early 1970s. Its success as a televised sport had more to do with circumstance than with anything specific about the sport itself. There's no reason to assume that other women's sports, such as basketball, wouldn't achieve a similar level of success if given the same kind of network coverage.

Professional women's sports also still lag far behind men's when it comes to pay. Even though female athletes' earnings have increased overall in the past few decades, they haven't kept pace with those of their male counterparts, and in many cases the income disparity is larger now than it was twenty or thirty years ago. In the early 1980s, the top male golfers earned about $400,000 per year on the PGA tour, while the top golfers on the LPGA tour earned about $300,000. Today, the male golfers' annual earnings are in the $5 million to $10 million range, whereas the best women golfers only get $1 million to $2 million a year. Meanwhile, the average annual salary for a professional men's basketball player in the late 1970s was around $200,000, about eighteen times higher than the $11,000 per year that the average player in the first women's professional basketball league earned. Since then, however, the average NBA player salary has increased to about $5 million per year, nearly seventy times the WNBA's average annual salary of $72,000.

The media also persists in treating women's sports as a novelty, as if basketball, soccer, and hockey somehow turn into different games when women are playing them. In articles, the WNBA is often portrayed as being analogous to non-mainstream sports that are trying to gain a foothold in the US sports market, such as rugby and lacrosse. Basketball isn't non-mainstream, though—it's one of the most popular sports in the United States and the world—and so, by all rights, women's basketball shouldn't be non-mainstream, either. It seems absurd to suggest that the sight of women playing basketball is so different that it's akin to watching a new and unfamiliar sport.

Female athletes also continue to get stereotyped based on physical appearance. Those with more traditional feminine looks—makeup, long hair, slender build—tend to be taken less seriously as athletes. Even when they receive praise for their athletic skills, it's usually presented in relation to their looks. "Young men like her because she plays to win and looks good doing so," the *Chicago Tribune* wrote about Jennie Finch in 2005. A 2015 article on the FIFA website described US soccer star Alex Morgan as "a goal-scorer with a style that is very easy on the eye and good looks to match."

Meanwhile, female athletes with shorter hair and more muscular builds tend to get labeled as masculine and are presumed to be lesbians, often starting at a young age. A lot of progress has been made since the days when just wearing jeans was enough to get a woman branded as mannish, but a lot of room for growth remains. And the day when it's considered as normal for women and girls to play sports as it is for men and boys still seems a long way off.

No doubt, many Americans today would find it hard to believe that it was once commonplace for entire towns to rally around women's sports teams. Yet, it happened. More than fifty years ago, women's fastpitch teams, such as the Lionettes, the Brakettes, the Florists, and the Ramblers captured fans' attention not just for a few weeks or even a few years, but for decades. People didn't go to their games out of the goodness of their hearts or to show their support for women. They went because they enjoyed the games and because it was the popular thing to do.

If it could happen in the forties, fifties, and sixties, when women were typically regarded as second-class citizens and didn't have half the opportunities that they do now, it must be possible for it to happen again. Maybe the sport will be different and the audience will be sitting at home instead of at a park or stadium. The specific details don't matter that much as long as they achieve the general desired outcome: the mainstream support and acceptance of competitive women's team sports. It may seem like a trivial goal to some, but considering the outsize role that team sports occupy in nearly every society, the impact would be monumental.

ACKNOWLEDGMENTS

Working on this book has been an immensely rewarding experience. It has introduced me to some of the most amazing people I've ever met and has given me a new way to relate to the world. Nearly everyone I spoke to in the past three years, in both my personal and professional life, seemed to have some sort of connection with fastpitch: they either played the sport themselves or had relatives who did; many also fondly recalled watching the US team play at the Summer Olympics or seeing Eddie Feigner's King and His Court act perform at their local ballpark. I was surprised and heartened by the overwhelmingly positive responses I received whenever I told people that I was writing about the history of softball.

Many people contributed to making this book a reality. I have to start by thanking my agents, Gillian MacKenzie and Allison Devereux, of the Gillian MacKenzie Agency and Wolf Literary Services, respectively, for helping me get this project off the ground and for their indispensable ideas and advice. I'm also hugely indebted to Michelle Howry, my initial editor at Touchstone, and to Miya Kumangai, who later took the reins and who, as a former fastpitch player herself, was an ideal collaborator for this book. Other members of the Touchstone team to whom I'm grateful include editorial assistant Lara Blackman, managing editors Ffej Caplan and Emily Fanelli, production editor Katie

Rizzo, copy editor Steve Boldt, art director Cherlynne Li, designer Kyle Kabel, and publicist Jessica Roth.

Most of all, I'm thankful to the softball players, coaches, and family members who were kind enough to share their stories with me. Janice Nelson, Bertha Tickey's daughter, was particularly generous with her time. She talked to me on the phone for hours and hours and welcomed me into her home. Her recollections helped fill in countless blanks and breathed life into what was previously just a rough sketch. I absolutely couldn't have written this book without her.

I must also thank John and Micki Stratton, Joan Joyce, Edna Fraser, Billie Harris, Jeanne Contel, Gloria May, Beverly Hollis, Millie Marchi, Margie Wright, Mary Lou Pennington, Stormy Irwin, Irene Shea, Jo An Kincaid, Shirley Topley, Dot Wilkinson, Marge McIntire, Edwina Bryan, Pete and Nancy Petinak, Morgan Melloh, Joe Palladino, Bob Ito, Lisa Wetselline, Katie Burkhart-Gooch, Joann McLaughlin, Kay Rich, Anita DeFrantz, Don Porter, and Jane Blalock, each of whom provided crucial bits of information that helped me weave this story together. Other people, such as Karen Mischlispy, Anne Barr, and Kathy Gage, provided the invaluable service of putting me in touch with former players.

For secondary sources, I was greatly aided by the Stratford Historical Society; the Stratford public library; the websites of the Brakettes and the Arizona Softball Foundation; the Orange, California, History Center; and the University of Arizona library. Lastly, I would like to thank all of my supportive friends and family members, especially my husband, Josh.

NOTES

Prologue

The description of the Memorial Field site in Stratford is drawn from an in-person visit during 2013 and from photographs. Descriptions of Bill Simpson are informed by articles in the *Bridgeport Post*. The accounts of the pollution at Memorial Field and other sites around Stratford are informed by reports by the Environmental Protection Agency and articles in newspapers, including the *Connecticut Post*, the *Stratford Bard*, and the *New York Times*. In March 2015, state and federal officials announced a $100 million plan to finish the Stratford cleanup effort.

Chapter 1

The epigraph is from Arthur Noren's *Softball with Official Rules* (New York: Ronald Press, 1959), 21. The story of Bertha's move to Connecticut relies on material drawn from interviews with her daughter, Janice Ragan Nelson, and her former teammates Jo An Kammeyer Kincaid, Edna Fraser, Beverly Mulonet Hollis, and Micki Macchietto Stratton; and from Bertha's own recollections, as chronicled in various newspaper and magazine articles, including "The Fabulous Career of Bertha Ragan Tickey," *Softball Illustrated*, Spring 1968; "In Stratford, Nobody Beats the Brakettes," *Sports Illustrated*, September 1967; an article in the *Bridgeport Post* about her presentation to the Stratford

Exchange Club, October 8, 1966; and a 1990 article in the *Bridgeport Post* about the Raybestos softball teams.

The descriptions of what Bertha was like as a pitcher come from a combination of interviews with former players and recollections posted on the Ultimate College Softball forum, available at robocoach. websitetoolbox.com, and in the *Women in Softball* newsletter, available at https://sites.google.com/site/softballnationalnews. Bertha's pitching records were described in several newspaper articles, such as "Bertha Ragan Is Softball's Answer to Outlawing Women," by the NEA syndicate, July 8, 1952; "Lionette Registers 107 No-Hit Games," in the *Van Nuys (CA) Valley News*, August 21, 1955; and in Morris Bealle's *The Softball Story* (Washington, DC: Columbia Publishing, 1957).

The accounts of Bertha's childhood and early adulthood, which are briefly mentioned here and are described in more detail in chapter 4, are derived from interviews with Janice Nelson and Pete Petinak, Bertha's youngest brother, and from Bertha's own recollections, as recounted in the 1968 *Softball Illustrated* article and in "Making Her Pitch: Tickey, an Ex-Lionette Shined on the Diamond," in the *Los Angeles Times*, October 21, 1991. Figures related to the Lionettes team, such as the approximate number of games played per season, come from Janice Nelson and newspapers that covered the team regularly, such as the *Santa Ana Register*.

For more on the "Play for play's sake" motto and the general anti-competition attitude that governed women's sports in schools during the first half of the twentieth century, see "The Controlled Development of Collegiate Sport for Women, 1923–1936," by Ellen Gerber, *Journal of Sport History*, Spring 1975; "A History of Women in Sport Prior to Title IX," by Richard Bell in the *Sport Journal*, March 2008; and Allen Guttmann's *Women's Sports: A History* (New York: Columbia University Press, 1991), 137–42.

The descriptions of air travel in 1956 are informed by "Six Golden Ages of Air Travel," published on smartertravel.com, September 29, 2013; and "The Golden Age of Flight," in the *Wall Street Journal*, July 22, 2010. The *San Bernardino County Sun* and the *Bridgeport Post* were the sources of the weather descriptions for Los Angeles and Stratford that week. For more background on the history of the US freeway system and the 1956 Federal Highway Act, see https://www.fhwa.dot.gov/interstate/history.cfm.

For more on the history of Stratford, Connecticut, see *In Pursuit of Paradise: History of the Town of Stratford, Connecticut*, by Lewis Knapp (Phoenix Publishing, 1989); and townofstratford.com. The population figure for Stratford in the 1950s comes from the "Connecticut Population by Town, 1900–1960," from the State of Connecticut website ct.gov. Those interested in learning more about Igor Sikorsky's helicopter-manufacturing facility can check out http://connecticuthistory.org/igor-sikorsky-and-his-flying-machines/ or consider visiting the National Helicopter Museum (nationalheli coptermuseum.org), located next to the Stratford train station. The history of the Stratford Raybestos plant can be found in *In Pursuit of Happiness* and on the Raybestos website (http://www.raybestos powertrain.com/history.aspx). The Raybestos ads featuring Mario Andretti appeared in magazines and other print publications during the late 1960s and early 1970s.

The descriptions of William (Bill) Simpson are drawn from a mixture of newspaper accounts, such as "Playing for Simpson's Brakettes 'a Privilege,'" from the *Connecticut Post*, July 10, 2011; and personal recollections of former Raybestos employees and their family members. For a comparison of the Brakettes' uniforms before and after Bertha's arrival, see the 1955 and the 1956 team photos, which can be found at http://brakettes.com/archive_1955.htm and http://brakettes.com/archive_1956.htm. Further descriptions of the uniforms and the Brakettes' initial reactions to wearing them come from interviews with Edna Fraser, Micki Macchietto Stratton, and other former players.

The Brakettes' regular-season record and a copy of the letter that Simpson gave each of the Brakettes before the national tournament in Florida can be found at http://brakettes.com/archive_1956.htm. The $10 for "incidental expenses" figure comes from interviews with Edna Fraser and other players. The figures on seating capacity and attendance at Raybestos Memorial Field, where the Brakettes played, are from articles in the *Bridgeport Telegram*, June 10, 1951; and the *Bridgeport Sunday Herald*, May 25, 1952, and August 24, 1958. Material related to the games from the 1956 national tournament comes mostly from the *St. Petersburg Times*.

Chapter 2

The epigraph is from *The Softball Story*, 192. George Hancock's impromptu invention of softball at the Farragut Boat Club has been recounted in numerous places, including *The Softball Story*; several newspaper articles, such as "To Play Ball Indoors," in the *Chicago Tribune*, October 25, 1896; and on the Amateur Softball Association website (http://www.teamusa.org/usa-softball/about/about-us/history). The score of the Harvard-Yale Thanksgiving game and Harvard's win-loss record for the 1887 season are from http://www.gocrimson.com/sports/fball/1887-88/Schedule.

For more on the early history of baseball, see John Thorn's *Baseball in the Garden of Eden* (New York: Simon & Schuster, 2011); "Play Ball: Colonial Games and America's National Pastime," by Ed Crews in the *Colonial Williamsburg Journal*, Spring 2008; and "The Early Years of Philadelphia Baseball," by Rich Westcott in *The National Pastime*, 2013. For more background on Elysian Fields and the history of baseball in New York City, see "Cooperstown? Hoboken? Try New York City," in the *New York Times*, October 4, 1990; and James Terry's *Long Before the Dodgers: Baseball in Brooklyn, 1855–1884* (Jefferson, NC: McFarland, 2002).

The descriptions of Chicago's urbanization and population growth during the late 1880s are primarily drawn from the University of Chicago Library's "Before and After the Fire: Chicago in the 1860s, 1870s, and 1880s," available at http://www.lib.uchicago.edu/e/collections/maps/chifire/. The Library of Congress's "Rise of Industrial America, 1876–1900: City Life in the Late 19th Century," at http://www.loc.gov/teachers/classroommaterials/presentationsandactivities/presenta

tions/timeline/riseind/city/, was a source of general information on America's industrial transformation.

Softball's appeal to city dwellers and factory workers in the early 1900s is documented in *The Softball Story* and various newspaper articles. The Connecticut newspaper story that mentioned prominent New York men playing the game "even in the snow" is from the *Day*, September 6, 1915. Hancock's rules for indoor baseball were originally published in Chicago in 1890 and then nationally in 1903, when the American Sports Publishing Company issued the first *Spalding's Official Indoor Baseball Guide* (the story of the sport's invention is recounted here as well).

More details on Lewis Rober, the Minneapolis fireman who popularized "kitten ball," can be found in *The Softball Story* and in "Area Man's Kin Invented Softball," in the *Allentown (PA) Morning Call*, February 17, 1995. Rober's game later came to be known as diamond ball, as chronicled in "Half a Million Minneapolitans to Watch 10,000 Diamond Ball Players This Year," in the *Minneapolis Tribune*, May 24, 1936. The various other names for softball before the 1930s are described in *The Softball Story* and *Softball with Official Rules*. The "playground ball" baserunning rule is from *Spalding's Official Handbook of the National Amateur Playground Ball Association of the United States* (New York: American Sports Publishing Company, 1908), 26–27.

The struggles of early softball teams from different states or sometimes just different towns to agree on the rules have been recounted in numerous newspaper articles, such as the *Muscatine (IA) Journal and News-Tribune*, May 21, 1931; and the *St. Petersburg Times*, September 9, 1971. As Arthur Noren put it in *Softball with Official Rules* (11), "A dozen sizes of balls were in use, as well as many different bat lengths, every conceivable base length, and a bewildering array of variations in rules." According to Noren and other softball historians, the name *softball* was first introduced by Walter Hakanson, a Denver YMCA director and eventual Amateur Softball Association president, at a Colorado state meeting in 1926 but wasn't adopted nationally until after a National Recreation Congress meeting in the late 1920s.

For more background on the YMCA and its influence on American sports in the late 1800s and early 1900s, see http://www.ymca .net/history and Charles Howard Hopkins's *History of the Y.M.C.A. in North America* (New York: Association Press, 1951). Early baseball's association with drinking, gambling, and general "rowdyism" has been well documented in historical publications, such as Harold Seymour's *Baseball: The Early Years* (New York: Oxford University Press, 1960). In his report "Disputed Diamonds: The YMCA Debate over Baseball in the Late 19th Century," in the *Journal of Sport History*, Winter 1992, William Baker mentions an Ohio YMCA official who denounced baseball for its "pernicious habits, such as Sabbath playing, betting, drinking, and the like."

The softball rules that the YMCA, American Physical Education Association, and other groups agreed upon were eventually published in 1934 under the title *Official Rules of Softball, Playground Ball, and Diamond Ball* (New York: American Sports Publishing Company, 1934). For more on the history of the Chicago version of the game played with a sixteen-inch ball, see "16-Inch Softball Comes Back," in the *Chicago Tribune*, September 4, 1970; and https://chicagology .com/baseball/16insoftball/.

The full reference for the Stuart Chase essay mentioned is "Play," in *Whither Mankind: A Panorama of Modern Civilization*, edited by Charles Beard (New York: Longmans, Green, 1928), 332–53. The National Humanities Center's *The Twenties in Contemporary Commentary: The "Machine Age,"* available at http://americainclass.org/sources/ becomingmodern/machine/text1/colcommentarymachine.pdf, was another resource for this section. Softball's growth during the Great Depression, particularly in cities, was chronicled in newspaper articles, such as the *Oregonian*, August 18, 1935; and in several sports history books, including *The Softball Story* and *Baseball: The People's Game* by Dorothy Seymour Mills and Harold Seymour (New York: Oxford University Press, 1990). It is also reflected in scholarly reports, such as "The Evolution and History of Softball in the United States," by Irvin Kawarsky, 1956, in which the Tennessee softball commissioner recounted how the Memphis recreation department had organized softball games in "its many playgrounds" during the Depression to help get unemployed young men off the streets.

The descriptions of the 1933 Chicago World's Fair are informed by newspaper articles, the University of Illinois at Chicago's collection on the subject at http://www.uic.edu/depts/lib/specialcoll/services/rjd/findingaids/COP16f.html, and the official program of the fair, which includes maps and full listings of the attractions and events that were offered. The Chicago unemployment rate cited comes from John McDonald's *Chicago: An Economic History* (New York: Routledge, 2015), 91; and other sources.

Details of the World's Fair softball tournament and the subsequent formation of the Amateur Softball Association are from "Softball Becomes American Game of New Importance," in the *New Orleans Times-Picayune*, December 30, 1940; "Softball Rules Author Visits in Clearwater," in the *St. Petersburg Times*, February 21, 1958; and Leo Fischer's *How to Play Winning Softball* (New York: Prentice Hall, 1940). The World's Fair horseshoe tournament was covered by the *Chicago Tribune*, July 20, 1933; and *Time* magazine, August 7, 1933.

Eastman Kodak's Harold "Shifty" Gears was one example of a baseball player who preferred softball, but there were many others. It's important to remember that the majority of sports were still amateur in the 1930s, at least in name. The professional football and basketball leagues were just getting started, which meant baseball, boxing, and horse racing were the main professional sports of the period. Even though public attitudes toward professional sports were starting to improve, the opinion that playing sports for money was crass and uncouth, as expressed in the 1903 *Harper's Weekly* (47: 915–16) editorial "Why Should Amateurs Imitate Professionals?" still prevailed.

The "tens of thousands" of softball teams in the United States by the late 1930s comes from the Amateur Softball Association, which publicized these figures in the softball rule books it published and in newspaper and magazine articles, including Lowell Thomas's 1937 piece "The Sport of 15,000,000," which I found in the September 5,

1937, edition of the *Milwaukee Journal*, but it was nationally syndicated and so appeared in many newspapers. Thomas mentions President Roosevelt's softball team in his article. Film footage of Roosevelt's team in action during a 1936 charity game is at https://archive.org/details/AFP-128R.

A pitcher from Arizona named Paul Watson introduced the windmill windup to the ASA national tournament in 1934, according to *Softball with Official Rules*, 40. Mary Littlewood's *The Path to the Gold: An Historical Look at Women's Fastpitch in the United States* (Columbia, MO: National Fastpitch Coaches Association, 1998) has excellent descriptions of the different softball pitching techniques, complete with illustrations, 116–23. The various pitching distances used in the 1930s and '40s, which ranged from thirty-seven to forty-three feet for men and thirty-four to thirty-eight feet for women, were chronicled in the ASA rule books and were also often noted in newspaper articles.

Descriptions of the rise ball and other softball pitches can be found in *Softball with Official Rules*, 42–45. For a more recent primer on how fastpitch pitching differs from baseball in delivery and batter reaction time, see ESPN's "Sport Science: How Pitches Move," at http://espn.go.com/espnw/video/12926694/how-pitches-move. The newspaper comic referenced is from the *Spartanburg (SC) Herald-Journal*, June 8, 1936. The story of John "Cannonball" Baker's striking out Babe Ruth in 1937 comes from *The Softball Story* and articles in the *Bridgeport Sunday Herald*, April 9, 1961; the *Bridgeport Telegram*, April 23, 1961; and the *Norwalk Hour*, December 29, 1997. The importance of bunting and fast baserunning in softball has been well documented in books, such as *Softball with Official Rules*, and newspaper and magazine articles. Morris Bealle's quote about the wiry player being the star of softball is from *The Softball Story*, 193.

Harold "Shifty" Gears, the pitcher for the Eastman Kodak fastpitch team, was the first player inducted into the ASA Hall of Fame when it opened in 1957 (his Hall of Fame bio can be found at http://www.teamusa.org/USA-Softball/About/National-Softball-Hall-of-Fame/Members). He was also written about in newspaper articles, such as "Shifty Gears, Softball's Greatest," by the NEA newswire service, June 4, 1940; and "Harold 'Shifty' Gears Was Softball Legend," in the *Rochester (NY) Democrat & Chronicle*, December 27, 2014. The Ke-Nash-A team, sponsored by Kenosha, Wisconsin's Nash Motors, won the 1934 men's national tournament and remained a top Midwestern team until the 1940s, as evidenced by articles in the *Ironwood (MI) Daily Globe*, September 13, 1938; the *Hammond (IN) Times*, June 18, 1939; and the *Kenosha Evening News*, May 12, 1944.

The Carpenter Steelies were mentioned in an article in the *Reading (PA) Eagle*, July 26, 1936. Examples of championship-winning teams sponsored by small businesses include the Cleveland, Ohio, Weaver Walls, who were sponsored by a local roofer and won the 1935 women's tournament, and the Pohler's Café men's team from Cincinnati, Ohio, which won the 1938 national title. The price of admission to community softball games, if there was one at all, was often listed in newspapers, along with the game schedules. In *Baseball: The People's Game*, the average softball-ticket price in Chicago during the 1930s is listed as between "fifteen to thirty-five cents" (370), while twenty cents or less was common in other parts of the country. Minor league baseball tickets usually cost about $1 during that time, according to newspaper articles, such as the *Pittsburgh Press*, July 24, 1987, and movie tickets cost about twenty-five cents, according to Box Office Mojo, at http://www.boxofficemojo.com/about/adjuster.htm. The information regarding the softball scene in Portland, Oregon, and the quote about whether it was still accurate to call baseball America's national sport are from "What About Softball?" in the *Sunday Oregonian*, July 24, 1938.

Chapter 3

The epigraph is from Viola Mitchell's *Softball for Girls* (New York: A. S. Barnes, 1943), vii. The numbers of men's and women's teams participating in the national softball tournament each year were chronicled in the Amateur Softball Association rule books and in newspaper articles. The 1903 *Spalding's Official Indoor Baseball Guide* includes a section called "Indoor Baseball for Women," which claims that female students at Chicago high schools had been playing the game since the 1890s (85). A photo dated from about 1920 in the Library of Congress collection shows a woman pitching a softball outdoors.

The Amateur Athletic Union (AAU) held the first national men's basketball tournament in 1897, according to Adolph Grundman's *The Golden Age of Amateur Basketball: The AAU Tournament, 1921–1968* (Lincoln: University of Nebraska Press, 2004), xiv. The AAU reportedly held its first women's basketball tournament in 1926—a team from Pasadena was said to have won—but regular tournaments weren't held until 1929, according to Margaret Costa and Sharon Guthrie's *Women and Sport: Interdisciplinary Perspectives* (Champaign, IL: Human Kinetics, 1994), 119. Both tournaments were held in Kansas, but unlike the softball tournament, the men's and women's basketball competitions took place in separate cities: Wichita for the women's and Kansas City for the men's. Then in 1935, the men's tournament moved to Denver, according to *The Golden Age of Amateur Basketball*, xiv.

The quote from Leo Fischer about allowing women to compete in the 1933 World's Fair softball tournament is from Frank Menke's *Encyclopedia of Sports* (New York: A. S. Barnes, 1960), 874. For more on the history of six-player basketball, which became the official women's version of the game in the 1930s, see Robert Ikard's *Just for Fun: The Story of AAU Women's Basketball* (Fayetteville: University of Arkansas Press, 2005). The *Esquire* article referenced was entitled "Belles of the Ball" and was published in the June 1940 issue.

The Madison Square Garden women's softball games, which were hugely popular in 1938 and 1939 but had disappeared by the early forties, were chronicled by many newspapers, including the *Arizona Independent Republic*, September 16, 1938; the *Reading (PA) Eagle*, September 20, 1938; and the *Brooklyn Eagle*, June 9, 1939. Attendance at these games was frequently reported as exceeding ten thousand. The seventy-five-cent ticket price is from the *New Yorker* article mentioned, which appeared in the August 6, 1938, issue.

An article in the *Norwalk Hour*, August 19, 1938, described one of the games Freda Savona played with the Num Num team at Madison Square Garden. The article referred to her as "the outstanding feminine softball player in the country." For more on Num Num Food and the history of the potato-chip industry, see Dirk Burhans's *Crunch! A History of the Great American Potato Chip* (Madison, WI: Terrace Books, 2008), 25–29.

Freda Savona's height was usually listed as five feet six inches in newspapers, such as the *Deming (NM) Headlight*, April 27, 1951. The story about Freda's throwing balls from the outfield to home at Madison Square Garden is from "Touring Glamour Girls Shoot for United States Softball Title," a newswire article about the Jax Maids published on July 17, 1940. The Tris Speaker quote is from the 1940 *Esquire* article. The *Times-Picayune* article mentioned was published on May 21, 1939, shortly after Freda and Olympia Savona began playing with the Jax Maids. The story about the Jax coach recruiting Olympia is from "You Have to Be a Lady to Play on the Ball Team of These Champs," in the *Milwaukee Journal*, August 3, 1948.

The Jax Maids' travels during the 1939 season were chronicled in the *Times-Picayune*. The descriptions of female employment in the United States during the thirties are informed by "Working Women in the 1930s," in the Gale Group's *U.S. History in Context* (2001) and the National Women's History Museum's "A History of Women in Industry," at https://www.nwhm.org/online-exhibits/industry/13.htm. The reference to softball giving women the opportunity to visit relatives and see landmarks, such as Radio City Music Hall and Niagara Falls, comes from a combination of newspaper articles and interviews with former players, such as Dot Wilkinson, who started playing for the Phoenix Ramblers in the thirties.

The Jax Maids' schedule the week of the 1939 national tournament was described in an article in the *Times-Picayune*, September 3, 1939. In the article, the team's manager stated that he had arranged for the team to arrive in Chicago three days before the tournament began so that the players would be well rested and could get a feel for the field they would be playing on. The national softball tournament had been held at Soldier Field since 1936, as evidenced by newspaper articles and the official tournament program. An article in the *Oakland Tribune*, September 16, 1939, mentions that it took two men to lift the tournament trophy. Benny Goodman and Jack Dempsey, a famous boxer, attended the 1938 tournament finals, according to the *Ogden (UT) Standard-Examiner*, September 7, 1938. The Chicago city council also officially designated that week of September as "Softball Championship Week" earlier that summer, according to city records, adding, "The citizens of Chicago should be urged to do all within their power to assist and support these championships to make them the outstanding sports event of the year."

The number of teams competing in the 1939 tournament was chronicled in articles in the *Chicago Tribune* and other newspapers. The rain delays during the '38 tournament were also well documented in the newspapers. The '39 tournament was the first year that the event featured a "parade of states" during the opening ceremonies, according to *The Softball Story*. Former players frequently described participating in the opening ceremonies before the tournament as a significant, proud moment in their lives.

The Jax Maids' 1–0 loss to the Phoenix Ramblers and the three-game series that they played against them earlier that month were described in the *Arizona Independent-Republic*, September 10, 1939. Most of the material pertaining to the J. J. Kriegs team from Alameda, California, comes from articles in the *Oakland Tribune*. Additional information is from articles in the *Berkeley Daily Gazette*, September 23, 1939; the *Lodi News-Sentinel*, June 5, 1939; and "Girl Softball Players Aren't Tomboys—They Cry Sometimes," a newswire article about the team from April 19, 1939.

For more background on California leisure culture in the 1930s, see Kevin Starr's *Dream Endures: California Enters the 1940s* (New York: Oxford University Press, 2002). The Los Angeles Rams football team, which joined the NFL in 1946, is generally regarded as California's first major professional sports team, but the state had a long history of strong minor league baseball teams, such as the San Francisco Seals and the San Diego Padres, where future legends Joe DiMaggio and Ted Williams got their starts, respectively.

The 1896 women's basketball game between Stanford and UC Berkeley, which most basketball historians consider to be the first intercollegiate women's basketball match, is described in Lynne Emery's "First Intercollegiate Contest for Women: Basketball, April 4, 1896," in the *North American Society for Sport History Proceedings*, 1979, and "Cal vs. Stanford in 1896: Women's Game Is Born," in the *San Francisco Chronicle*, January 10, 1992. The game wasn't quite as progressive as it might sound: no male spectators were allowed, lest they ogle the players (women even guarded the gym windows to make sure no one looked inside), and there wasn't any running or dribbling to speak of (the final score was 2–1). Women's basketball at Stanford also proved to be short-lived; three years later, the school's faculty committee banned female students from competing in intercollegiate contests.

For more on UCLA's racially integrated football team in the late 1930s, see Lane Demas's *Integrating the Gridiron: Black Civil Rights and American College Football* (New Brunswick, NJ: Rutgers University Press, 2011), 28–45; and "Forgotten Story of Four Who Broke Color Barrier in Pro Football to Screen at Royce," by the UCLA newsroom, August 24, 2014. The ASA's decision to split California fastpitch into two regions (north and south) during the 1940s was chronicled in *The Softball Story* and the ASA rule books.

Chapter 4

The epigraph is from *The Softball Story*, 167. Nearly all of the details regarding Bertha's parents and her childhood in Dinuba come from looking at family photographs and from interviews with Janice Nelson (her daughter) and Pete Petinak (her youngest brother). Some of the material was also informed by an article Janice wrote about the Petinaks for *Serb World*, March/April 2010.

Without an official record, determining Bertha's birth year proved difficult. Her age varied in newspaper articles, especially by the 1960s. Even her obituaries, published in local newspapers, listed different ages: she was ninety-one in some, ninety-two in others. I knew from Janice that she celebrated her birthday in mid-March, and after going through hundreds of newspaper articles and other materials, such as the Petinaks' listing in the 1930 census, I'm reasonably confident that she was born in March 1922 and have calculated her age at different points in the book based on that.

Bertha's mother's death was chronicled in the *Fresno Bee*, May 21, 1937. I was unable to find an obituary for her father, but the date on his headstone is February 19, 1936. Other details pertaining to their deaths came from interviews with Janice Nelson and Pete Petinak and Bertha's recollections in "The Fabulous Career of Bertha Ragan Tickey" article from 1968, although that article incorrectly stated that her mother had died before her father. The story of the Petinaks' neighbor, Obren Vuich, pleading with a judge so that Bertha and her brothers could remain together in their family home, is from interviews with Janice and Pete and is also recounted in Janice's *Serb World* article.

The descriptions of Bertha's experience playing for the Alta Chevrolet softball team are drawn from her comments in articles such as "The Fabulous Career of Bertha Ragan Tickey," photographs, and from articles in the *Fresno Bee*, which covered the team regularly. The novelty of softball fields having electric lights in the 1930s is described in *The Softball Story* and was often mentioned in newspapers. A variation of men's softball played in the Los Angeles area was even called nightball precisely because of the field lights (the games were chronicled in newspaper articles, such as in the *San Bernardino County Sun*, September 11, 1938).

The first Major League Baseball night game was played in 1935, but it was an anomaly; in 1939, most major league ballparks still didn't have electric lights, and the majority of games were played during the day. Expense was only part of the issue, as many major league executives found the idea of playing baseball under artificial lights "repugnant," according to "Under the Lights," by Oscar Eddleton in the Society of American Baseball Research's journal, September 1980. The death of Ruth Hanson—the Alta Chevrolet pitcher whom Bertha replaced—in a car accident was reported in the *Fresno Bee*, May 5, 1938, and was also the subject of a 1941 lawsuit, *Hanson vs. Reedley School District* (her parents sued the school for relying on a student, driving his personal car, to transport players on the girls' tennis team).

Lois Terry, the pitcher whom Bertha replaced on the Lionettes, was written about quite a bit in the 1930s. Newspapers that referred to her as the Blonde Bomber included the *Santa Ana Register* and the *Orange Daily News*, and she was called the Blonde Terror by the *Pampa (TX) Daily News* and other papers in 1937, when she toured the country with the Hollywood all-star team. Her shoulder injury originally occurred during the California players' tour of Japan in the fall of 1938, according to newspaper articles, and was then aggravated the next spring while she was driving.

The *Orange Daily News* article about Bertha's first tryout with the Lionettes was published on May 15, 1939. In the "Fabulous Career of Bertha Ragan Tickey" article, she recalled that she had been so nervous that she felt she was going to throw up. An article in the *Fresno Bee*, March 2, 1938, chronicled her brother Sam's brief stint pitching for the San Francisco Seals' farm team in Arizona. The description of Bertha's second game with the Lionettes is also from an *Orange Daily News* article, this one published on May 20, 1939. Melitas Forster, former catcher for the Lionettes, recalled Elwood Case's hiring her and other players to work at his dry-cleaning service, Spic and Span Cleaners, and sending them to secretarial school, on her blog, at http://thememoircoach.com/writing/mondays-with-melitas-february-20-2012/, which she recently published as a memoir, *What a Life!* (Campbell, CA: FastPencil, 2015).

Orange's population in 1940 is from the 1940 US census, at http://www.ocalmanac.com/Population/po26.htm. Dinuba's population according to the 1940 census was 3,790, but the "total census area labelled as Dinuba" was apparently closer to 7,000, according to "Farm Size and Community Quality: Arvin and Dinuba Revisited," by Michael N. Hayes and Alan L. Olmstead in the *American Journal of Agricultural Economics*, November 1984. Hollywood's enthusiasm for softball during the 1930s was chronicled in newspaper articles and in books, such as *Baseball: The People's Game*, 374. Bertha and other former Lionettes players, including Joann McLaughlin, whom I interviewed, recalled getting fitted by "Suzie from Hollywood," the movie-studio seamstress, for their team uniforms.

The four-month-long 1938 Pacific tour, organized by sports promoter Marty Fiedler, was chronicled in several newspaper articles, including "Feminine Softballers Will Tour Japan," by the Associated Press, September 8, 1938; and "Four Lionettes Off for Games in Japan," in the *Santa Ana Register*, September 23, 1938. The description of the *Chichibu Maru* ship was informed by "Launching of the N.Y.K. Motor Ship 'Chichibu Maru' at the Yokohama Dockyard," in the *Malayan Saturday Post*, September 14, 1929.

The Orange Public Library has more information on the history of Orange, including the town's founding, at http://www.cityoforange .org/depts/library/history/old_towne/default.asp. The description of Orange as the kind of place where everyone knew one another on a first-name basis comes from Bertha, via the 1991 "Making Her Pitch" *Los Angeles Times* article. Details about the Orange City Park, known today as Hart Park, are from "The New Deal in Orange County," in the Orange County Historical Society's February 2011 newsletter; Charles Epting's *New Deal in Orange County* (Stroud, UK: History Press, 2014), 87–88, and "Old-Style Park's Perfect Setting for Summer Fun," in the *Los Angeles Times*, August 4, 1986. Descriptions of the park were also informed by an in-person visit (the softball park, bandstand, swimming pool, and pool house are still there today and have largely been preserved in their 1930s state).

The material about Bertha's living with Leo and Ollie Mathis and working as a lifeguard at the Plunge is drawn from her recollections in "The Fabulous Career of Bertha Ragan Tickey" article, interviews with Janice Nelson, and family photographs that show her on the job, sitting in the lifeguard chair. Articles in the *Santa Ana Register* from around that time confirm that Leo Mathis was the manager of the Plunge. Pete Petinak confirmed that he and his siblings used to swim in the farm's irrigation ditches. Bertha's love of sunbathing was well-known and was confirmed by Janice Nelson, Jo An Kammeyer Kincaid, Millie Dixon Dubord Marchi, and other acquaintances.

The descriptions of the Lionettes' intensity and their after-game strategy meetings came from Janice Nelson and Barbara Galt, the daughter of Ruth Sears, former Lionettes first baseman (Leroy "Chub" Sears, Ruth's husband, later became the Lionettes' coach). The Lionettes and the other top women's softball teams from the Los Angeles area during the late thirties and early forties were widely covered by regional newspapers, such as the *Santa Ana Register*, the *Orange Daily News*, and the *Los Angeles Examiner*, which sponsored the Southern California tournament. Descriptions of Bertha's psychological pitching style, which she developed while playing for the Lionettes, comes from a combination of newspaper articles and interviews with former players who later faced her as batters. She was called the "poker-faced miss" by an *Orange Daily News* reporter.

Details of the 1938 Southern California softball championship, which was held at Wrigley Field (not to be confused with the one in Chicago, although both fields were built by and named after William Wrigley, Philip Wrigley's father), are from "Career Game," in the *Los Angeles Times*, February 6, 1998; and "Lionettes Gun for S.C. Title Tonight," in the *Santa Ana Register*, September 12, 1938. The Lionettes' semifinal loss in the 1939 Southern California tournament was chronicled in "Lionettes Lose, Out of So. Cal. Tourney," in the *Santa Ana Register*, September 27, 1939. They lost, 3–0, to the Goodrich Silvertowns, who were led by future All-American Girls pitching star Dottie Wiltse.

Accounts of the Lionettes' 1940 season and the Southern California tournament in Long Beach came mostly from articles in the *Orange Daily News*. The *Los Angeles Times* sports columnist who called

Bertha the city's best softball pitching prospect since Lois Terry was Bob Ray (his column was called Sports X-Ray). Terry pitched that season for the Marshall-Clampetts, who were named after their car-dealership sponsor. Their three losses against the Lionettes were recorded by the *Orange Daily News*.

The information about the Dinuba Peppers softball team that Bertha's brothers played on that summer came from articles in the *Fresno Bee*. The description of Bertha's uncle Marko Petinak came from Janice Nelson. His books, most of which were self-published but are now part of the University of California's collection, include *Foundation of Correct Living* (1938), *Dates as Food: How to Use Them* (1939), and *Scenic Wonders of the World* (1940), which covers his hiking adventures throughout North America, Europe, Asia, and the Middle East.

Bertha's struggles with pitching accuracy during the 1941 season were chronicled by the *Santa Ana Register* and the *Orange Daily News*. The article calling her a "slow starter who has not yet rounded into shape" was in the *Orange Daily News*, April 26, 1941. On July 1, the *Santa Ana Register* described a no-hit game that Bertha almost lost because of walks. A similar situation occurred later that month in a game against the Dr Pepper team, except that time the Lionettes lost (*Santa Ana Register*, July 31, 1941). Both the *Santa Ana Register* and the *Orange Daily News* reported on games during July and August when Martha Cooper pitched and Bertha played in right field.

The description of Jim Ragan comes from interviews with Janice Nelson and articles in the *Orange Daily News*, which regularly reported on Jim's father, John, and uncle James, the deputy sheriff. I was unable to track down Jim Ragan's exact army enlistment date, but articles in the *Orange Daily News*, such as "Jas. Ragan Graduates as Aircraft Mechanic," November 6, 1943, state that he joined the army in January 1942 and had worked as an aircraft mechanic in Burbank before enlisting. Christmas and New Year's celebrations and holiday sales following the Pearl Harbor attack were chronicled in newspapers, such as the *Chicago Tribune* and the *St. Petersburg Times*.

The location and date of Bertha's marriage to James (Jim) Ragan were noted in the *Bridgeport Sunday Herald*, December 1, 1963, and were confirmed by Janice Nelson. The Lionettes' abbreviated season that summer was noted by the *Orange Daily News* and the *Santa Ana Register*. Information pertaining to Bertha's brothers' military service came from interviews with Janice Nelson and Pete Petinak and newspaper articles and, when possible, was confirmed using the US National Archives database.

Articles about Orange's scrap-metal drives appeared in the *Orange Daily News* throughout August and September of 1942. The quote about a discarded kettle furnishing eighty-four rounds of ammunition came from an editorial in the August 12, 1942, paper. The advertisement from the regional telephone company asking callers to keep their conversations brief appeared in the *Orange Daily News*, August 11, 1942. The bank war bonds ads proclaiming that "War has made your Christmas shopping easy!" began appearing in the paper later that fall.

Articles about food and gasoline rationing dominated American newspapers during the fall of 1942. The Ames, Iowa, Historical Society has compiled an online list of all the products that were rationed at various points throughout the war, at http://www.ameshistory.org/exhibits/ration_items.htm. For more background on the victory gardens that the US government urged women to grow during the war, see the National World War II Museum's "Fun Facts about Victory Gardens" page, at http://www.nationalww2museum.org/learn/education/for-students/ww2-history/at-a-glance/victory-gardens.html. The USC student newspaper article about pleasure driving being prohibited is from the *Daily Trojan*, September 22, 1942. By October and November, advertisements in the *Orange Daily News* and other West Coast newspapers were discouraging people from taking the bus, even for holiday travel.

Nightly dimouts were common in California during the late summer and fall of 1942. Newspapers would explain the details in articles with headlines such as "Dim-Out in Effect Tonight: Civilian Defense Head Asks Cooperation of Citizens," in the *Highland Park Post-Dispatch*, August 20, 1942; and "OCD [Office of Civilian Defense]

Continues Dim-Out Tips," in the *San Francisco News*, October 17, 1942. Newspapers would also report on businesses that violated the dimout rules and left their electric signs on. Such merchants "cannot expect public sympathy and do not deserve it," wrote the *Brooklyn Daily Eagle*, August 22, 1942 (dimouts were common in New York at that time, too).

Descriptions of the February 23, 1942, attack by a Japanese submarine on the Santa Barbara oil refinery and the panic that followed in Los Angeles are informed by the American Oil & Gas Historical Society's "Petroleum in War" page, at http://aoghs.org/petroleum-in-war/wwii-sub-attacks-oilfield/; and "Los Angeles Metropolitan Area During World War II," by the California State Military Museum, at http://californiamilitaryhistory.org/LAWWII.html.

More background on the internment of Japanese Americans during the war can be found in the Library of Congress's primer on the subject, at http://www.loc.gov/teachers/classroommaterials/primary sourcesets/internment/pdf/teacher_guide.pdf. "Half a Century Later, Relocation Pain Persists," in the *Los Angeles Times*, February 16, 1992, also proved a useful resource. This article and other sources, including the National Japanese American Memorial Foundation, list the total number of internees at 120,313. Kazui Oshiki Masuda's participation with the Lionettes in the summer of 1938 and the Pacific tour that fall were chronicled in the *Santa Ana Register*. The site japanese relocation.org lists Oshiki Masuda as having been detained at the Jerome Relocation Center in Arkansas along with her husband, Hiroshi, and other family members.

The US military's reshaping of California during the war has been written about extensively. The National Park Service's "World War II in the San Francisco Bay Area," at http://www.nps.gov/nr/travel/wwiibayarea/intro.htm, has more information about the transformation of San Francisco. For more on how the military used the state's desert areas, see "Desert Deployment: Southern California's World War II Desert Training Center," by Sarah McCormick Seekatz for KCET Los Angeles, March 16, 2015. The Tustin Area Historical So-

ciety has photos of the Santa Ana Naval Lighter-Than-Air Station at
http://www.tustinhistory.com/photos-lta.htm. The *Los Angeles Times*,
on April 13, 1991, also published a time line of events at the base. For
more on Los Angeles aircraft manufacturers, such as Douglas Aircraft,
becoming more influential than the movie studios, see Kevin Starr's
Embattled Dreams: California in War and Peace, 1940–1950 (New
York: Oxford University Press, 2003), 134.

Chapter 5

The epigraph is from *The Softball Story*, 5. The Jax Maids' record of six
losses out of a total of ninety-eight games in 1942 is from an Associated
Press article that appeared in newspapers across the country beginning
on September 16, 1943. Descriptions of the 1943 Mardi Gras celebration were drawn from "Mardi Gras Made Bond Day Rally: Glamor
Affair Turned into Patriotic Event," a newswire article that appeared
in the *Panama City (FL) News-Herald*, March 9, 1943; and from Jerry
Purvis Sanson's *Louisiana During the War: Politics and Society, 1939–
1945* (Baton Rouge: Louisiana State University Press, 1999), 262.

Data from the US Brewers Association, as used in "A Concise History of America's Brewing Industry," by economist Martin Stack, at
https://eh.net/encyclopedia/a-concise-history-of-americas-brewing
-industry/, show that beer consumption in the United States increased
by 50 percent during the war. "Beer parties" at US military bases, including the Santa Ana army base in California, during the war years
were also well documented. The Historic New Orleans Collection
has photos of the original Jax brewery, at http://www.hnoc.org/vcs/
property_info.php?lot=18332. For more on the history of the Jax
brewery and the German family that owned it, see Ellen Merrill and
Don Tolzmann's *Germans of Louisiana* (New Orleans: Pelican Publishing, 2014), 169–70.

The quote about the Jax Maids being the best-dressed softball
team, with three sets of uniforms and two different jackets, is from
the 1940 "Touring Glamour Girls Shoot for United States Softball

Title" newswire article. The detail about the Jax having to give up their private train car during the war comes from "The Batter Half: The Ladies Have Taken the Soft out of Softball," in *Collier's Weekly*, August 12, 1944. Articles in the *Times-Picayune* and other newspapers reported that attendance at the Jax team's home games usually ranged in the thousands. In "Jax Girls Recall Triumphant Years," in the *Times-Picayune*, May 27, 1979, former player Hazel Gill recalled people saying that visitors wanted to see two things in New Orleans: Mardi Gras and the Jax Maids. Freda Savona claimed that the team regularly outsold the Pelicans, New Orleans's minor league baseball team, in "You Have to Be a Lady to Play on the Ball Team of These Champs," in the *Milwaukee Journal*, August 3, 1948.

The material about Nina Korgan comes from "Korgan, World's Greatest Woman Softball Hurler, Could Have Been Tops in Any Sport," in the *Council Bluffs (IA) Nonpareil*, June 4, 1944; the 1944 *Collier's Weekly* article; the 1979 "Jax Girls Recall Triumphant Years" article; and "On the Ball: Star Pitcher Cherishes Softball Memories," in the *Tulsa World*, March 11, 1998. (Korgan died in 2009, at the age of ninety-three, according to her obituary.)

Descriptions of the national softball tournament games in this chapter are informed by articles in the *Chicago Tribune* and other newspapers. The Jax coach's telegram warning the players that they "may have to walk" after the 1943 tournament, depending on results, was described in the 1943 Associated Press article. More background on Philip Wrigley and the founding of the All-American Girls league can be found on the league's website, aagpbl.org. Wrigley's involvement with Marty Fiedler's women's softball league in the late 1930s is described in Harold Seymour's *Baseball: The People's Game* (374). Stuart Shea, author of *Wrigley Field: The Long Life and Contentious Times of the Friendly Confines* (Chicago: University of Chicago Press, 2014), and other historians have described Philip Wrigley as an art lover who primarily saw the Cubs as a business entity and as a way to preserve the legacy of his father, William, who founded the team.

The All-American Girls league starting salary of $45 to $85 per week was reported in newspaper articles, such as "Girls' Softball Loop, with Money and Brains, Bids for Big Popularity," by the Associated Press, May 29, 1943, and "Accent on Face and Figure in New Ladies' Loop," in the *Belvidere (IL) Daily Republican*, May 28, 1943. More details about how the league's playing style resembled and differed from standard fastpitch softball can be found on the AAGPBL's "League History" page, http://www.aagpbl.org/index.cfm/pages/league/12/league-history. The league's rules regarding conduct and appearance can be found at http://www.aagpbl.org/index.cfm/pages/league/18/league-rules-of-conduct.

The "embody the highest ideals of womanhood" quote is from "All but Forgotten Now, a Women's Baseball League Once Flourished," in *Sports Illustrated*, June 10, 1985. The phrase is also mentioned in Merrie Fidler's *The Origins and History of the All-American Girls Professional Baseball League* (Jefferson, NC: McFarland, 2010), 36. The full references for the Bloomer Girls articles mentioned are "Bloomer Girls Play Baseball: Salt Lake Professionals Have Lots of Fun with Them," in the *Deseret Evening News*, May 28, 1901; and "Bloomer Girls from Boston Beaten by Bushnell's Boys," in the *San Francisco Call*, July 15, 1901.

A quote, attributed to Arthur Meyerhoff, Wrigley's advertising executive, about the "amazing spectacle of beskirted girls throwing, catching, hitting, and running like men" is in Susan Cahn's *Coming on Strong: Gender and Sexuality in Women's Sport*, 2nd ed. (Champaign: University of Illinois Press, 2015), 149. The story of the chaperone yelling at a batter about not having her lipstick on has been recounted in numerous places, including Ken Burns's *Baseball* documentary, but "Belles of the Game," in *Smithsonian*, July 1989, appears to be the original source. A blog post by Lois Browne, author of *Girls of Summer: In Their Own League* (self-published, 1992), features a 1943 newspaper photo of All-American Girls player Ann Harnett making coffee. *The Origins and History of the All-American Girls Professional Baseball League* also mentions an article that described outfielder Clara (Claire) Schillace as enjoying sewing and cooking spaghetti (60). The May 28,

1943, "Accent on Face and Figure in New Ladies' Loop" article noted that shortstop Terrie Davis's husband worked in a "war plant." Photos of the All-American Girls players forming the *V*-for-"victory" symbol can be found on the aagpbl.org site and in various newspaper and magazine articles.

For more background on Dottie Wiltse, see Carolyn Trombe's *Dottie Wiltse Collins: Strikeout Queen of the All-American Girls Professional Baseball League* (Jefferson, NC: McFarland, 2005). Faye Dancer was the inspiration for Madonna's character in the movie *A League of Their Own*, according to her obituary in the *New York Times*, June 9, 2002. Most of the details pertaining to the National Girls Softball League, later called the National Girls Baseball League, are from articles in the *Chicago Tribune*, which regularly covered the league's teams during the 1940s and early 1950s.

The descriptions of Bertha's experiences during the war are informed by "The Fabulous Career of Bertha Ragan Tickey" article and interviews with Janice Nelson. Her brother Sam's death in 1944, after being held in a German prisoner-of-war camp, was reported in the *Fresno Bee*, August 24, 1944. His US military record confirms that he was captured in Italy that January and then held in Germany until his death in February. In Orange, where he had briefly pitched for the Cubs fastpitch team when Bertha first joined the Lionettes, his death made the front page of the paper. The article, in the September 2, 1944, edition of the *Orange Daily News*, said that the Petinak family had held out hope that the announcement of Sam's death had been a mistake and that Bertha had received the news in Laredo, "where she is residing with her husband Pfc. James Ragan, who is attached to the ground crew at the fighter plane base."

The Jax Maids' surprising loss to the Erin Brews was chronicled in newspaper articles, such as "Erin Brews Trip New Orleans," in the *Cleveland Plain Dealer*, September 17, 1944. The national softball tournament's switch to a double-elimination format was noted in newspaper stories and later in books, such as *Softball with Official Rules* and *The Softball Story*. The number of teams competing in the

'44 tournament—fifteen men's and fifteen women's—was listed in the 1945 ASA rule book. Some newspapers, including the *Plain Dealer*, initially reported that sixteen men's and women's teams would be participating, but it wasn't unusual for a team or two to drop out of the tournament last minute because of travel difficulties.

Information about the Phoenix Ramblers team came from "National Girls Softball Champs Stress Youth, Versatility, and Fight," by the Associated Press, August 9, 1941; and from my interview with Dot Wilkinson. The team and their coach, Ford Hoffman, were also frequently written about in Arizona newspapers, such as the *Arizona Republic*. The Jax Maids' loss to the Ramblers at the '44 tournament was described in "Jax Lassies Eliminated," in the *Times-Picayune*, September 18, 1944. A former All-American Girls player recalled that Freda and Olympia Savona were offered up to $325 per week to play in the league in "A Long Way to Go," on espn.go.com, August 10, 2009. The "fairly well fixed" comment from Freda is from a letter she wrote to a *Globe and Mail* sportswriter in 1943.

The descriptions of the 1945 national softball tournament mostly come from articles in the *Plain Dealer*. The rivalry between the Zollner Pistons and M&S Orange was discussed in Rodger Nelson's *Zollner Piston Story* (Fort Wayne, IN: Allen County Public Library Foundation, 1995), 47–49; and in the program for the 1992 Greater Flint Area Sports Hall of Fame inductions, which included the M&S team. The team's absence from the '45 tournament was explained in a newswire article about the competition from August 31, 1945. The quote about softball's being the game of choice for American soldiers during the war is from *Softball with Official Rules*, 18. Descriptions of the various softball sponsors in the late 1940s in the United States are informed by city and state game listings that were commonly published in newspapers at the time.

The Amateur Softball Association's claim that 250,000 men's and women's fastpitch teams were competing for spots in the national tournament is from a newswire article from August 31, 1945. The national survey that found softball was the widest-attended sport in the United States in the late 1940s with 125 million spectators was conducted by the US Rubber Company and was referenced in Frank Menke's *Encyclopedia of Sports* and several newspaper articles. Coca-Cola's involvement with the tournament as a sponsor and trophy provider starting in 1944 is mentioned in *The Softball Story* and in articles, such as "Sunshine City World Headquarters for Softball," in the *St. Petersburg Evening Independent*, May 25, 1948. Articles, such as "All Hail the Bombers," in the *St. Petersburg Times*, September 19, 1950, reported that the tournament's first-place trophy was four-feet tall. The May 25, 1948, *Evening Independent* article also mentioned that "Olympic competition" was a goal of the Amateur Softball Association.

Chapter 6

The epigraph is from *The Softball Story*, 169. Articles in the *Orange Daily News* confirm Bertha was back with the Lionettes by March 1946, although the softball season didn't start until the next month. The descriptions of Bertha's jobs and general mind-set following the war come from interviews with Janice Nelson. The population figures for Los Angeles and Orange County before and after the war are from the US Census Bureau and "From 1940 Census: How Has Orange County Changed?" in the *Orange County Register*, April 15, 2012. Photos of the Orange May Festival parades can be found in the Calisphere digital collection, at http://calisphere.cdlib.org/.

Bertha recalled her experiences working on the film *Cass Timberlane* in the 1991 *Los Angeles Times* article "Making Her Pitch: Tickey, an Ex-Lionette, Shined on the Diamond." Janice Nelson also remembers Bertha's working on the movie and maintains that it's actually her pitching during the softball game, not Lana Turner. It very well could be—the pitching style used is definitely the same as Bertha's—but I was unable to confirm it.

A newswire article about players from Marty Fiedler's Los Angeles softball league being used in the movie *Girls Can Play* appeared on

June 20, 1937. Kay Rohrer was perhaps the most notable softball player to have signed a movie-studio contract. The announcement that she had signed with MGM in November 1940 was reported nationally in an article entitled "Diamond Starlet Meets First Stars." It proved to be a short-lived arrangement, though. She broke her wrist in a softball game during the filming of her first movie. Studio officials demanded that she quit the sport, but she refused, according to her obituary in the *Chicago Tribune*, March 18, 1962. Like many of the Los Angeles players, she joined the Midwest professional softball leagues during the war, playing one season with the Rockford Peaches in the All-American Girls league, then switching to the National Girls league in Chicago.

Lana Turner's quote about only having to "brush up" on her softball skills because she hadn't forgotten any of the plays from when she'd played in high school is from "Tracy Is Flautist in 'Timberlane' While Lana Turner Pitches Curves," in the *Montreal Gazette*, May 7, 1948 (the movie was originally released in the fall of 1947, as evidenced by reviews in newspapers, such as the *New York Times*, but came out in theaters again in June of 1948). I viewed the photo of Bertha and Carole Landis during a visit with Janice Nelson. Landis's niece also featured the photo on her blog, carolelandisofficial.blogspot.com, in 2012 and labeled it the last picture taken of the actress before she died.

The description of Bertha's experiences in Balboa, California, is from Janice Nelson. The story of the Lionettes' breakup in 1948 is recounted in "The Fabulous Career of Bertha Ragan Tickey." The Monrovia Red Gals played in the Western States Girls Softball League, as it was called in the 1940s (the name later changed to the Pacific Coast Softball League), which first formed in 1946, according to the *Medford (OR) Mail Tribune* and other newspapers. By July 4, 1948, when the Red Gals played the Salt Lake City Shamrocks, Bertha was leading the league in strikeouts, with 172 (an article published in the *Salt Lake Tribune* that day referred to her as "iron man Bertha Ragan").

The *Santa Cruz (CA) Sentinel*, September 12, 1948, was one of the newspapers that described Portland's new softball stadium as the country's "most modern." Other details about the field, including the number of seats and the plans to expand it into a community park, were described in "World Series of Softball: Tournament Starts at New City Park with Night Games," in the *Sunday Oregonian*, September 12, 1948. The descriptions of the 1948 national tournament came from Associated Press coverage of the games and from articles in the *Bakersfield Californian* and the *Bend (OR) Bulletin*.

Betty Evans was written about frequently in the 1940s, starting in 1944, when she led the Portland Florists to a national title at age eighteen. Her "double windmill" pitch was described in an article in the *Roseburg (OR) News-Review*, August 28, 1948. The ASA rule book restricted windmill pitchers to one arm revolution in 1952. The Portland Beavers' win-loss record was 89-99 in 1948 and 85-102 in 1949, according to baseball-reference.com. Kip Carlson and Paul Andresen's *Portland Beavers* (Mount Pleasant, SC: Arcadia Publishing, 2004), 51, calls 1948 the beginning of "a half-dozen year streak where the Beavers were simply an average team."

The story of how Erv Lind wound up sponsoring and coaching the Florists is from the 1948 *Sunday Oregonian* article referenced above. Robbie Mulkey was one of the Florists players who grew up in a logging camp. She didn't grow up playing softball, according to an article in the *Vancouver (WA) Columbian*, November 4, 2008, but picked up the game quickly, and the record she set for most home runs during the women's national tournament (4) in 1949 stood for forty-four years, according to her ASA Hall of Fame page.

Dorothea McCullough Lee, Portland's mayor in 1949, was the second female mayor of a major US city, according to the Oregon Historical Society's *Oregon Encyclopedia*, oregonencyclopedia.org. Nicknamed No Sin Lee, she pledged to rid the city of gambling halls and brothels. For more background on Dorothea Lensch, Portland's parks director at the time, see her profile on Portland State University's "Portland's Walk of the Heroines" site, at http://www.woh.pdx.edu/heroine/2422. The article describing Bertha's near-perfect pitching against the Baton Rouge team at the '49 tournament was in the *Rose-burg (OR) News-Review*, September 13, 1949. Bertha was selected as Miss Softball on the night of September 16, 1949, according to newspapers such as the *Orange Daily News*.

Bertha described attending the Anaheim secretarial school in the aforementioned 1991 *Los Angeles Times* article about her. Descriptions of her training there and her work with the addressograph at the Orange Water Department come from Janice Nelson. The details about American women transitioning into clerical jobs after World War II are informed by "Women's Work: The Feminization and Shifting Meanings of Clerical Work," by Kim England and Kate Boyer in the *Journal of Social History*, Winter 2009. The quote from the secretarial textbook that warned readers against viewing the profession as a "rose-hued dream picture" is from Bernice Turner's *Private Secretary's Manual: A Practical Handbook for Secretaries and Executives* (New York: Prentice-Hall, 1947), 2. The description of addressographs and their importance to Los Angeles area utility services was informed by "The Addressograph Section" and "Early Commercial Organization" pages of the Water and Power Associates website, at waterandpower.org.

The announcement that the 1950 national men's and women's softball tournaments would be held in Austin and San Antonio, respectively, appeared in the *Freeport (TX) Facts*, March 2, 1950. Descriptions of the Lionettes' Greyhound bus trip to Texas are informed by Bertha's recollections in "The Fabulous Career of Bertha Ragan Tickey" and "The Girls of Summer," in the *Orange County Register*, March 19, 2014; an interview with former player Joann McLaughlin; and photos of the team and the bus from the Calisphere collection.

Details of the 1950 women's tournament, including game descriptions and the weather conditions, were reported in multiple newspapers, including the *Corpus Christi Caller-Times*, the *Brownsville Herald*, the *Tucson Daily Citizen*, and the *San Bernardino County Sun*. The description of Bertha's stomach injury during the tournament finals was drawn from newspaper articles and Dieselette pitcher Marie Wadlow's recollections in her ASA Hall of Fame profile (she described that final as the most thrilling one she'd witnessed).

Descriptions of the 1954 national women's tournament, which was held in Orange, are informed by newswire articles and the program for the event. Bertha's appearance in the *Ripley's Believe It or Not!* comic that year was noted by the *St. Petersburg Times*, September 8, 1954. Janice Nelson also possesses a clipping of the illustration of Bertha that accompanied the comic. The description of Bertha's appearance on *You Bet Your Life* was drawn from footage of the episode, which aired on November 18, 1954.

The "Mrs. Homemaker" cookware advertisement appeared in 1950s women's magazines, such as *Ladies' Home Journal*. The quote from the home economics textbook advising wives not to complain if their husbands arrived late for dinner is from a section of the book entitled "How to Be a Good Wife," at https://web.archive.org/web/20100127103858/http://jade.ccccd.edu/grooms/goodwife.htm.

The article that reported that Bertha stayed fit by dusting the house—the headline was "Softball Champ Stays Fit Caring for Family" and featured a photo of her dusting her trophies—appeared in the *Fresno Bee* in 1954 but may have been a newswire story (unfortunately, the clipping I viewed was incomplete). The article that said Bertha darned her husband's socks in the dugout was in the *Cumberland (MD) Evening Times*, March 25, 1952. The "No Spinning Wheel for This Granny" article in the *Fresno Bee* appeared during the 1954 national tournament. The quote about the "hot diamond" outdrawing the "hot stove" is from "Girls Know Their Softball," in the *St. Petersburg Times*, June 1, 1952.

The excerpt from Adlai Stevenson's commencement speech at Smith College that was published in *Woman's Home Companion*, September 1955, can be found at http://coursesa.matrix.msu.edu/~hst306/documents/stevenson.html. Mamie Eisenhower's quote about turning the lamb chops while her husband, Ike, ran the country is from a profile of her by the Miller Center at the University of Virginia. The results of Gallup's annual Most Admired men and women were published in newspapers every January. Eleanor Roosevelt topped the women's list nearly every year during the 1950s. For more background on Marian Anderson, the first African American to perform with the Metropolitan Opera, see the Library of Congress's profile of her, at http://www.americaslibrary.gov/jb/modern/jb_mod ern_anderson_1.html.

The story of telegrams and flowers pouring in from around the country (the world, actually) following Babe Didrikson Zaharias's death from cancer was reported in the *Deadwood (SD) Pioneer-Times*, September 28, 1956. The quote from President Eisenhower about her death comes from her obituary in the *New York Times*, September 27, 1956.

Chapter 7

The epigraph is from *Softball with Official Rules*, 17. Softball's addition to the Merriam-Webster dictionary was noted in "Softball Comes of Age in Portland," in the *Oregonian Sunday Magazine*, 1946. By 1955, newspapers, such as the *Bridgeport Telegram*, were reporting that half a million men's and women's teams were competing for spots in the ASA's national tournament. Most of the details related to Fred Zollner and his Zollner Pistons team are from *The Zollner Piston Story*.

Players or even entire teams were frequently penalized for violating the ASA's residence rules. For example, an article in the *Kokomo (IN) Tribune*, July 7, 1950, reported that the manager/coach of a local team called the Speedettes had been suspended for two games for using a player who had allegedly lived in Indianapolis for more than ninety days and was thus ineligible. Four days later, the same newspaper revealed that the player hadn't in fact lived in Indianapolis—the coach of a rival team had forged the document indicating that she did (the coach was suspended from the league indefinitely).

Descriptions of the National Softball Congress are informed by newspaper articles, such as "National Softball Congress Making Rapid Progress," in the *Lewiston (ME) Evening Journal*, July 12, 1951; and

"State ASA Outlaws All Connected with National Softball in Orlando," in the *St. Petersburg Independent*, August 24, 1948. The story of the Jax Maids being stripped of their national tournament title in 1947 was chronicled by the *Chicago Tribune* and other papers. The quote from Michael Pauley about the ASA's having an easier time getting teams to participate in the tournament "now that the Jax are out" appeared in a newswire article published on September 25, 1947.

Ray Johnson, executive secretary of the ASA, was the official who claimed the NSC's prize money made players professional and said, "To us, softball is a recreation and not a profession." The quote appeared in an Associated Press article published on January 17, 1948. The ASA had been down this road before. In 1940, the organization called out the American Softball Association, a smaller league founded in St. Louis by former baseball star George Sisler, for being professional, similarly for offering prize money at its end-of-season tournament. Sisler's league disbanded a few years afterward, according to the 1955 National Softball Congress rule book. A year before that, in 1939, the ASA had barred its members from participating in a nascent professional indoor baseball league that players tried to form in New York. "The association has no difference with any group endeavoring to organize professional groups to play softball. However, any athlete signing to play with one of these pro teams or competing with or against pro teams definitely will be suspended from competition in amateur softball," the ASA president said in a newswire article published on November 22, 1939.

In the 1950s, sitting out a year was the standard for softball players with "professional" experience. Betty Evans, Ginny Busick, Tiby Eisen, and other players who had joined the All-American or National Girls softball leagues during the 1940s and early 1950s had to sit out a season before returning to the ASA league. A few men's fastpitch players had played baseball professionally, including Ed Tickey, Bertha's second husband (he spent a few years in the minor leagues, playing for New York Giants and Brooklyn Dodgers farm teams, according to baseball-reference.com). One of the more interesting of these cases was that of Bob Fesler, a pitcher who started in softball, then in 1955 switched to the Seattle Rainiers, which played in the famed Pacific Coast minor league and was the city's only professional baseball team at the time. The team allowed Fesler to continue pitching underhand—indeed, it was the main reason the Rainiers hired him—but apart from one impressive strikeout in a game against San Francisco, the transition didn't go well. He was moved to a lower-tier minor league team the next season and was dropped from that team by late April. He was ineligible to return to the ASA that summer or the next one because he had played professionally that year, however briefly, but he was pitching for fastpitch teams by 1958, according to "The Bob Fesler Experiment," on *Sportspress Northwest* (sportspressnw.com), April 10, 2012.

The story of Olympic medalist Lee Calhoun's losing his amateur status in 1957 after appearing on *Bride and Groom* was chronicled by United Press and other newswire services. An article in *Jet*, December 24, 1953, reported that Mal Whitfield, another American Olympic track star, almost lost his amateur status after someone in Europe suggested in "hush-hush fashion" that he had asked race organizers to pay him to race. Whitfield denied the accusations, but as *Jet* put it, the AAU "accepted hearsay as fact." (He was later cleared of any wrongdoing.) That same year, the AAU reportedly investigated Wes Santee, who'd competed with Whitfield in Europe, after he told the *Saturday Evening Post* that he hoped to "collect enough [travel] expenses to finance a farm," according to Joseph Turrini's *End of Amateurism in Track and Field* (Champaign: University of Illinois Press, 2010), 37–38.

Althea Gibson announced that she was retiring from competitive tennis "for at least one year" after winning the US Open on September 7, 1958. Her quote about reigning over an empty bank account is from her International Tennis Hall of Fame profile page, at https://www.tennisfame.com/hall-of-famers/inductees/althea-gibson/.

Freda and Olympia Savona's time playing in the National Girls league in Chicago during the early 1950s was chronicled by the *Chicago Tribune* and other newspapers. The umpire threatening to quit if the Harrisburg minor league team allowed Eleanor Engle to play, and the coach saying, "This is no-woman's land and believe me, I mean it," are from "Rookie's Curves Not Appreciated by Harrisburg," by the Associated Press, June 23, 1952. The subsequent ban on professional baseball teams signing female players was reported in the *Harrisburg Evening News* and other papers and was recounted in "Engle Nearly Made History," in the *Indiana (PA) Gazette*, June 28, 2002. The "Women Players in Organized Baseball" essay on the Society for American Baseball Research site (sabr.org) presents evidence that a few women had played on minor league baseball teams before Engle, however, often with little fanfare.

Althea Gibson's stint playing tennis before Harlem Globetrotters games has been mentioned in books and articles about her athletic career. Joe Louis's Punchers fastpitch team was fairly well-known and was covered by newspapers regularly. The Brown Bombers, the team Louis sponsored and sometimes played with in the 1930s and '40s, was even more famous. He seemed genuinely fond of the game and was said to want to give African American players more opportunities to compete. Details about the traveling women's fastpitch team that Jim Thorpe sponsored came from "Jim Thorpe Once Owned a Women's Baseball Team," in the *Lehighton (PA) Times News*, July 13, 2013. For more background on the Sioux City Ghosts, see the profile of the team on siouxcityhistory.org.

The descriptions of Eddie Feigner and his King and His Court act are drawn from a combination of newspaper and magazine articles, such as "A King Without a Crown," in *Sports Illustrated*, August 21, 1972; "Eddie Feigner Is Speed King of Softball," in the *Tuscaloosa News* (via a syndicated *Los Angeles Times* article), August 25, 1976; and "Old King Eddie Is Still Courting Fans," by the NEA newswire service, July 20, 1988. The Queen and Her Maids was a family act, consisting of teenage pitcher Rosie Beaird and her two sisters (plus another player to round out the infield) and organized and run by their father, Royal Beaird. Metro Szeryk, originally from Ontario, pitched for several top ASA teams before touring with the Silver Six group in the early 1960s. He started the act when his hometown refused to let him play in its league because his pitching was too dominant, according to an article in the *Bridgeport Post*, April 4, 1965.

Descriptions of the Fresno Rockets in this chapter are informed by interviews with former players Jeanne Contel and Gloria May and from articles in the *Fresno Bee*. The descriptions of the 1957 national tournament in Buena Park are drawn from newspaper accounts and recollections of former players, including Contel, May, and Beverly Mulonet Hollis from the Brakettes.

Bertha's participation in the *Sports Illustrated* festival in Yonkers later that week was chronicled in the magazine's September 16, 1957, issue. Her appearance on the game show *To Tell the Truth* was mentioned in the *Bridgeport Post*, October 6, 1957. Details about the appearance were obtained from watching the episode. It has been suggested in later articles that Bertha also appeared on *What's My Line?*—a similar show that aired during the same time period—but I was unable to find any record of this, and it would have been strange for her to appear on both shows because they were so much alike and overlapped in audience.

The announcement that the 1958 national women's tournament would be held in Stratford was reported in the *Bridgeport Post*, February 9, 1958. Bill Simpson's desire to bring the tournament to Connecticut and to end the West Coast teams' dominance of the event were chronicled in an article in the *Bridgeport Sunday Herald*, January 19, 1958. The *Bridgeport Telegram* article predicting that the tournament would be the "greatest sports spectacle conducted in the state" that year appeared on April 16, 1958.

Jo An Kammeyer's engagement and subsequent wedding in 1958 were chronicled by the *Bridgeport Post* and confirmed in an interview with her. The schedule of Bertha's return to Stratford in June of that year and the Brakettes' victories over the New Jersey Debs were reported in the Bridgeport newspapers.

Chapter 8

The epigraph is from *Softball for Girls*, 57. Most of the details of the 1958 tournament, such as game attendance figures and the weather conditions, are from articles in the *Bridgeport Post* and the *Bridgeport Telegram*, which, not surprisingly, covered the '58 tournament extensively. The "Bertha Ragan Ace in Thrilling Game" article referenced appeared in the *Bridgeport Telegram*, September 5, 1958. Bertha's hip injury during the tournament final was described in newspaper articles, such as "Pleasure and Pain Mark Brakettes' Title Win," in the *Bridgeport Sunday Herald*, September 14, 1958; and in "The Fabulous Career of Bertha Ragan Tickey." The description of it was also informed by interviews with Beverly Mulonet Hollis, Micki Macchietto Stratton, and Janice Nelson.

The description of Joan Joyce's taking over for Bertha in the '58 final was informed by newspaper articles and interviews with Joyce and other players who participated in that game, including Mulonet Hollis, Macchietto Stratton, Edna Fraser, Jeanne Contel, and Gloria May. The congratulatory telegrams and town celebrations that followed the Brakettes' tournament victory that year were chronicled in the *Bridgeport Telegram*, September 22, 1958; and the *Bridgeport Post*, September 23, 1958.

Descriptions of Joan's early years in Waterbury are drawn from articles, such as "It's an Underhanded Trick," in *People*, August 11, 1975; and "Joan Joyce: The Best Ted Williams Ever Faced," from espn .go.com, August 5, 2011; and from interviews with her and Beverly Mulonet Hollis. The story of Joan's struggling to find her pitching style until she learned the slingshot delivery from John "Cannonball" Baker is from interviews with her. The *Bridgeport Post* was the newspaper that called Joan the Waterbury Whiz Kid and Bertha the California Comet. The 1975 *People* article about Joan quoted her as saying that she idolized Mickey Mantle growing up. Descriptions of her various sports-related jobs after she graduated from high school are from interviews with her.

The *Saturday Evening Post* article that featured Mary Hartman was entitled "Lady at the Plate" and appeared in the September 5, 1959, issue. The comparatively deluxe travel arrangements that the Brakettes enjoyed during the 1950s and '60s were described in newspaper articles and in interviews with former players, such as Beverly Mulonet Hollis, Micki Stratton, and Millie Dixon Dubord Marchi. Descriptions of the Brakettes' 1960 trip to the Caribbean are informed by articles, such as "Poised for Conquest of the Caribbean," in the *Bridgeport Post*, September 11, 1960; and interviews with Hollis, Fraser, and Marchi.

The reports that Bertha was going to accompany the Florists on their 1959 Pacific tour and then wound up not going appeared in the *Bridgeport Sunday Herald*, September 20 and October 11. The description of the Lionettes' experiences during their 1960 Pacific tour are from an article in the *Long Beach Independent*, December 17, 1960.

Marge McIntire, who played with the Brakettes in 1961, recalled in an interview that Simpson promised to take the team on a big trip—"anywhere they wanted to go," he reportedly said—if they won the national title that year. Descriptions of the games from that tournament, including the marathon finals against the Whittier Gold Sox, are informed by articles in the *Bridgeport Telegram* and Littlewood's *The Path to the Gold*, 73–74. The women's tournament trophy was described as being six feet tall in the program for the 1961 championship.

Bertha's new blond hairstyle in 1962 is apparent in photos of her from that year. Millie Dixon Dubord Marchi recalled in an interview that she helped Bertha dye her hair. Other details about Millie mentioned in this chapter are from interviews with her. Descriptions of Janice Nelson's wedding and Bertha's longer stays in Connecticut are from interviews with Janice and from "The Fabulous Career of Bertha Ragan Tickey."

The Brakettes' victories over the Florists, Ramblers, and Lionettes during their West Coast tour in July 1962 were described in the *Bridgeport Post*. An article in the *Bridgeport Post*, April 12, 1962, reported the shortage of "choice seats" for the national tournament that was to begin in August that year. The need for additional bleachers for the tournament was noted in the *Bridgeport Post*, August 10, 1962. The claim that the national tournament was more popular than the Stratford Shakespeare Festival is from a newswire article published on August 31, 1962.

The "Osaka Girls Add Orient's Spice to Softball Tourney" article was in the *Bridgeport Post*, August 24, 1962. Other details about the team and the US tour they embarked on before the tournament are from a newswire article published August 27, 1962. Bertha's lingering pain from her 1958 hip injury was often mentioned in Bridgeport newspapers that season.

Chapter 9

The epigraph is from *The Softball Story*, 168. The *Bridgeport Post* was the newspaper that sometimes referred to Bertha and Joan as the Big Two. Dan Parker, a columnist for the *New York Mirror*, was one of the sportswriters who wrote favorably about Joan after her appearance on the CBS *Sports Spectacular* in 1961. On July 18, 1962, a newswire reporter wrote that she had "achieved every one of the dream goals and more. She has won 20 straight games, pitched two successive perfect games. The works . . . After a while, it just doesn't pay to count. Not when you've got a record like Joanie's."

The description of Joan pitching to Ted Williams in August 1963 is drawn from ESPN's "Joan Joyce: The Best Ted Williams Ever Faced"; an article in the *Waterbury Republican-American*, August 13, 1963; and from interviews with Joan. The exact details of what transpired are somewhat difficult to pin down. Williams appeared in Waterbury for a charity event to benefit a foundation called the Jimmy Fund nearly every August during the 1960s (he retired from professional baseball in 1960), as did the Brakettes and the Raybestos Cardinals, who usually played a doubleheader against two of their New England rivals. Sometimes other baseball players showed up to pitch to Williams, but the focus of articles in newspapers, such as the *Bridgeport Post*, was on the softball games rather than Williams and the other celebrity guests, such as the actor Jerry Lewis.

Articles in the *Waterbury Republican-American* confirm that Joan pitched to Williams at the Jimmy Fund event in 1963 and 1966. The articles also reveal that Bertha pitched against him in 1962 (Joan was supposed to, but she had suffered an arm injury and didn't want to aggravate it before the national tournament). There doesn't seem to be any newspaper coverage of Joan pitching to Williams in 1961, as some later articles have suggested she did, but it's possible that she did and that it wasn't written about at the time. She had also pitched to him at a summer baseball camp in Massachusetts that he was involved with, complicating matters further. After reviewing the available evidence, though, I believe that August 12, 1963, was most likely the first time Joan pitched against Williams in front of an audience (the crowd was seventeen thousand, according to the *Waterbury Republican-American* and the *Bridgeport Post*, which only covered the Brakettes game).

The article that suggested there was "something peculiar" about Joan's decision to move to California and join the Lionettes appeared in the *Bridgeport Sunday Herald*, September 15, 1963. The explanation of wanting to play in the Pacific Coast softball league and not wanting to take classes with students she knew from teaching and refereeing high school basketball games came from interviews with Joan, as did the details about her driving out to California that fall and having her own apartment there. Bill Simpson's assurance that she was welcome to rejoin the Brakettes anytime also came from interviews with Joan.

The two shutouts that Bertha pitched in July 1963 were chronicled in the *Bridgeport Post*, July 21, 1963. This was also the article that called the performance "another remarkable demonstration of her softball skill." Bertha petitioned for a divorce at the Bridgeport Superior Court on July 22, 1963, according to the *Bridgeport Telegram*. California became the first state to offer no-fault divorce in 1969, when Ronald Reagan, the state's governor at the time, signed the Family Law Act. The 1965 law journal paper referenced is "Domestic Relations:

Single Act of Cruelty as Grounds for Divorce," by Michael Rick in the *Marquette Law Review*, November 1965. The details described in Bertha's divorce hearing were reported in articles in the *Bridgeport Post* and the *Bridgeport Sunday Herald* and were confirmed by Janice Nelson. The "Girl Softball Ace Strikes Out Mate" article appeared in the *Bridgeport Sunday Herald*, December 1, 1963.

The description of Brakettes fans booing Joan at the July 1964 all-stars game is from the *Bridgeport Post*, July 26, 1964. "We will hope that they were booing what seemed at the time as the Brakettes' last opportunity to score . . . not showing displeasure at Joan's decision last winter to move to the West Coast," the reporter wrote.

The rise in slowpitch softball during the 1960s was chronicled by the ASA and has been recalled in articles such as "Slowpitch Puts Fastpitch in Slump," in the *Orlando Sentinel*, July 13, 1987. An article in Santa Clara University's alumni magazine, May 24, 2012, noted that female students were banned from the school's pool until the 1970s because the men wanted to swim nude. A 2009 discussion on the US Masters Swimming Forum, at http://forums.usms.org/archive/index.php/t-13275.html, also suggests that males-only nude-swimming pools at YMCA and university facilities were common in the 1950s and '60s.

The Olympics figures cited are from olympic.org, the official site of the Olympics. The site's page for the 1964 Summer Olympics notes that the addition of women's volleyball to the program that year marked the first women's team event. Accounts of women moving to different towns—for example, from Portland to Orange or Fresno—to join new competitive fastpitch teams after their old ones folded were commonplace in the 1960s, especially later in the decade as more teams started to struggle financially. Interviews with former players confirmed their involvement with girls' youth teams, such as the Cubettes and the Robins. These teams were also frequently written about in local newspapers.

For more information about the history of softball in Australia, see Softball Australia's history page, http://softball.org.au/extra

.asp?ID=19501. The organization of the 1965 international tournament in Melbourne is also chronicled in the International Softball
Federation's recent "Five Decades of International Softball" report.
Descriptions of the tournament and the Brakettes' international tour
are drawn from articles in the *Bridgeport Post* and the *Bridgeport Telegram* and interviews with former players, including Beverly Mulonet
Hollis and Edna Fraser.

The descriptions of Bertha's experiences during the tour are in-
formed by interviews with Janice Nelson and her recollections in
"The Fabulous Career of Bertha Ragan Tickey." Bertha often spoke of
wanting her sport to be in the Olympics, and her desire to compete
in the Olympics herself was confirmed by Janice. She also confirmed
Bertha's marriage to Ed Tickey following her divorce from Jim Ragan.
By the start of the 1964 softball season, she was referred to as either
Bertha Ragan Tickey or Bertha Tickey in the Bridgeport newspapers.
John Stratton, Micki's husband and a former Brakettes coach, confirmed in an interview that Micki's mother went along on the 1965
international tour. Meanwhile, Beverly Mulonet Hollis confirmed that
the other players, save Bertha, who brought Ed, had to leave their
loved ones at home.

Film footage of the tournament final between the Brakettes and
Australia is at https://youtube.com/watch?v=uY7vGe_IOLM. The
game was also covered by the Associated Press, February 22, 1965.
Some of the questionable calls by the umpires during the tournament were on Bertha, for illegal pitches. "I think those decisions stank.
Bertha almost invented pitching in women's softball, and she's never
been called for that before," Wee Devitt said in a newswire article
published in the *Fresno Bee*, February 14, 1965.

Descriptions of the 1965 national tournament are informed by
articles in the *Bridgeport Post* and the *Bridgeport Telegram* and interviews with Beverly Mulonet Hollis. Descriptions of the 1966 national
tournament were also mostly drawn from the Bridgeport newspaper
coverage. That about five hundred fans waited in the rain on a Sunday
night to greet the Brakettes after they got back from Orlando comes

from the *Bridgeport Telegram*, September 5, 1966. Bertha's appearance on *I've Got a Secret* was reported in the *Bridgeport Telegram*, October 10, 1966. I wasn't able to obtain footage of the episode, but a description of it on carsoncrafts.com mentions that Bertha pitched to host Steve Allen while Ed served as her catcher.

The article in which Wee Devitt said that he knew Bertha's retirement was inevitable but still difficult to accept was in the *Bridgeport Post*, September 18, 1966. Bertha's talk at the Stratford Exchange Club luncheon was chronicled in the *Bridgeport Telegram*, October 8, 1966.

Chapter 10

The epigraph is from *Softball for Girls*, 9. The Associated Press article with the line about the US women's Olympic track team running like startled gazelles while also being as lithe and graceful appeared on October 14, 1964, under the headline "How Feminine Are Women Athletes?" The *Sports Illustrated* article referenced is "In Stratford, Nobody Beats the Brakettes," September 11, 1967.

The account of Jock Semple's trying to push Kathrine Switzer off the course at the 1967 Boston Marathon and yelling, "Get the hell out of my race!" has been described in numerous places, such as "How Kathrine Switzer Paved the Way," on espn.go.com, April 12, 2012. A newswire article from April 20, 1967, described Switzer as a "dark blond." The *New York Times* article that asked what a former beauty contestant was doing in a marathon is "Lady with Desire to Run Crashed Marathon," April 23, 1967. That article also noted that Switzer had "big, brown eyes."

The description of Dot Wilkinson chasing the announcer out of a ballpark with a bat is from interviews with former Fresno Rockets players Jeanne Contel and Gloria May. Details about the estrogen treatments pediatricians used to administer to tall girls are from "Tall Girls: The Social Shaping of a Medical Therapy," by Joyce Lee and Joel Howell in the *Archives of Pediatric Adolescent Medicine*, October 2006.

The description of doctors prescribing amphetamines for weight loss during the 1960s was informed by "America's First Amphetamine Epidemic, 1929–1971," by Nicolas Rasmussen in the *American Journal of Public Health*, June 2008. The *Seventeen* magazine book that said a woman's smile mattered more than the words she said is *The Seventeen Book of Fashion and Beauty* (New York: Macmillan, 1967).

The story of Beverly Mulonet Hollis's parents driving around in the middle of the night to listen to radio coverage of a Brakettes game is from interviews with her. The description of Gloria May's daughter Jamie accompanying the Rockets on road trips is from interviews with May and Jeanne Contel. An article in the *Bridgeport Post*, August 28, 1963, also featured a photo of Jamie kissing her mom's bat for good luck.

The account of Tiby Eisen's not being able to join the Los Angeles Bank of America softball team is from an article about her on the Jewish Women's Archive, at http://jwa.org/encyclopedia/article/eisen-thelma-tiby. The account of the African American Boeing employee who started her own women's team when she wasn't allowed to join the company fastpitch team is from an article in the *Afro American*, June 10, 1944. Lionette catcher Nancy Ito was recruited from her Denver Japanese American team at age fourteen, according to an article in a Japanese American magazine from the 1950s that was passed on to me by Bob Ito, Nancy's nephew. (I was unable to determine the exact publication information, but it was written by Bill Hosokawa, a reporter for the *Denver Post*.) The account of Mary "Toots" Edmonds and her sisters playing on Native American teams in their hometown before getting recruited to play on the Oklahoma City Rufnex team that played in the 1963 national tournament is from an interview with Edmonds's daughter, Lisa Wetselline.

Descriptions of the prejudice Charlie Justice and the two other African American players on the Toronto Tip Top Tailors team encountered at the 1949 national tournament in Arkansas are informed by "The Sultans of Softball: Transcendent 1949 Team to Receive Long Overdue Acclaim When It Enters Hall Next Month," in the *Toronto*

Sun, October 10, 2009. The descriptions of Billie Harris's experiences playing for the Phoenix Ramblers and the Yakima Webb Cats are from an interview with her. For more background on the St. Augustine, Florida, hotel manager who dumped acid in the pool after African American protesters jumped in, see National Public Radio's "Remembering a Civil Rights Swim-In: 'It Was a Milestone,'" published on npr .org, June 13, 2014. The Las Vegas casinos were desegregated in 1960, according to news sources.

The dissolution of the Ramblers due to financial troubles in 1966 was reported in the *Phoenix Gazette* and other area newspapers. The death of Erv Lind, coach and sponsor of the Portland Florists, in 1964 shortly after the team won their second national title was reported by the Associated Press, November 20, 1964. The account of Bobbie Bailey's promising Hollie Lough she would keep the Atlanta Lorelei Ladies team going only to find out after his death that the money he'd set aside for the team was gone is drawn from an interview with her conducted by Kennesaw State University in 2007 as part of the school's oral history project and an interview with former Lorelei player Edwina Bryan. Descriptions of the 1967 national tournament are informed by articles in the *Bridgeport Post* and the *Bridgeport Telegram*. A clipping of the newspaper column that compared the Netherlands softball team to awkward swans can be found in the September 1967 issue of the *Women in Softball* newsletter, available at sites.google.com/site/womeninsoftball/.

The Brakettes' trip West and to Canada for softball's debut as a demonstration sport in the Pan American Games was chronicled by the *Ogden (UT) Standard-Examiner* and the *Salt Lake Tribune* in addition to the Bridgeport newspapers. Bertha's problems with back spasms were reported in the *Bridgeport Post*. Descriptions of Bertha and Ed enjoying golf and trips to Puerto Rico are from "The Fabulous Career of Bertha Ragan Tickey" and were confirmed by Janice Nelson. The account of Bertha's returning to the Brakettes for the 1968 season after Donna Lopiano went to graduate school in California and Donna Hebert had to undergo surgery is from the *Bridgeport Post*, May 3 and May 19, 1968. The Bertha Tickey Night celebration during the national tournament that August was also covered by the *Bridgeport Post*. Janice Nelson also confirmed details from the event, such as that Simpson paid for her and Bertha's other family members to fly East.

Chapter 11

The epigraph is from *The Softball Story*, 6. Descriptions of Bernice Sandler's and Edith Green's efforts to end sex discrimination in schools, which led to the passage of Title IX, are informed by the profile of Sandler on the Maryland Women's Hall of Fame page, http://msa.maryland.gov/msa/educ/exhibits/womenshall/html/sandler.html. The quoted text from the Title IX amendment is from the US Department of Justice's "Equal Access to Education: Forty Years of Title IX," June 2012. The figure of nearly half as many US women having college degrees as men before Title IX is also from this report. The figure of women holding fewer than 20 percent of university faculty positions prior to Title IX is from "Title IX at 30: Report Card on Gender Equity," by the National Coalition for Women and Girls in Education, June 2002.

A transcript of President Nixon's statements during the signing of the education amendments of 1972, which included Title IX, is available at http://www.presidency.ucsb.edu/ws/?pid=3473. A time line chronicling the passage of Title IX and the NCAA's resistance can be found at http://www.equalrights.org/title-ix-timeline/.

The various name and sponsor changes experienced by teams, such as the Florists and Ohse Meats, during the 1970s were chronicled by local newspapers and in the *Women in Softball* newsletter. Descriptions of the Brakettes' switch to polyester uniforms in 1974 are informed by team photos and interviews with former player Irene Shea. Bertha's appointment as assistant director of the Barnum Festival was reported in the *Bridgeport Post*, September 19, 1973. (She was promoted to executive director in 1980, according to an article in the *New London Day*, June 20, 1980.)

Descriptions of the abandonment and eventual rehabilitation of the Jax brewery are drawn from "Jax Beer Plant Becomes Hottest Spot in New Orleans' Old French Quarter," in the *Dallas Morning News*, February 17, 1985. Morris "Munny" Sokol actually sold his Alabama furniture stores in late 1968, according to the *Tuscaloosa News*, October 10, 1968, but he was still running the company then. Less than a year later, though, he and the national company he'd sold out to parted ways, and the stores changed hands again, this time without Sokol's involvement, which is why 1969 is generally recognized as the year the stores were sold. Details pertaining to Harold "Shifty" Gears's career at Eastman Kodak are from the *Rochester (NY) Democrat & Chronicle*, December 27, 2014.

The Brakettes' 1972 trip to Italy for a small international tournament was chronicled by the *Bridgeport Telegram* and the Associated Press. Irene Shea and other former players confirmed that the Brakettes always flew to long-distance games and stayed in nice hotels, never more than two to a room. Descriptions of the 1974 international tournament that was held in Stratford are informed by "The Early Birds Squirmed," in *Sports Illustrated*, August 26, 1974; articles in the *Bridgeport Post*; and interviews with Irene Shea and Joan Joyce. Baseball has been part of the Pan American Games since the competition began in 1951, according to web.usabaseball.com, the official site of USA Baseball.

The description of Joan's diminished running abilities in the 1970s because of knee injuries is based on interviews with Irene Shea and John Stratton. Joan first joined the Brakettes in the spring of 1955, when she was fourteen (her birthday is in August), making 1973 her nineteenth year playing softball. Bertha and the Old-Timers' victory over the Brakettes, minus Joan, was chronicled in the *Bridgeport Post*, July 14, 1973. The new record that Joan set during the '73 tournament, with 134 strikeouts, was reported in the *Bridgeport Post*, August 26, 1973. The "it is so rare that one person so dominates a sport" line is also from that article. The "I've seen eleven women's and three men's tournaments, but never a performance to match Joyce's in the

1973 event," is from a different article in that same edition of the *Bridgeport Post*.

Descriptions of Joan being the first female recipient of the Connecticut Sports Writers' Alliance's Gold Key award are drawn from "Softball Great Joan Joyce Wins Writers' Gold Key," in the *Bridgeport Post*, January 29, 1974. Bertha won the same award in 1982, and the *Norwalk Hour*, December 8, 1981, noted that she was the second female recipient, after Joan. Joan's win-loss record was said to be 375–27 in the *Bridgeport Post*, July 28, 1974. The description of the 1974 national tournament finals and of Micki Stratton's RAYBESTOS IS NUMBER ONE IN THE WORLD AND THE USA sign are from an article that appeared in the *Orlando Sentinel Star*, September 1, 1974.

The first asbestos-related lawsuit against Raybestos was filed in 1971, according to a timeline published by the *Connecticut Post*, October 30, 2011, as part of a series of articles about the Raybestos pollution in Stratford. Sumner Simpson's 1930s letters, which were uncovered in a file box in the 1970s, provided some of the first evidence that companies, such as Raybestos, that used asbestos in their manufacturing knew about the potential health hazards of the substance and sought to keep that information quiet. Excerpts of the letters can be found on the Harvard University Law School site, at http://www.presidency.ucsb.edu/ws/?pid=3473; and in Barry Castleman's *Asbestos: Medical and Legal Aspects* (New York: Aspen Publishers, 2005), 152–53. Mesothelioma was first discovered in the 1960s, and that was when medical researchers realized that the health hazards of asbestos exposure were likely more serious than previous studies had suggested, according to "History of Asbestos Related Disease," by P. W. J. Bartrip in *Postgraduate Medical Journal*, February 2004.

The Raybestos plant physician's assertion that there had never been a case of mesothelioma at the factory is from an article in the *Bridgeport Post*, March 15, 1972. Other studies have found the disease in employees who worked at the Stratford plant in the 1930s to the 1980s, as illustrated in "Malignant Mesothelioma among Employees of a Connecticut Factory That Manufactured Friction Materials Using

Chrysotile Asbestos," by Murray Finkelstein and Christopher Meisen-kothen in the *Annals of Occupational Hygiene*, June 2010. The finding that Stratford residents had slightly higher rates of bladder cancer and mesothelioma compared to other parts of Connecticut is from a 1993 review by the Centers for Disease Control and Prevention.

A more detailed description of the pollution from Raybestos (called Raymark after 1982) at Memorial Field and other sites in Stratford can be found on the Environmental Protection Agency's site, epa.gov/superfund/raymark. Pollution in Rochester, New York, from the Eastman Kodak facility has been described in "Pollution by Kodak Brings Sense of Betrayal," in the *New York Times*, March 8, 1989; and "Kodak Taking Steps to Hand Off Environmental Concerns," in the *Rochester (NY) Democrat & Chronicle*, May 30, 2013. The site http://www.corp-research.org/dowchemical chronicles some of Dow Chemical's pollution issues in Midland, Michigan. The quote from the DuPont spokesperson following the pollution lawsuit settlement is from "With Pollution Suit Settled, Town Awaits DuPont Millions," in the *New York Times*, July 3, 1997.

Chapter 12

The epigraph is from *Softball for Girls*, 21. Billie Jean King's milestone of becoming the first female athlete to earn $100,000 a year was chronicled by the Associated Press, October 4, 1971. She was still grossly underpaid compared to the top male tennis players, as she pointed out in a news story published in *Sports Illustrated* that same day, saying, "Nine out of every ten people there [at the US Open tournament] came to see the women. So why didn't the women get nine-tenths of the prize money [instead of 25 percent]?" Descriptions of Joan's travel agency and the house she shared with her sister are from "It's an Underhanded Trick," in *People*, August 11, 1975; and interviews with her.

Joan's announcement that she would compete in the Women's Superstars event was reported in the *Bridgeport Post*, September 22,

1974. Descriptions of the Houston portion of the Women's Superstars competition are informed by "Superstars Set for Astrodome Contest," in the *Port Arthur (TX) News*, December 20, 1974; and "Recognition, Money Goals of Women Superstars," in the *Chicago Tribune*, December 22, 1974. Details of the finals, held in Florida a month later, including the quote from Peppler after she won, are from newswire articles and "Super Mary Jo Cashes In," in the *Chicago Tribune*, January 30, 1975.

Descriptions of Billie Jean King's experiences playing softball before she switched to tennis and her interest in promoting women's team sports are informed by articles about her on PBS, ESPN, and biography.com. Her father's obituary in the *Los Angeles Times*, June 18, 2006, mentioned that he was once a scout for the Milwaukee Brewers. Joan's prediction that the pro league would help softball players get more respect and media coverage is from "Joyce Is Leaving Brakettes to Join Pro Softball League," in the *Bridgeport Post*, September 30, 1975.

The additional professional basketball and hockey leagues that existed during the 1970s—the American Basketball Association and the World Hockey Association—were also founded by Dennis Murphy. He had a reputation as a sort of sports disrupter and was still going strong in 1998, when the *Los Angeles Times* published an article about a new pro roller-hockey league (the headline was "New Venture Just Another Case of Murphy's Leagues"). World Team Tennis started in 1974. Professional surfing competitions started in the 1960s, but a full-time pro surfing tour didn't get going until the mid-1970s. The National Lacrosse League, the pro indoor lacrosse league, started in 1974. Pelé played his first season with the North American Soccer League in 1975. The National Women's Football League is the fledgling pro women's football league referenced in this chapter. The coed International Volleyball Association league started in 1975.

Details of the professional softball league's first season, such as player salaries and game attendance figures, are drawn from "Women's Professional Softball: Here We Are . . . 120 Games Later," in *Sports-*

woman, November 1976; and coverage by newspapers, such as the *Meriden (CT) Morning Record-Journal* and the *San Jose Mercury News*. Descriptions of players' attitudes about the league are from articles and interviews with former players, including Mary Lou Pennington, Irene Shea, Edwina Bryan, and Shirley Topley. Rosie Beaird Black's comment that playing against women would be like a day off for her is from an article in the *San Jose Mercury News*, June 1, 1976. Murphy's quote about Royal Beaird being "colorful" is from a different article in that same edition of the *Mercury News*. Other details about the Gems, including Royal Beaird's departure from the team, are from articles in the *San Bernardino County Sun*.

Descriptions of the league's 1977 season are informed by interviews with former players and articles in newspapers such as the *Fullerton (CA) News Tribune* and magazines such as *Women's Sports*. Many of these articles, along with clippings of newspaper advertisements for some of the teams' games—for example, the Santa Ana Lionettes' "Battle of the Sexes" event with Bobby Riggs—can be found on Mary Lou Pennington's excellent International Women's Professional Softball page, at sites.google.com/site/iwpsoftball/. The new Sunbirds manager's comment about cutting down on bunting and getting more action into the game is from the team's 1977 program. The *California Today* article on Karen Ambler appeared in July 1977; and the quote from Sunbirds manager John Bruno about "gorgeous" players being a plus appeared in the *Mercury News* that summer.

For more background on the important role softball played in the lesbian community during the 1960s and '70s, see Yvonne Zipter's *Diamonds Are a Dyke's Best Friend* (Ithaca, NY: Firebrand Books, 1988), 45. Descriptions of softball's role in gay and lesbian history in Atlanta and Memphis are informed by "Discursive Memorials: Queer Histories in Atlanta's Public Spaces," by Wesley Chenault, Andy Ditzler, and Joey Orr in *Southern Spaces*, February 2010; and Daniel Buring's *Lesbian and Gay Memphis: Building Communities Behind the Magnolia Curtain* (New York: Garland Publishing, 1997), 140–43. Newspaper and magazine articles, including the 1975 *People* article about Joan, show that female athletes were commonly asked about their opinions on feminism, or women's lib, as it was often called at the time.

Debbie Ricketts was the Santa Ana Lionettes player who joined the Michelin basketball team, according to an article in the *Fullerton (CA) News Tribune*, August 17, 1977. The rumor that the pro softball league would be expanding in 1978, with about twenty cities, including Denver and Tulsa, supposedly interested in starting teams, is from the *Women in Softball* newsletter, November 1977. Billie Jean King's press conference quote about the league's requiring a lot of hard work and money is from a 1976 article in the *Royal Oak (MI) Daily Tribune*. Descriptions of the Bic pens sponsorship deal for the league's 1979 season are drawn from newspaper articles and interviews with Joan Joyce and Jane Blalock. The *People* article about the Falcons' China trip was published on June 25, 1979.

Descriptions of the Golden Apples team are from newspaper articles and interviews with Mary Lou Pennington, who didn't play in 1978 after the Lionettes folded (she would have had to quit her job), but agreed to join the New York team to help the league. Pennington's personal photos from that season, available on sites.google.com/site/iwpsoftball/, also informed the descriptions. The account of Bic pens withdrawing its sponsorship of the pro softball league in February 1980 was chronicled in the *Meriden (CT) Morning Record-Journal*. Descriptions of the younger players' uncertainty about what to do after the league went "on hold" that season are drawn from newspaper articles and interviews with Margie Wright and other former players.

The account of the New York Stars pro women's basketball team going on hiatus after winning the 1980 league championship was reported in the *New York Times*, November 23, 1981; and in other papers. The American Basketball Association, World Hockey Association, and National Lacrosse League all folded in the 1970s. Pelé left the North American Soccer League in 1977. ESPN's coverage of the Falcons in 1979, its first year on the air, was mentioned in "For Falcons, a Reunion of Pioneers," in the *Hartford Courant*, August 12, 1999. Descriptions of Joan's transition into professional golf are drawn from interviews with her and Jane Blalock and from newspaper articles, such as "Joan Joyce Leaves Softball Glory Behind; Turns to Pro Golf," in the *Christian Science Monitor*, August 23, 1982. She and Nancy Lopez went through the LPGA's qualifying school in 1977.

Chapter 13

The epigraph is from *The Softball Story*, 166. Ivan Lendl and Dan Marino's attempts to play in professional golf tournaments have been chronicled by the *Guardian* and the Associated Press, among other news outlets. Descriptions of Joan's performance on the LPGA tour are drawn from newspaper articles and her player profile on the LPGA website, at http://www.lpga.com/players/joan-joyce/81009/ bio. Her first time leading an LPGA tournament was chronicled in "Joan Joyce Enjoys Moment of Glory," in the *New York Times*, May 30, 1981. The LPGA record she set for lowest number of putts (seventeen) was reported by the Associated Press, May 17, 1982. "Regrets? Not really," she told the *Philadelphia Inquirer* in 1985. "If I had been a man with my skills . . . I would have made a ton of money, but money doesn't mean that much to me. As long as I have enough in my pocket right now to have dinner."

Newspaper coverage of the 1982 NCAA softball tournament was scant, but a television sports guide in the *Seguin (TX) Gazette-Enterprise*, May 30, 1982, revealed that at least part of a game was shown on TV that afternoon. For more background on how Title IX applies to high school and college athletics, see the Women's Sports Foundation's "Title IX Myths-Facts" page, at http://www.womens sportsfoundation.org/home/advocate/title-ix-and-issues/what-is -title-ix/title-ix-myths-and-facts. The NCAA also has a "Title IX Frequently Asked Questions" page, at http://www.ncaa.org/about/ resources/inclusion/title-ix-frequently-asked-questions#dollars. Stories of college softball coaches from the 1980s putting in extra hours and spending their own money to ensure their teams had good playing opportunities are commonplace; in fact, it would be unusual to find a coach who wasn't putting in extra effort during this time. Descriptions of the AIAW and its demise are informed by "AIAW Struggling," in the *New York Times*, January 7, 1981; and "A History of Women's Sports Prior to Title IX," in the *Sport Journal*, March 14, 2008.

The *Sports Illustrated* article about Ty Stofflet appeared in the May 28, 1979, issue. Mike White, the University of Oregon softball coach, is one of several New Zealand players who came to the United States during the 1980s and '90s to pitch for men's fastpitch teams. Descriptions of California's dominance of college softball in the 1980s are drawn from articles in the *Los Angeles Times* and other papers and records available on the NCAA website. Former Rocket player Jeanne Contel and former Fresno State coach Margie Wright confirmed that Bertha attended Fresno State softball games after she moved back to the area in the late 1980s. The description of her triumph at the Old-Timers' game is from Brakettes coach John Stratton. The *60 Minutes* episode referenced was actually a rebroadcast: it originally aired in the fall of 1981 and was then shown again in the spring of 1982.

Shawn Andaya Pulliam is an example of a softball player for whom going to college was life-changing. She grew up in Stockton, California, in an area plagued by poverty and crime and hadn't considered college as an option until schools started recruiting her in high school. She wound up being one of the California players at Texas A&M and pitched the team to their second NCAA title in 1987. In an article in the *Lodi (CA) News-Sentinel*, June 29, 2012, she called balancing playing softball with college academics one of the most rewarding challenges of her life. She stayed in Texas after graduation, working as an assistant coach for her alma mater for about ten years, then becoming a fund-raiser for a local nonprofit. "I'm still competitive in my profession," she told the *Waco Tribune*, January 30, 2012. "I guess it's just how I'm made." Other articles, such as "Amateur Softball a Draw for Women," in the *New York Times*, May 30, 1982, illustrate the frustrations that many college softball players experienced when they realized their lack of playing options after they graduated.

Twenty-three teams competed in the 1982 women's international tournament in Taipei, according to the International Softball Federation's "Five Decades of International Softball" report. Descriptions of the legal battles over high school softball in Florida and other states during the 1980s and '90s are drawn from articles in the *Gainesville Sun* and other newspapers. The Florida high school coach's comment that he wouldn't "sit and watch fifteen to eighteen strikeouts" is from the *Orlando Sun-Sentinel*, May 13, 1993. The quote from Kentucky legislator Anne Northup is from the *Kentucky New Era*, February 24, 1994.

The accounts of the Iowa and Oklahoma high schools' resistance to transitioning to five-player girls' basketball are from articles in *Education Week*, September 14, 1983; the *New York Times*, February 5, 1993; and the *Oklahoman*, March 30, 2008. The comment from the coach who suggested lengthening high school girls' cross-country distances to match national standards would lead to programs going under appeared in the *Orlando Sun-Sentinel*, December 8, 1996. Evidence presented in articles from espn.go.com, May 14, 2012, and the *Wisconsin State Journal*, May 8, 2014, suggest that lengthening the race distances and making the teams more competitive actually increases participation.

Descriptions of the rivalry between UCLA and the University of Arizona are informed by articles in the *Los Angeles Times*, the *Salt Lake City Deseret News*, and other newspapers. The Arizona team's reputation as a pioneer in slap hitting was confirmed by former college coaches Margie Wright and Shirley Topley. The history of slap hitting has also been recounted in articles, such as "Slap Happy," in the *Chicago Tribune*, April 4, 1998; and "Slap-Hitting Trend Strikes Oklahoma City," on espn.go.com, July 12, 2005. Descriptions of Tanya Harding pitching for UCLA at the 1995 college championship and the NCAA investigation that followed are drawn from articles by the *Los Angeles Times*, Associated Press, and other publications. The "UCLA's Ringer from Down Under" story appeared in the *New York Times*, June 1, 1995; and the *Sports Illustrated* article referenced was in the June 12, 1995, issue. The comment from the college coach about not thinking women's athletics was "win-at-all-costs" like the men's is from the *Los Angeles Times*, May 31, 1995.

Joan started coaching softball at Florida Atlantic University in 1995. The details about her golf record are from her player profile on the LPGA website. The account of her not always having sponsorship and staying with friends while traveling to tournaments to save money is from "A Softball Great Struggles on Links," in the *Philadelphia Inquirer*, June 8, 1986. Descriptions of her move to Boca Raton and employment as a golf pro there are from "Joyce Has All the Right Moves," in the *Orlando Sun-Sentinel*, April 13, 1990; and from interviews with her. Descriptions of her transition into coaching and her involvement with every aspect of the team, including painting the dugout, are drawn from "FAU Softball Coach Joan Joyce Crafted Her Legendary Career with Her Competitive Will," in the FAU *University Press*, February 28, 2013; and from interviews with her. The account of Joan's softball team's encounter with the US national team is from interviews with her and with Irene Shea, who helped coach the national team that year.

Interviews with Shea and Margie Wright also informed the descriptions of the tryouts for the 1996 Olympic softball team. Descriptions of the final week of Olympic tryouts in Oklahoma City are drawn from "Historic First: Olympic Softball Team Announced," in the *Oklahoman*, September 5, 1995. Former UCLA pitcher Debbie Doom recalled her disappointment about not getting to realize her childhood dream of competing in the Olympics in "Debbie Doom's Day Far from Being Over," in the *Las Vegas Sun*, June 3, 1990.

Chapter 14

The epigraph is from *Softball with Official Rules*, 21. Descriptions of the first Olympic softball game are drawn from a combination of newspaper articles, such as "It's Not the Heat, It's the Humility," in the *Los Angeles Times*, July 22, 1996; and interviews with former players who were in attendance, including Joan Joyce, Jeanne Contel, and Edwina Bryan. Descriptions of the long campaign to get softball into the Olympics are informed by "Athletes in Excluded Sports Seek Olympic Acceptance," in the *Chicago Tribune*, June 10, 1990; the International Softball Federation's "Five Decades of International Softball" report; and an interview with Don Porter, former president of the ISF. The description of the ASA's pre-Olympics national tour was drawn from articles in the *Bloomington (IL) Pantagraph*, May 15, 1996; and the *Tulsa World*, March 11, 1998.

Details from the US team's games during the 1996 Olympic tournament are primarily from articles, such as the *New York Daily News*, and the box scores available on the ISF website. Figures from olympic .org were used to calculate the increase in female participation between the 1988 and 1996 Olympics. Figures related to softball's global growth following the 1996 Olympics are from the ISF's "Five Decades of International Softball" report. Dick Ebersol's quote about regretting not broadcasting any of the 1996 Olympic softball games appeared in the *Atlanta Journal-Constitution* that August and were the subject of "Softball Gets Boost from NBC," by the Scripps Howard news service, August 11, 1996.

Descriptions of the pro softball league that started up after the '96 Olympics are informed by "Calm Belies Dawson's Fiery Spirit," in the *Orlando Sun-Sentinel*, July 2, 1997; and "A Game of Their Own: Women Softball Players Are Making a Pro Try," in the *Philadelphia Inquirer*, July 16, 1997; among other articles. The ASA's initial resistance to Olympic players participating in the league is discussed in "Sponsor on Deck for Women's Softball," in *Sports Business Daily*, December 7, 1998.

Descriptions of the planned professional women's soccer league that was supposed to start in 1998 but never got off the ground are from "U.S. Pro League Is Set to Spring into Action," in the *Los Angeles Times*, September 29, 1997; and "Women's League Falls Short of Goal," in the *Washington Post*, April 17, 1998.

Descriptions of the tryout process for the 2000 US Olympic softball team and the grievances that followed are drawn from articles in the *Los Angeles Times*, *St. Petersburg Times*, and other newspapers. Details regarding the US team's games at the 2000 Olympics were derived from coverage by the Associated Press and other news outlets. The account of Eddie Feigner's throwing out a ceremonial pitch at one of the 2000 Olympic softball games is drawn from "The King and His Court Reign Down Under, Too," in the *Washington Times*, September 18, 2000; a fan's description in the *Allentown (PA) Morning Call*, October 19, 2000; and the International Softball Federation. The "certain countries" phrase is from "Review of the Olympic Programme and the Recommendations on the Programme of the Games of the XXIX Olympiad, Beijing 2008," August 2002.

Chapter 15

The epigraph is from *The Softball Story*, 7. The quote from Samaranch about the 2000 Olympics being the "best ever," is from "Samaranch Calls These Olympics 'Best Ever,' " by the Associated Press, October 1, 2000. The figures that showed the 2000 Summer Olympics were the largest ever are from the Olympic Games Study Commission's "Interim Report to the 114th IOC Session," November 2002. The "somebody's got to get off the bus" phrase is from an interview with US IOC member Anita DeFrantz. The Program Commission report referenced is the August 2002 "Review of the Olympic Programme." The account of the Program Commission's wanting to vote on eliminating baseball, softball, and modern pentathlon in November 2002 and the resulting backlash were reported in "Is This an Olympic Sport?," in *Sports Illustrated*, June 6, 2005.

Descriptions of Sue Candrea's death shortly before the 2004 Olympics are drawn from articles such as "Grieving Candrea to Coach at Olympics," in the *Tucson Citizen*, July 27, 2004; "U.S. Team Plows through Tragedy to Win Gold Medal," in the *Savannah Morning News*, August 24, 2004; and "Schedule Revives Memories of Coach's Emotional Journey," in the *New York Times*, June 7, 2008. Descriptions of the US softball team's performance at the 2004 Olympics are informed by articles in the *Los Angeles Times* and by the Associated Press. The *Sports Illustrated* cover story on the US Olympic softball team appeared on August 30, 2004. The team received the Arete Courage in Sports award on October 24, 2004, and Candrea was awarded the Olympic Shield on January 5, 2005.

Jennie Finch actually appeared in *People*'s 50 Most Beautiful People a few months before the Olympics, in May 2004. She struck out Mike Piazza and Albert Pujols at the 2004 Pepsi All-Star softball game. After the Olympics, she appeared regularly on Fox's *This Week in Baseball* and appeared in *Sports Illustrated*'s 2005 swimsuit issue. She later appeared in commercials for Gatorade and other products. The 2006 Women's College World Series final drew more viewers than Game 1 of the Stanley Cup Finals, according to the *San Diego Union-Tribune*, June 9, 2006; and "Softball Series Worth Watching," in the UCLA *Daily Bruin*, May 30, 2007. Descriptions of the 2005 IOC vote that led to softball's and baseball's getting eliminated from the Olympic program are informed by articles by the Associated Press and other news outlets, the Program Commission's "Review of the Olympic Programme" report, and interviews with Don Porter and Anita DeFrantz. Concerns that the US softball team may have been too dominant at the 2004 Olympics were expressed in articles, such as "No Mercy: Dominant U.S. Captures Gold with 79th Straight Win," in the *San Francisco Gate*, August 24, 2004.

The IOC's issues with baseball were frequently brought up in articles by the *Los Angeles Times* and other news publications. After baseball and softball were voted out of the Olympics in 2005, Jacques Rogge said, "The message is clear. The IOC wants clean sport, the best athletes, and universality," according to the Associated Press, July 10, 2005. Descriptions of the ISF's bid for a revote after it was revealed that a single vote had led to softball's elimination from the Olympic program are drawn from articles, such as "Baseball Cut from Olympics by Three Votes," by the Associated Press, October 7, 2005; and "Baseball, Softball Done after 2008," in the *Los Angeles Times*, February 10, 2006. The account of Jim Easton's decision to recuse himself from the

2005 vote was reported in the *Chicago Tribune*, July 9, 2005. Reactions from Finch and other players from the US softball team were also reported in these articles.

The decrease in funding for national softball programs in China and other countries following the sport's elimination from the Olympics has been reported by the ISF, as was the decreased participation in the 2010 World Cup of Softball competition. Descriptions of the 2012 Summer Olympics, including the security costs, are informed by articles in the *Guardian* and by CBS News, and other news publications. Examples of press coverage that termed the 2012 Games the "women's Olympics" include "London 2012: The Women's Olympics?," by CNN, August 10, 2012. Other examples can be found in "Women in the Olympic and Paralympic Games: An Analysis of Participation and Leadership Opportunities," by the SHARP Center for Women & Girls and the Women's Sports Foundation, April 2013.

The debate over whether the women's Olympic boxers should wear skirts was reported by the Associated Press, March 1, 2012; and the *Washington Post*, July 12, 2012. The list of male and female Olympic events can be found on olympic.org. The 2013 "Women in the Olympic and Paralympic Games" report lists three countries—Barbados, Nauru, and St. Kitts—as not having sent any female athletes to the 2012 Olympics, but an article by Reuters, July 29, 2012, confirmed that St. Kitts did send a female athlete: sprinter Tameka Williams, who traveled to London and was staying at the Olympic village, but withdrew from the competition after admitting to using a banned substance.

Tiger Woods was the main golfer mentioned in articles about golf's campaign to get into the Olympics. "Who is one of the major icons of the world? Tiger Woods. This is a very important sport," Jacques Rogge said in an Associated Press article, August 13, 2009, about the selection of golf and rugby as the two candidate sports for the 2016 Olympics. Rogge also touted the 204 spots for female athletes that golf and rugby would add in this article. "This is an upside of eighty-four," he said. Wrestling's removal from the Olympic program in 2013 and subsequent reinstatement that same year were chronicled by the *Chicago Tribune*, the BBC, and many other news outlets. The IOC voted to end its one-in/one-out policy regarding new Summer Olympic sports in December 2013.

Chapter 16

The epigraph is from *Softball for Girls*, 4–5. Descriptions of the history of company-sponsored sports in Japan are informed by articles such as "In Japan, It's Sayonara for Corporate-Sponsored Sports Teams," in the *New York Times*, November 11, 1999, and "Top-Floor Tokyo," in the *Japan Times*, May 18, 2003; and by Toyota Global's company sports page, at http://www.toyota-global.com/company/history_of_toyota/ 75years/data/company_information/personnel/welfare/toyota_clubs/ achievements.html.

Descriptions of US softball players' experiences playing on Japanese company-sponsored women's softball teams are drawn from interviews with current and former players and from "Loving Softball Is Easier Than Living It," in the *New York Times*, August 31, 2013, which is also the source of the salary figure for American players referenced in this chapter. Michele Smith's experiences playing for the Toyota Shokki team are described on her website, michelesmith.com, and in a profile of her on the New Jersey Sports Heroes site, at http://www.njsportsheroes.com/michelesmithbb.html.

The descriptions of prestige trumping profitability when it comes to ownership of teams in high-profile professional sports, such as men's basketball, are informed by "A Billion Bucks for the Cubs? It's Only Money," in the *New York Times*; *Forbes*'s annual list of most valuable NBA teams; and other articles. MLS's $75 million per year television deal was reported in *Sports Business Daily*, May 12, 2014. The WNBA's $12 million per year deal, despite having higher ratings than MLS in 2012, which was actually one of the WNBA's lowest ratings season (viewership increased again in 2013, though), was reported in *Sports Business Daily*, November 11, 2013. The hundreds of millions of dollars lost by MLS has been chronicled in articles such as "Soccer: Time to Kick It Up a Notch," by *Bloomberg*, November 21, 2004.

Magic Johnson's purchase of the Los Angeles Sparks WNBA team in February 2014 was reported by ESPN and other news outlets. The US national soccer program's rescue of the professional women's soccer league was chronicled by the Associated Press, November 21, 2012. More information about the National Pro Fastpitch league, including the league's history and a list of current teams, can be found on the organization's website, profastpitch.com. Descriptions of experiences of softball players who attended college after softball was eliminated from the Olympics are drawn from articles, such as "Loving Softball Is Easier Than Living It," and interviews with former players, such as Katie Burkhart-Gooch, who won the NCAA title with Arizona State University in 2008.

Figures regarding the percentage of female and male athletic coaches at US colleges are from "Women in Intercollegiate Sport: A Longitudinal, National Study, 37 Year Update," by Vivian Acosta and Linda Carpenter, 2014. Additional findings and observations in this section are informed by the Women's Sports Foundation's "Do Female Athletes Prefer Male Coaches" report and "The Decline of Women Coaches in Collegiate Athletics," by the University of Minnesota's Tucker Center for Research on Girls & Women in Sport, 2012. The observation that many of the national women's softball players' "favorite athletes" were men came from the player profiles on the team website, teamusa.org/usa-softball/team-usa/women. Bertha's preference for male coaches was confirmed by Janice Nelson.

Descriptions of college softball coaching being a full-time, year-round job are from interviews with Margie Wright and Joan Joyce. Descriptions of college softball players contemplating staying with the sport longer now that it will likely be back in the Olympics for 2020 are from interviews with Burkhart-Gooch and current NPF player Morgan Melloh and from articles, such as "USA Softball Sees a Path out of the Wilderness," on espn.go.com, July 20, 2015. Details about the Women's College World Series attracting more television viewers than the college baseball championships are from "2015 WCWS Viewership Easily Eclipses Baseball's College World Series," by the National Fastpitch Coaches Association, 2015; and from figures posted on sportsmediawatch.com. The claim that the yellow ball currently used in college softball originated in the 1970s pro league comes from "For Falcons, a Reunion of Pioneers," in the *Hartford Courant*, August 12, 1999.

Epilogue

The account of Bertha pitching to Melitas Forster at her Dinuba field dedication ceremony in 2009 is described in an article in the *Visalia (CA) Times Delta* that year and was confirmed by Janice Nelson. Bertha's death in March 2014 was reported by the *Dinuba Sentinel* and the *Orange County Register* and was also confirmed by Janice Nelson. The *Bridgeport Post* article about Bertha referenced is from August 14, 1968. The dedication of the Joan Joyce softball field in Waterbury in August 2015 was chronicled in the *Waterbury Republican-American*. Her 800th victory as Florida Atlantic University's softball coach was recorded in February 2015. A full list of ASA Hall of Fame members can be found on the organization's website, http://www.teamusa.org/USA-Softball/About/National-Softball-Hall-of-Fame/Members.

The study of women on *Sports Illustrated* covers is "Where Are the Female Athletes in *Sports Illustrated*? A Content Analysis of Covers, 2000–2011," by Jonetta Weber and Robert Carini in the *International Review for the Sociology of Sport*, January 30, 2012. The study about the lack of women's sports coverage on *SportsCenter* and other TV programs is "It's Dude Time: A Quarter Century of Excluding Women's Sports in Televised News and Highlight Shows," by Cheryl Cooky, Michael Messner, and Michela Musto in *Communication & Sport*, June 5, 2015. The "I tend to point the finger at the fans" quote is from "Women's Teams Still Struggle for Fans," in the *New York Times*, June 29, 2015. Women accounted for 47 percent of medical school graduates in the United States in 2014, according to the Kaiser

Family Foundation (for a breakdown by state, see http://kff.org/other/ state-indicator/medical-school-graduates-by-gender/). The 7 percent to 40 percent figures for female athletic participation in American high schools in 1971 and today are from the National Coalition for Women and Girls in Education's "Title IX at 40" report.

Figures for male and female golfer earnings are from the PGA and LPGA leaderboard listings. The figure for average salaries in the NBA during the 1970s is from "No End in Sight as Athletes' Salaries Skyrocket," in the *Chicago Tribune*, January 1, 2000. The salary figure for professional women's basketball players in the 1970s is from the Texas State Historical Association's page on the Women's Basketball League, at https://tshaonline.org/handbook/online/articles/xowuf. The present-day figures regarding average NBA and WNBA salaries are from "Top WNBA Salaries vs. NBA Salaries: Who Gets Paid More?," in *Black Enterprise*, December 28, 2012; and "Average MLB Salary Nearly Double NFL's but Still Trails NBA's," in *Forbes*, January 23, 2015.

The *Chicago Tribune* article about Jennie Finch is "Softball's Golden Girl Brings Star Power Here," May 29, 2005. The FIFA article that called Alex Morgan "easy on the eye" is from June 30, 2015.

INSERT PHOTOGRAPH CREDITS

1–2: Library of Congress

3–7, 12: Janice Nelson

8–9: Jeanne Contel

10: Billie Harris

11, 14: Brakettes Softball Photo Archive

13: *Bridgeport Post*/Hearst Connecticut Media

15–16: Joan Chandler/Women's Sports Foundation